AN IRISH GENEALOGICAL SOURCE

GUIDE TO
CHURCH RECORDS

Published 1994
by the Ulster Historical Foundation
Balmoral Buildings
12 College Square East
BELFAST
BT1 6DD   14ᵉ ℓₐₙ

on behalf of

Public Record Office of Northern Ireland
66 Balmoral Avenue   01232 661621.   9.15.
BELFAST
BT9 6NY

This book has received financial assistance under the Cultural
Traditions Programme which aims to encourage acceptance
and understanding of cultural diversity.

ISBN   0-901905-59-3

Printed by W & G Baird Ltd, Greystone Press,
Caulside Drive, Antrim, BT41 2RS

Cover illustration shows an elevation of Drumboo Church (*sic* Drumbo,
Belfast), architect Charles Lilley, 1789, [**PRONI reference DIO.4/22/7/6**],
reproduced by kind permission of the Deputy Keeper of the Public Record
Office of Northern Ireland and the Provincial Registry of Armagh.

Department of the ENVIRONMENT
for Northern Ireland

AN IRISH GENEALOGICAL SOURCE

GUIDE TO
CHURCH RECORDS

PUBLIC RECORD OFFICE OF NORTHERN IRELAND

FOREWORD

The steady growth of family and local history as an area of research and leisure interest over the last decade has placed increased demand on the relevant sources - principally Church records recording baptisms, marriages and deaths. PRONI's response to this demand has included the recent opening of a self-service microfilm reading room specifically for researchers into Church records. However, the need for a comprehensive *Guide to Church Records*, their availability and location, has also long been clear.

In 1983, the History Department of the University of Ulster at Coleraine initiated a project to compile an accurate all-embracing guide to Church records held by PRONI in both the original and in copy form. At that time, the examination of almost 1000 churches was carried out by the project researcher, Paul Lalor, and PRONI gratefully acknowledges his contribution to the present *Guide* which drew upon his meticulously recorded findings. For the past two years, PRONI has gladly committed its own time and staff resources to the continuation and conclusion of this project and in this the expertise of Miss Valerie Adams, assisted by Mrs Jean Kyle, should be recognised and commended. It is fitting that for Mrs Kyle this is a signing-off task for PRONI as she is shortly to retire after many years of dedicated service to the Record Office.

Miss Adams, Principal Records Officer, an acknowledged authority on Irish Church records, their creation, history and use, researched and wrote the Introduction, which sets out and interprets how the various denominations kept their records over the generations. Based upon a considerable mass of information, the Introduction is condensed for the purpose of this *Guide* and is a valuable and informative starting-point for the researcher.

It is a pleasure to have this opportunity of making acknowledgement to the individual churches of various denominations which have deposited their records or allowed records to be copied by PRONI. Thanks should also be expressed to the Presbyterian Historical Society, the Wesley Historical Society and the Representative Church Body Library for their assistance in compiling the *Guide*.

The *Guide to Church Records* is published by the Ulster Historical Foundation on behalf of PRONI, from a text prepared as part of PRONI's series of Guides. In view of its appeal to the wider, genealogical audience in which the UHF specialises, this was thought to be the appropriate way to target this particular publication. Both institutions hope that it will prove a useful and informative resource.

A P W MALCOMSON   B TRAINOR
Director, PRONI   Director, UHF
September 1993

INTRODUCTION

General

Of all the many and varied sources held in the Public Record Office of Northern Ireland (PRONI) which are useful to the genealogist, the most important must surely be church records, particularly the registers of baptisms, marriages and burials. These were kept by most of the main religious denominations in Ireland and, as this *Guide* indicates, many of those for the nine counties of Ulster and indeed elsewhere in Ireland have been copied by PRONI or, in some cases, are deposited in PRONI. Civil registration of births and deaths and of Roman Catholic marriages began in 1864 in Ireland, though Protestant marriages were registered from 1845. Church records are therefore of particular importance before these dates, and so most of the copying undertaken by PRONI has concentrated on the pre-civil registration period. The local historian will also find church records a useful source to consult since churches played an important part in the life of the community, particularly in education and welfare, much of which is documented in the minute books of the churches.

Identifying churches in an area

A major problem in using church records is identifying which records exist in a particular area and for what dates. The most obvious way of conducting a search is on a civil parish basis as every townland in Ireland belongs to a civil parish. In origin, the parish is an ecclesiastical administrative unit which then also became the territorial division for civil or government purposes. The townlands, and the parishes they belong to, can be traced through the topographical indexes, which are available in PRONI and in many libraries. Both the Church of Ireland and Roman Catholic parishes have well defined boundaries. In general, the Church of Ireland parish and the civil parish are the same and bear the same name, but throughout the 18th and 19th centuries new Church of Ireland parishes were carved out of existing parishes or parishes united to form a new parish and hence the variation between the present civil and Church of Ireland parishes. Roman Catholic parishes less often correspond with a civil parish and frequently are called by different names. They are usually more difficult to define and the composition of many has changed over the years.

Presbyterian, Methodist and other denominations do not have a parish structure at all and so in producing this *Guide* the site of the church building has largely determined which parish it is placed in. Some denominations do have their own defined church areas such as the circuits of the Methodist Church. In some cases a Methodist circuit has only one chapel in it but more usually contains a number of chapels which have moved from one circuit to another over the years. Circuits also straddle several civil parishes. It is therefore very difficult to attach a Methodist circuit to a particular civil parish. This *Guide* attempts to locate each church within a civil parish, but it has to be said that such location, particularly for Roman Catholic and Methodist churches, presents difficulties both for the reasons just highlighted and because of conflicting evidence in the sources researched.

Scope and arrangement of the Guide

Some years ago PRONI produced a 'Sectional List' of church records of all denominations based largely on the civil parish and including, for each church, details of the types of records and their covering dates, and whether they had been copied by PRONI, the PRONI reference code where appropriate and which records not copied were in the custody of the church. So much copying has been done since the list was produced that it has become very much out of date. This completely revised version includes everything copied or deposited up to September 1993. It includes the same type of information but has attempted to locate more accurately churches within each civil parish and to check that all dates are as accurate as it is possible to make them. This has involved extensive research, including an examination of Ordnance Survey maps to locate the sites of churches, and the checking of the content of many films and copies.

The *Guide* is organised alphabetically by civil parish and within each civil parish the churches are arranged alphabetically by denomination (*see* **Appendix 1** for a list of abbreviations for denominations) which are in turn arranged alphabetically. Where the name of the church is different from the civil parish, a cross-reference is given to the civil parish where the church is located. Certain churches in the Irish Republic have simply been listed under the name of the town or the church rather than the civil parish (*see* **Appendix 2** for a list of these). No attempt has been made to locate churches in Belfast within a civil parish since most of Belfast fell within one parish and in a built-up area a parish is less meaningful - these have been listed under 'Belfast' and no cross-references have been made to these churches.

The records of any particular church will not always be found under the same PRONI reference code. Where there is more than one reference code it sometimes signifies that the records exist simply in different forms (for example, on microfilm and in xerox form). The detailed lists on the shelves in PRONI's Public Search Room should be consulted to obtain the exact details of what is under each reference code. A list of the reference codes used in the *Guide* and what they stand for can be found in **Appendix 3**. There are some church records, in original and copy form, scattered among the records from private individuals and institutions (under 'D' and 'T' PRONI references) and these will be indicated in the *Guide*.

Baptism, marriage and burial registers

The amount of detail one can extract from registers varies enormously even though many registers are in a printed format which encouraged consistent record-keeping. The most comprehensive baptism register would indicate besides the name of the child, the date of baptism and of birth, as well as the name of the father, the maiden name of the mother and the townland where they lived. Sometimes the occupation of the father is also given. Less detailed entries will give only the date of the baptism and the name of the father.

From 1845, church marriage registers are the same as the civil registers, and always contain the date of the marriage, the names of the two parties, their age (often just whether they are over the age of majority), the names of the fathers of each party and their respective occupations, and the townland where each party resided.

Pre-1845 marriage entries are as varied in content as the baptism entries. In addition to the names of the parties and the date of marriage, the townland where each resided is often given but rarely the names of the fathers. Burial registers are more standardised, usually indicating not only the name and the date of burial (or sometimes that of death) but also address and age.

Finally, it should be said that churches did not generally maintain contemporary indexes to their baptism, marriage and burial registers, although some do exist (for example, St Anne's Cathedral, Belfast). Some indexes have been prepared by family history societies or by the Society of Genealogists in London; others have been done in recent years by churches employing people under government employment schemes and using computers. A list of all those known and available in PRONI can be found in **Appendix 4**.

Church of Ireland Records

Until 1871 the Church of Ireland was the state church in Ireland. Following disestablishment, the Parochial Records (Ireland) Act, 1875, declared baptism and burial registers prior to 1871 and marriage registers prior to 1845 to be public records which should be deposited in the then Public Record Office of Ireland in Dublin. However, the opposition of the parishes resulted in a further Act of Parliament in 1876 which permitted these records to remain in local custody provided there was adequate provision for their safe-keeping. Nevertheless, by 1922 the records of 1006 parishes in Ireland had been deposited in the Public Record Office leaving the records of only 637 parishes in local custody. Although the intention of the 1875 Act was to preserve the parish records, it was nullified by the destruction of the Public Record Office in 1922 when the records of all but four parishes were burnt.

Such widespread destruction has left a huge gap in the archival heritage of Northern Ireland and of the Irish Republic, making it difficult not only to trace families who belonged to the Church of Ireland but also those of other denominations because, in the 17th and 18th centuries, the Church of Ireland registers often contain baptisms, marriages and burials of Protestant dissenters and Roman Catholics who were baptised, married or buried within the state church. This practice arose from conditions in Ireland where the Penal Laws against Dissenters, among other things, gave to the Church of Ireland an exclusive right to administer baptism, marriage and burial ceremonies. Although the destruction of the Church of Ireland registers was catastrophic, it must not be exaggerated. For example, 65 parishes in Northern Ireland have records going back to 1800. A complete list of all parish registers which were held in the Public Record Office in Dublin can be found in the *28th Report of the Deputy Keeper of the Records in Ireland, 1896*, which lists all the parishes in alphabetical order, identifies those parishes whose records were sent to the Public Record Office and those which retained them locally. It also indicates for each parish the covering dates of all registers of baptisms, marriages and burials. This source has been used to check if the records of a particular Church of Ireland parish were destroyed and the information has been noted in the *Guide*.

The Parochial Records (Ireland) Act, 1875 excluded from its provisions other Church of Ireland records which may be earlier in date than the public records: for example, vestry minute books, which sometimes contain baptism, marriage and burial entries, particularly in the late 17th and early 18th centuries. Frequently vestry minutes contain items such as the names of church wardens, of the confirmed, of cess applotters and cess payers (cess being a local tax levied by the general vestry for the repair of the roads etc.,), of the poor, the widowed and the orphaned receiving relief, and of overseers of the poor and of the roads. The local historian and the gene-alogist will both find much useful material buried in the vestry minutes.

Other types of Church of Ireland non-public records of interest are: confirmation registers; account books recording the names of those who gave money to the church or who were paid for their services and even the names of those who received financial and other assistance from the parish; registers of vestrymen which list for each year those who served on the vestry (though they generally date from 1870). Occasionally there is a census for a parish identifying the members of each family, such as that for Christ Church, Belfast, in 1852.

PRONI's copying programme of Church of Ireland records covers mainly the pre-1871 baptisms and burials, pre-1845 marriages and early vestry minute books for churches in Northern Ireland. More recently all pre-1900 records for churches in counties Cavan, Monaghan and Donegal were filmed. Original records and paper copies can be found under the PRONI reference code C.R.1, paper copies only under T.679 and the microfilm copies under MIC.1. At the beginning of the catalogues of T.679 and MIC.1 there is an alphabetical index to all the records listed. The *Guide* also notes those records not copied or not deposited but which are available in local custody according to the periodic returns of parish records sent to the Representative Church Body Library.

Methodist Church Records

Methodism grew out of the Established Church. When John Wesley came to Ireland in the mid-

18th century, people joined the Wesleyan Methodist Society from all denominations but remained in their own churches. In 1804 the Irish Conference of the Methodist Church stated that no Methodist preacher in Ireland should perform the office of baptism. Methodists were expected to go to the parish church for the administration of baptism, and hence the importance again of the Church of Ireland records in the 18th century. However, in 1816 there was a split in Methodism between the Primitive Wesleyan Methodists who retained their link with the Established Church, and the Wesleyan Methodists who allowed their ministers to administer baptisms. This explains the fact that the earliest baptism registers date from 1816 (those for Donegall Square, Belfast) and also that the Primitive Wesleyans did not have any separate baptism registers until the 1860s, and then only until 1878 when the two branches of Methodism were united.

Another breakaway branch of Methodism to be found in Ireland was the Methodist New Connexion, which wanted to move even further away from the Established Church than the Wesleyan Methodists. Their churches were largely confined to counties Down and Antrim. For example, Zion at Newtownards, Co. Down, Broomhedge, Co. Antrim, and Priesthill, Co. Down, were such churches. They eventually united with the Irish Methodist Conference in 1905.

The Society of Primitive Methodists, which began in England in 1812 as part of the revivalist movement, was also to be found in Ireland. It began its Irish mission work in 1832, but only ever had a few congregations in the Shankill and Donegall Road areas of Belfast. In 1910 the Irish Methodist Conference took over responsibility for the Irish Primitive Methodist churches.

The majority of Methodist baptism registers do not begin until the 1830s and the marriages until 1845. There are few Methodist burial registers because most Methodist churches simply did not have their own burial grounds. However, an important record is a large volume of baptism entries for Methodist churches throughout Ireland which is in among the administrative records of the Methodist Church in Ireland (MIC.429/1) and which may have been the product of an attempt to compile a central register of baptisms. Although incomplete, it contains baptisms from 1815 to 1840 and often pre-dates existing individual church baptism registers.

Other classes of records are useful to the genealogist and the local historian. Membership registers or quarterly class rolls, dating mainly from the mid-19th century (a few go back to 1819, such as those for Lurgan), are an important source for researching the growth and the decline of Methodism in an area. Circuit schedule books, dating mainly from the 1870s, give the names of Methodist societies, the number in each, the numbers of new members received, of members removed elsewhere, of emigrations and of deaths, as well as details of Temperance associations, returns of Sunday schools and chapels, and accounts. They are an invaluable source for the history of Methodism.

Many Methodist churches in Northern Ireland and in counties Cavan, Monaghan and Donegal have had their records copied by PRONI and these are to be found under reference codes MIC.1E and C.R.6. At the beginning of the MIC.1E catalogue there is an alphabetical index to all circuits and churches mentioned in the catalogue. Records not copied by PRONI will be in local custody or will be held by the Wesley Historical Society [*see* **Appendix 6** for address].

Methodist baptism registers are generally for a circuit; for marriages each individual church usually has its own registers from 1845 onwards. Because the composition of circuits has changed from time to time, it is important to note that the records of any Methodist church may be found in several different circuits.

Presbyterian Church Records

Presbyterianism came to Ulster from Scotland in the 17th century but its freedom was severely curtailed by penal enactments to the extent that it was illegal until 1782 for Presbyterian ministers to perform marriages even of Presbyterians and only from 1845 could they legally marry a Presbyterian and a member of the Church of Ireland. Religious and civil persecution resulting from the Penal Laws meant that many Presbyterian baptisms, marriages and burials are to be found in the registers of the Church of Ireland, albeit sporadic, until well into the 18th century. Burial registers for Presbyterian churches are uncommon as there were few Presbyterian burial grounds. Although Presbyterian registers and those of other denominations were not subject to state control and therefore there was no requirement to place them in the Public Record Office of Ireland for safe-keeping, there are still few registers going back into the 18th century.

A feature of Presbyterianism is the number of places which have more than one Presbyterian church and are referred to as 1st, 2nd and 3rd. Frequent disputes over doctrine or the choice of a minister, or just the need for more accommodation, led to the creation of new congregations, and building of new churches. Many of the churches now known as 1st, 2nd or 3rd began as seceding congregations which broke away from the original Synod of Ulster in 1733. The Seceders took a strong evangelical stand and in particular objected to an Act of Parliament in 1712 which accepted patronage as an accepted method of appointing ministers. However, as the Synod of Ulster and Secession Synod gradually resolved their differences and eventually came to hold the same doctrines, the secession congregations were re-united in 1840 into the Synod of Ulster. Another complication arises from changes in the designation of churches. For example, a new congregation was formed in Ballymoney in 1834 and was known as 2nd Ballymoney but, when the Seceders joined the Synod of Ulster in 1840, the Seceding congregation was given the name 2nd Ballymoney and this new church (hitherto the 2nd) became 3rd Ballymoney. *A History of Presbyterian Congregations in the Presbyterian Church in Ireland, 1610-1982*, published by the Presbyterian Historical Society, is a useful tool when unravelling these problems.

Besides registers, there are other records of interest to the family and local historian. Instead of vestry minutes, Presbyterian churches have session and committee minutes. The former are usually the more interesting as they sometimes record baptisms and marriages, and the names of new communicants, of those who transgressed and those who left the church (whether to another congregation or emigrated and thus required a transfer certificate), as well as subscription lists. There are often separate communicants' registers which sometimes contain details of deaths, emigrations or transfers to other congregations. A common Presbyterian church record is the stipend book recording details of those who paid into the church. Seat lists or pew rent books are also common, listing the names of those who had seats rented in the church. There are also occasionally account books and censuses of congregations.

Presbyterian records copied by PRONI are almost exclusively for the nine counties of Ulster and are available under the PRONI reference codes MIC.1P and C.R.3. There are also alphabetical indexes to the churches appearing in the MIC.1P and C.R.3 catalogues. Where records have not yet been copied this is indicated in the *Guide*. Some records are held by the Presbyterian Historical Society including some for churches in the Irish Republic and particularly for churches no longer in existence. The most significant of these for the nine counties of Ulster are noted in the *Guide*.

Roman Catholic Records

The Penal Laws militated against the erection of chapels and regular record-keeping, and so Roman Catholic registers are generally later than Protestant registers, mostly dating from the 1820s. They are almost entirely for baptisms and marriages, though death or funeral entries do occur occasionally (these generally record only the name of the deceased and the date of death). Roman Catholic registers themselves are often closely written - although from the 1860s pro-forma registers are more common - and are sometimes in Latin. The baptism entries include the names of sponsors and marriage entries, the names of witnesses.

Roman Catholic parishes are often made up of parts of more than one civil parish and so searching under several parishes is necessary to find all the records of the Roman Catholic parish. Cross-references appear in the *Guide* where this is known to occur. Another complication arises from the fact that a Roman Catholic parish can be known by several names. Where known, the historical name is given in brackets in the *Guide*. However, the name in brackets may also indicate the registers of a particular church within the Roman Catholic parish. Most Roman Catholic parishes have more than one church. Sometimes only one register was kept for the entire parish, but at other times each church had its own registers. The registers themselves do not always make this clear and so it is often difficult to ascertain what is contained in a register.

The National Library of Ireland microfilmed almost all the pre-1880 registers in Ireland, but PRONI only has microfilm copies only for parishes in Northern Ireland, for most of those in counties Donegal, Cavan and Monaghan, and for some in counties Louth and Leitrim. They are to be found under the PRONI reference code MIC.1D. In addition there are some xerox copies under C.R.2. An alphabetical index to all names referred to in the MIC.1D list is to be found at the beginning of the MIC.1D catalogue.

Other Protestant Dissenting Records

(a) *Congregational Church*

Congregationalists came to Ireland in the 17th century but made little impact until the early 19th century. The setting up of the Irish Evangelical Society in 1814 resulted in many churches being built. From this date the earliest records exist, although most date from the 1880s. They are mostly baptism and marriage registers and minute books.

PRONI holds some records of Congregational churches in Dublin and of the church at Carrickfergus (which has baptisms from 1819 to the present). The only records copied are those of Straid. All of these will be found under the reference code C.R.7

(b) *Non-Subscribing Presbyterian Church (or Unitarians)*

The Non-Subscribing Presbyterian Church has its origins as far back as 1725 when a number of congregations refused to subscribe to the Westminister Confession of Faith and formed themselves into a separate Presbytery of Antrim. It retained links with the General Synod of Ulster until the 1820s when the issue of subscription having come to a head, the Non-Subscribers were forced out of the Synod of Ulster and formed the Remonstrant Synod of Ulster. Some of the early Non-Subscribing Presbyterian Church records, created before the split, are in fact Presbyterian records: for example, the early records of Scarva Street Presbyterian Church in Banbridge are to be found in Banbridge Non-Subscribing Presbyterian Church records. It is advisable to check the history of a congregation to find out if the early records might be elsewhere.

PRONI has copied some Non-Subscribing Presbyterian Church records and some have also been deposited, notably one of the earliest session minute books which is for Templepatrick, 1646-1743. The records can be found under the PRONI reference code MIC.1B or C.R.4.

(c) *Reformed Presbyterian Church (or Covenanters)*

Although the Reformed Presbyterian Church had its origins in the 17th century, when a minority of Presbyterians wished to adhere more strictly to the Covenants of 1638 and 1642, it was not until the mid-18th century that congregations were formed with their own ordained ministers. In 1763, the first Irish Reformed Presbytery was set up; by 1800 it had 28 congregations in counties Antrim, Armagh, Down, Tyrone, Donegal and Monaghan. However, the earliest records begin mainly in the mid-19th century, apart from some early 19th century session minutes for Cullybackey, Co. Antrim, and Drumbolg, Co. Londonderry. They are similar in type to Presbyterian Church records. Some have been copied by PRONI and can be found under the reference codes MIC.1C and C.R.5.

(d) **Baptist Church**

Although the Baptists were among the independent churches who came to Ireland in the mid-17th century, it was the early 19th century before they began to make progress. Although there are over 50 Baptist churches in Ireland today, less than a dozen have pre-1900 records. The earliest records begin in the 1860s and consist of marriages and minute books. As the Baptist church does not practice infant baptism, there are no baptism registers, but details of those who came into membership of the church are be found in the minute books. They do not have any burial grounds and hence the absence of burial registers. The documentary record is therefore very scanty. PRONI has not copied any Baptist Church records, but you will find them in the custody of the churches or with the Baptist Union of Ireland in Belfast [see **Appendix 6** for address].

(e) **The Religious Society of Friends (or Quakers)**

The Religious Society of Friends began in Ulster in the mid-17th century, settling mainly around Lisburn, Co. Antrim, and Lurgan, Co. Armagh. From the beginning there was a strong emphasis on record-keeping. George Fox, the founder of the Society, advised every meeting to keep a record of its business and to keep also registers of births, marriages and burials. The records are very complete and for most monthly meetings they exist almost continuously from the date of origin.

Apart from registers of births [not baptisms, as baptism was not practised by the Society of Friends], marriages and burials, the Society of Friends also maintained a number of other unique types of records. Records of sufferings detail the penalties endured for their religious beliefs (for example, they often suffered for non-payment of tithes). There are copies of removal certificates, given when members transferred to other societies, and testimonies of disunity from those who committed offences contrary to church rules (for example, marrying outside the Society, failure to pay debts or drinking to excess). Minutes record in great detail the work, organisation and oversight of meetings, including details about sufferings and records of births, marriages and deaths (sometimes arranged by family name). Wills and inventories throw a great deal of light on social conditions and on rural and domestic life because they list household and farm equipment.

PRONI has copied all the records at the Lisburn Meeting House which include not only those of Lisburn, but of Lurgan, Ballyhagen and Richhill in Co. Armagh, Grange near Charlemont, Co. Tyrone, Antrim, and Cootehill, Co. Monaghan. They are to be found under the reference code MIC.16. In the last century indexes were made of the early registers of monthly meetings and these contain abstracts of all births, marriages and deaths up to 1859. Thereafter, new abstract registers were kept. Another valuable search aid is a list [Jones Index] of every surname occurring in the registers of the Society of Friends in Ireland and showing the monthly meeting in which each name appears. All of these are available at the Dublin Friends' Historical Library [*see* **Appendix 6** for address].

(f)   ***The Moravian Church***

The Moravian Church was founded in the 18th century in what is now the Czech Republic. John Cennick introduced Moravian work into Ireland, arriving in Dublin in 1746 and founding the first Moravian Church there. Within two years there were societies in counties Antrim, Down, Armagh, Londonderry, Cavan and Monaghan. From these sprang the congregations making up the Moravian Church in Ireland - Ballinderry, Kilwarlin, Gracehill, Gracefield, Belfast (University Road and Cliftonville) and Dublin.

Like the Religious Society of Friends, the Moravians were excellent record-keepers, as illustrated by the fact that some series of records for Dublin and for Gracehill are virtually continuous from their date of origin in the mid-18th century. Apart from baptism, marriage and burial registers, the Moravian Church also maintains very detailed membership registers recording for each member date of birth, previous denomination (if appropriate), when deceased or left and the reason for leaving. Ministers' diaries contain births, marriages and deaths (often with biographical details), the names of those who joined the church and those who left, and lists of members.

PRONI has copied all the records held at Gracehill Moravian Church which compromise not only of those for Gracehill but also for other churches including the Dublin church. Kilwarlin and Ballinderry churches have their own records, and these too have been copied by PRONI. All these records can be found under the PRONI reference code MIC.1F.

APPENDIX 1

Key to Abbreviations

B.	-	Baptist Church
C.	-	Congregational Church
C.I.	-	Church of Ireland
M.	-	Methodist Church
MOR.	-	Moravian Church
N.S.P.	-	Non-Subscribing Presbyterian Church
P.	-	Presbyterian Church
R.C.	-	Roman Catholic Church
R.P.	-	Reformed Presbyterian Church
R.S.F.	-	Religious Society of Friends

APPENDIX 2

List of places not arranged under civil parish

Athlone

Belfast

Cork

Dublin

Galway

Kerry

Kilkenney

Limerick

Longford

Maryborough

Skibbereen

Sligo

Waterford

Wexford

Wicklow

APPENDIX 3

Church records in PRONI can mainly be found under the following codes:

Microfilm

MIC.1   -   Church of Ireland Records

MIC.1B -   Non-Subscribing Presbyterian Church Records

MIC.1C -   Reformed Presbyterian Church Records

MIC.1D -   Roman Catholic Church Records

MIC.1E -   Methodist Church Records

MIC.1F -   Moravian Church Records

MIC.1P -   Presbyterian Church Records

MIC.16 -   Religious Society of Friends' (Quakers') Records

Copies and Originals

C.R. 1   -   Church of Ireland Records

C.R. 2   -   Roman Catholic Church Records

C.R. 3   -   Presbyterian Church Records

C.R. 4   -   Non-Subscribing Presbyterian Church Records

C.R. 5   -   Reformed Presbyterian Church Records

C.R. 6   -   Methodist Church Records

C.R. 7   -   Congregational Church Records

C.R. 8   -   Religious Society of Friends' (Quakers') Records

T.679   -   Church of Ireland Records

APPENDIX 4

INDEXES AVAILABLE TO CHURCH RECORDS

CHURCHES	CONTENTS	REF. NO
CHURCH OF IRELAND		
Arboe, Co. Tyrone	Baptisms, 1775-1813 and 1824-71 Marriages, 1773-1812 and 1824-45 Burials, 1776-1813 and 1827-1906 Confirmations, 1828-33	D.1278 [Copy available in Public Search Room]
Badony Lower, Co. Tyrone	Baptisms, 1828-37 Marriages, 1828-37 Burials, 1828-37	T.679/76 [Copy available in Public Search Room]
Belfast (St Anne's)	Baptisms, 1745-1886 and 1872-84 Marriages, 1745-1823 Burials, 1745-1823	T.679/251 and 260; MIC.1/178A
Belfast (St George's)	Baptisms, 1817-70 Marriages, 1817-33	T.679/263-266 [Copy available in Public Search Room]
Belfast, Malone (St John's)	Baptisms, 1842-87 Marriages, 1842-4	D.231 [Copy available in Public Search Room]
Belfast (Trinity)	Baptisms, 1844-77	D.523A-B [Copy available in Public Search Room]
Donaghadee, Co. Down	Baptisms, 1771-1845 Marriages, 1772-1844	C.R.1/54; T.679/44
Donaghmore, Co. Tyrone	Baptisms, 1748-1870 Marriages, 1741-1883 Burials, 1741-1870	T.786; MIC.1/106/2; T.679/19; D.750/9-10
Dundalk, Co. Louth	Baptisms, 1803-41 and 1847-88 Marriages, 1803-28 Burials, 1803-44 and 1853-1901	MIC.1/204A & C
Kilkeel, Co. Down	Baptisms, 1816-47 Marriages, 1816-27 Burials, 1816-27	C.R. 1/15 [Copy available in Public Search Room]

APPENDIX 4

INDEXES AVAILABLE TO CHURCH RECORDS (contd)

CHURCHES	CONTENTS	REF. NO
Kilskeery, Co. Tyrone	Baptisms, 1767-1835, and extracts, 1837-44 Marriages, 1778-1841 Burials, 1796-1841	C.R. 1/22 [Copy available in Public Search Room]
Lisburn (Christ Church Cathedral), Co. Antrim	Baptisms and marriages, 1640-1806	D.1823/5
Lisnaskea, Co. Fermanagh	Baptisms, marriages, and burials, 1804-15	D.2896/1/1 [Copy available in Public Search Room]
Loughinisland, Co. Down	Baptisms, 1760-1806 and 1816-37 Marriages, 1760-1800 and 1815-94 Burials, 1760-93 and 1816-37	D.1407 (Copy available in Public Search Room]
Seagoe, Co. Armagh	Baptisms, 1672-1919 Marriages, 1676-1919 Burials, 1691-1919	MIC.1/73-74 [Copy available in Public Search Room]
Tullycorbet, Co. Monaghan	Baptisms, 1796-1831 Marriages, 1822-30 Burials, 1814-31	C.R.1/44 [Copy available in Public Search Room]

PRESBYTERIAN CHURCH

CHURCHES	CONTENTS	REF. NO
2nd Ballybay, Co. Monaghan	Baptisms, 1833-1918	C.R. 3/28
1st Bangor, Co. Down	Marriages, 1808-45	MIC.1P/23 [Copy available in Public Search Room]
Cahans, Co. Monaghan	Baptisms, 1752-1844	C.R. 3/25A/4
Killinchy, Co. Down	Baptisms and marriages, 1812-54	D.1759/1D/5A-B and 8
Killyleagh, Co. Down	Baptisms, 1693-1713 Marriages, 1692-1757	D.1759/1D/11

APPENDIX 4

INDEXES AVAILABLE TO CHURCH RECORDS (contd)

<u>CHURCHES</u>	<u>CONTENTS</u>	<u>REF. NO</u>
ROMAN CATHOLIC CHURCH		
Tullycorbet, Co. Monaghan	Baptisms, 1876-1918	C.R.2/16/1 [Copy available in Public Search Room]

APPENDIX 5

Bibliography of works which may be of use in tracing the history of churches and their records:

General

P Lalor - Church of Ireland Parish Registers in Ulster prior to Civil Registration: Some Preliminary Observations, in *Familia,* Vol. 2, No. 1, 1985

Church of Ireland

Rev. James B Leslie - *Clogher Clergy and Parishes* (Enniskillen, 1929)

Rev. James B Leslie - *Derry Clergy and Parishes* (Enniskillen, 1937)

Rev. James B Leslie and Very Rev. Henry B. Swanzy - *Biographical Succession Lists of the Clergy of the Diocese of Down* (Enniskillen, 1936)

Rev. James B. Leslie - *Armagh Clergy and Parishes* (Dundalk, 1911)

G O'Duill - Church Records after Disestablishment, in *Irish Archives Bulletin,* Vol. 5, 1975

Henry B Swanzy - *Succession Lists of the Diocese of Dromore* (Belfast, 1933)

Handbook of the United Diocese of Down, Connor and Dromore (Belfast, 1886)

Down, Connor and Dromore Library Committee - *Clergy of Connor from Patrician Times to the Present* (Belfast, 1993)

Kilmore Succession List (unpublished)

Methodist Church

C H Crookshank - *History of Methodism in Ireland,* Vols 1-3

F Jeffrey - *Irish Methodism* (Epworth House, Belfast, 1964)

Presbyterian Church (all branches)

A History of Congregations in the Presbyterian Church in Ireland, 1610-1982 (Presbyterian Historical Society of Ireland, Belfast, 1982)

John Campbell - *A Short History of the Non-Subscribing Presbyterian Church of Ireland* (Belfast, 1914)

Adam Loughridge - *The Covenanters in Ireland* (Outlook Press, Rathfriland, 1984)

Religious Society of Friends (Quakers)

P Beryl Eustace and Olive C Goodbody - *Quaker Records Dublin - Abstracts of Wills* (Dublin, 1957)

Olive C Goodbody and B G Hutton - *Guide to Irish Quaker Records* (Dublin Stationery Office for the Irish Manuscripts Commission, 1967)

Roman Catholic Church

Rev. James O'Laverty - *An Historical Account of the Diocese of Down and Connor, Ancient and Modern*, Vols 1-4 (Dublin, 1878-8)

APPENDIX 6

Useful addresses:

1. Irish Baptist Union, 117 Lisburn Road, Belfast, BT9 7AF.

2. Presbyterian Historical Society, Church House,
    Fisherwick Place, Belfast, BT1 6DW.

3. Religious Society of Friends, Ulster Quarterly Meeting,
    Archives Committee, Railway Street, Lisburn, Co. Antrim,
    BT28.

4. Religious Society of Friends in Ireland, Swanbrook House,
    Morehampton Road, Donnybrook, Dublin 4.

5. Representative Church Body Library, Braemor Park,
    Rathgar, Dublin 14.

6. Wesley Historical Society, Aldersgate House,
    13 University Road, Belfast, BT7 1NA.

ACTON CHURCH OF IRELAND PARISH, CO. ARMAGH
[*see under* **BALLYMORE**]

AGHABOG, CO. MONAGHAN

C.I. Aghabog (Clogher diocese)
[Earliest registers destroyed in Dublin]

Baptisms, 1877-1979; marriages, 1845-1953; preachers'
book, 1907-27.   **MIC.1/131; DIO.2/11/4**

Burials, 1878-; vestry minutes, 1814-.   **In local custody**

C.I. Newbliss
[Formed out of Aghabog and Killeevan parishes - *see
under* **KILLEEVAN**]

P. Drumkeen
Baptisms, 1856-1981; marriages, 1845-1956.   **MIC.1P/174**

R.C. [Aghabog parish forms part of Killeevan Roman
Catholic parish - *see under* **KILLEEVAN**]

AGHADERG, CO. DOWN

C.I. Aghaderg (Dromore diocese)
Baptisms, 1814-70; marriages, 1814-49; burials,
1814-1980; vestry minutes, 1747-1841.   **T.679/94-100; C.R.1/47**

C.I. Scarva (Dromore diocese)
[Earliest registers destroyed in Dublin]

Baptisms, 1877-; marriages, 1851-; burials, 1850-; vestry
minutes, 1850-.   **In local custody**

P. Glascar
Baptisms, 1780-1844 and 1885-1931; marriages, 1781-98
and 1822-32, with indexes, and 1845-1903; communicants'
roll, 1890-1940.   **MIC.1P/63**

P. Loughbrickland
Baptisms, 1842-1903; marriages, 1842-89; committee
minutes, 1842-1905, with accounts up to 1912; stipend
payers' book, 1862-83; communicants' roll, 1882-91.   **MIC.1P/181**

P. Scarva
Baptisms, 1807-1964; marriages, 1814-1936; lists of new
communicants, 1858-94 and 1924-7; communicants' roll,
1927-9.   **MIC.1P/182; C.R.3/53**

R.C. Aghaderg (Dromore diocese)
Baptisms, 1816-76; marriages, 1816-76; burials, 1838-75.   **MIC.1D/29**

AGHADOWEY, CO. LONDONDERRY

C.I. Aghadowey (Derry diocese)
[Earliest registers destroyed in Dublin]

Baptisms, 1882-; marriages, 1845-; burials, 1881-;
vestry minutes, 1774-; register of vestrymen, 1870-;
preachers' books, 1869 and 1881-.   **In local custody**

P. Aghadowey
Baptisms, 1855-1944; marriages, 1845-1923;
committee minutes, 1851-85; stipend lists, 1832-54;
communion rolls, 1903-13.   **MIC.1P/123**

Session minutes, 1702-61.   **In Presbyterian
                                                                  Historical Society**

P. Ballylintagh [dissolved in 1883]
Marriages, 1872-82.   **MIC.1P/381**

P. Killaig
Baptisms, 1860-1944; marriages, 1865-1903.   **MIC.1P/414**

Baptisms, 1805-56; communicants' roll, 1749-1918.   **In Presbyterian
                                                                  Historical Society**

P. Ringsend
Baptisms, 1871-1937; marriages, 1845-1902.   **MIC.1P/413**

R.C. [Aghadowey parish is in the Roman Catholic parish of
Coleraine - *see under* **COLERAINE**]

AGHADRUMSEE CHURCH OF IRELAND PARISH,
CO. FERMANAGH
[*see under* **CLONES**]

AGHAGALLON, CO. ANTRIM

C.I. Aghagallon (Connor diocese)
[*see under* **AGHALEE**]

M. Craigmore
    Baptisms, 1941-; marriages, 1940-.   **In local custody**

R.C. Aghagallon (Down and Connor diocese)
    [Includes the parishes of Aghagallon, Aghalee and part of
    Ballinderry]

    Baptisms and marriages, 1828-89; burials, 1828-48 and
    1873-81.   **MIC.1D/6, 63**

AGHALEE, CO. ANTRIM

C.I. Aghalee (Dromore diocese), **Aghagallon** (Connor diocese)
    and **Magheramesk** (Connor diocese)

    Baptisms, 1811-81; marriages, 1811-44 and 1864-6;
    burials, 1811-74.   **T.679/90-93**

R.C. Aghalee
    [*see under* **AGHAGALLON**]

AGHALOO, CO. TYRONE

C.I. Aghaloo or Caledon (Armagh diocese)
    Baptisms, 1791-5 and 1801-71; marriages, 1792-5 and
    1800-45; burials, 1792-5 and 1800-72; confirmation lists,
    1840-72; vestry minutes, 1691-1807.   **T.679/286, 290-294;**
                                                                          D.2602/1

    Baptisms, 1872-; marriages, 1845-; burials, 1873-.   **In local custody**

C.I. Brantry (Armagh diocese)
    [Formed out of Aghaloo, Carnteel and Clonfeacle
    parishes]

    Baptisms, 1844-71; burials, 1846-82; confirmation list,
    1873.   **T.679/276-277**

    Baptisms, 1871-; marriages, 1845-; burials, 1883-; vestry
    minutes, 1844-.   **In local custody**

M. Caledon
    Baptisms, 1815-.   **In local custody**

P. Ballymagrane
    Baptisms, 1851-1985; marriages, 1845-1921.   **MIC.1P/39**

P. Caledon
    Baptisms, 1870-1950; marriages, 1848-1932.   **MIC.1P/25**

P. Minterburn
    Baptisms, 1829-1950; marriages, 1830-1911.   **MIC.1P/26**

R.C. Aghaloo (Caledon) (Armagh diocese)
    Baptisms, 1846-81; marriages, 1832-82.   **MIC.1D/36**

    [Also includes details for the chapel at Aughnacloy in
    Carnteel parish]

AGHALURCHER, COS FERMANAGH AND TYRONE

C.I. Aghalurcher (Clogher diocese)
    Baptisms, 1788-1984; marriages, 1801-1924; burials,   **T.679/25, 81-82;**
    1802-1927.   **MIC.1/227**

    Vestry minutes, 1747-; registers of vestrymen, 1870-.   **In local custody**

C.I. Cooneen (Clogher diocese)
    [Partly in Aghalurcher parish and partly in Mullaghfad
    parish]

    Baptisms, 1872-1965; marriages, 1887-1937; register of
    vestrymen, 1871-.   **In local custody**

C.I. Kiltermon (Clogher diocese)
    Baptisms, 1861-5.   **MIC.1/6**

C.I. Fivemiletown (Clogher diocese)
    [Formed out of part of Aghalurcher - *see under*
    CLOGHER]

C.I. Lisnaskea (Holy Trinity) (Clogher diocese)
    Baptisms, 1804-1925; marriages, 1804-1909; burials,
    1804-88; banns, 1807-13; confirmations, 1929-42;
    vestry minutes, 1870-93 and 1922-42; accounts,
    1870-1958; preachers' books, 1866-1966; index to
    baptisms, marriages and burials, 1804-15.   **T.679/16; MIC.1/73;**
          D.2896

C.I. Maguiresbridge (Clogher diocese)
    Baptisms, 1840-1921; marriages, 1842-5 and 1882;
    burials, 1842-95; vestry minutes, 1870-1911.   **MIC.1/60**

    Burials, 1896-; registers of vestrymen, 1870.   **In local custody**

C.I. Mullaghfad (All Saints) (Clogher diocese)
    Baptisms, 1836-; marriages, 1837-; burials, 1850-78 and
    1921-; vestry minutes, 1870-; registers of vestrymen,
    1870-.   **In local custody**

M. Grogey
    Baptisms, c.1880-1954; circuit schedule books,
    c.1880-1909.   **MIC.1E/28**

M. Lisnaskea
Baptisms, 1873-1942 (In Newtownbutler register);
marriages, 1887-1935.   **MIC.1E/29-30**

M. Maguiresbridge
[Originally Primitive Wesleyan Methodists]

Baptisms, 1865-1925; marriages, 1873-1936; circuit
schedule books, 1865-93.   **MIC.1E/9, 28**

P. Cavanaleck
Baptisms, 1853-1953; marriages, 1871-1925; session
minutes, 1856; marriage notices, 1858 and 1860-83;
list of communicants, 1862.   **MIC.1P/80;**
                                                                           MIC.1P/230/4

P. Maguiresbridge
Baptisms, 1860-1985; marriages, 1845-1920.   **MIC.1P/69**

R.C. Aughalurcher (Lisnaskea and Maguiresbridge)
(Clogher diocese)

Baptisms, 1835-83.   **MIC.1D/12; CR.2/12**

AGHANLOO, CO. LONDONDERRY

C.I. Aghanloo (Derry diocese)
[Earliest registers destroyed in Dublin]

Baptisms, 1904-; marriages, 1845-; burials, 1883-;
vestry minutes, 1855-; registers of vestrymen, 1870-;
preachers' books, 1889-.   **In local custody**

R.C. [Part of Aghanloo parish is in the Roman Catholic parish
of Limavady along with Drumachose and Tamlaght
Finlagan - *see under* **DRUMACHOSE** and part is in
Magilligan - *see under* **MAGILLIGAN**]
[There is no chapel in Aghanloo parish]

AGHANUNSHIN, CO. DONEGAL

C.I. Aghanunshin (Raphoe diocese)
[Earliest registers destroyed in Dublin]

Baptisms, 1878-1975; marriages, 1845-1957; burials,
1878-1900; vestry minutes, 1788-1814; tithe
applotment book, 1834.   **MIC.1/214**

R.C. [Aghanunshin parish forms part of the Roman Catholic
parish of Aughnish- *see under* **AUGHNISH**]

AGHAVEA, CO. FERMANAGH

C.I. Aghavea (Clogher diocese)
Baptisms, 1815-1926; marriages, 1815-1907; burials,
1815-1986; vestry minutes, 1762-1947; list of payers,
1832 and 1834; list of clergy, 1762-87; lists of the poor,
1833-40.   **T.679/83-89;
                                                                            MIC.1/229**

Registers of vestrymen, 1870-.   **In local custody**

C.I. Tattykeeran (Clogher diocese)
Baptisms, 1857-78; marriages, 1874-8; burials, 1874-8.   **MIC.1/229**

M. Brookeborough [Wesleyan Methodists]
Baptisms, 1841-1954; marriages, 1867-1917; circuit
schedule books, 1865-1909.   **MIC.1E/28**

Baptisms, 1841-4.   **MIC.429/1/212**

R.C. Aghavea (Brookeborough) (Clogher diocese)
Baptisms, 1862-82; marriages, 1866-81 and 1896-7.   **MIC.1D/15**

AGHAVILLY CHURCH OF IRELAND PARISH,
CO. ARMAGH
[*see under* **LISNADILL**]

AGHERTON CHURCH OF IRELAND PARISH,
CO. LONDONDERRY
[*see under* **BALLYAGHRAN**]

AGHNAMULLEN, CO. MONAGHAN

C.I. Aughnamullen or Aughnamullan or Aghnamullen
(Clogher diocese)
[Earliest registers destroyed in Dublin]

Marriages, 1845-1954.   **MIC.1/129**

Baptisms, 1888-; burials, 1888-; confirmation register,
1856-.   **In local custody**

C.I. Crossduff (St Peter's Laragh) (Clogher diocese)
[Earliest registers destroyed in Dublin]

Baptisms, 1890-1946; marriages, 1845-65 and 1882-1946.   **MIC.1/130**

Baptisms, 1852-3 and 1876-89; burials, 1876-; vestry
minutes, 1870-.   **In local custody**

P. Corlea
Baptisms, 1836-1982; marriages, 1835-1955; list of
elders, 1880; lists of communicants, 1860 and 1876-8.   **MIC.1P/158**

P. Crieve
Baptisms, 1819-1953; marriages, 1845-1944; deaths, 1883-97; notes on the ordination of ministers, 1797-1915. **MIC.1P/194**

Typed list of marriages, 1846-92, and deaths, 1883-97. **C.R. 3/33**

P. Loughmourne
Baptisms, 1847-1965; marriages, 1851-1945; lists of communicants, 1847-65 and 1880-1916. **MIC.1P/193**

R.C. Aughnamullen East (Clogher diocese)
Baptisms, marriages and burials, 1857-81. **MIC.1D/19**

R.C. Aughnamullen West (Clogher diocese)
Baptisms and marriages, 1841-81. **MIC.1D/18**

AGIVEY CHURCH OF IRELAND PARISH, CO. LONDONDERRY
[Incorporated with Aghadowey - *see under* **AGHADOWEY**]

AGLISH, CO. MAYO

M. Castlebar
Baptisms, 1829-46. **MIC.429/1/155**

AHOGHILL, CO. ANTRIM
[Cullybackey used to be in Ahoghill parish but is now in Craigs parish - *see under* **CRAIGS**]

C.I. Ahoghill (Connor diocese)
Baptisms, 1811-70, with the McKinney family details from 1802; marriages, 1811-45; burials, 1811-70; banns, 1829-39. **T.679/101-105**

Vestry minutes, 1811-27, 1847-61 and 1870-; account books, 1811-30 and 1874-94; preachers' books, 1849-64, 1868-1920 and 1929-. **In local custody**

MOR. Gracehill
Diaries which record baptisms, marriages and deaths and the movement of members, 1750-1899; baptisms, 1749-1986; marriages, 1758-1862; burials, 1766-1987; Elders' Conference minutes, 1755-1892; Congregational Committee minutes, 1788-1927; Congregational Council minutes, 1790-95 and 1833-93; Lot Conference minutes, 1755-91; register of members, with an index, 1755-91; register of pupils and teachers at Gracehill Academy, 1805-83; reviews of the years' activities, including details of births, marriages and deaths, 1863-91 etc. **MIC.1F/3**

P. 1st Ahoghill
Baptisms, 1841-1922; marriages, 1841-1920; session
minutes, 1845-78.   **MIC.1P/64**

P. Brookside or 3rd Ahoghill
Baptisms, 1859-1962; marriages, 1845-1911.   **MIC.1P/95**

P. Cunningham Memorial, Cullybackey
[*see under* **CRAIGS**]

P. Trinity or 2nd Ahoghill
Baptisms, 1835-1901; marriages, 1836-1920.   **MIC.1P/136**

Typescript history of the church from the 17th century
to c.1900.   **MIC.43/B**

R.C. Ahoghill (Down and Connor diocese)
Baptisms and marriages, 1833-81; some deaths,
1833-47.   **MIC.1D/68**

[Includes Ahoghill and Craigs parishes and part of
Kirkinriola parish - *see also under* **KIRKINRIOLA**]

AHOREY PRESBYTERIAN CHURCH, CO. ARMAGH
[*see under* **KILMORE**]

ALBANY PRESBYTERIAN CHURCH, CO. TYRONE
[*see under* **BALLYCLOG**]

ALL SAINTS, CO. DONEGAL

C.I. All Saints (Raphoe diocese)
[Earliest registers destroyed in Dublin]

Baptisms, 1877-1937; marriages, 1845-97; burials,
1820-1955.   **MIC.1/176**

Vestry minutes, 1773-; preachers' books, 1857-;
register of vestrymen, 1870-.   **In local custody**

C.I. Newtowncunningham (Raphoe diocese)
Baptisms, 1877-; burials, 1820-; marriages, 1845-;
registers of vestrymen, 1870-; vestry minutes, 1873-.   **In local custody**

P. Crossroads
Baptisms, 1811-1906; marriages, 1819-40 and 1845-1956;
deaths, 1854-1903; communicants' lists, 1854-1904;
session minutes, 1859-85 and 1902-03; stipend account
book, 1815-20; church history, c.1780-1885.   **MIC.1P/259**

P. Newtowncunningham
Baptisms, 1830-1974; marriages, 1830-1944; deaths,
1880-1901.   **MIC.1P/188**

R.C. All Saints (Newtowncunningham, Drumoghill)
(Raphoe diocese)

[All Saints parish forms part of the Roman Catholic
parish of Taughboyne,Killea and Raymochy]

Baptisms, 1843-81; marriages, 1843-70.   **MIC.1D/85**

ALL SAINTS (EGLANTINE) CHURCH OF IRELAND
PARISH, CO. DOWN
[*see under* **BLARIS**]

ALT PRESBYTERIAN CHURCH, CO. DONEGAL
[*see under* **URNEY, COS TYRONE AND DONEGAL**]

ALTEDESERT CHURCH OF IRELAND PARISH,
CO. TYRONE
[Partly in Pomeroy parish and partly in Desertcreat parish -
see under **POMEROY**]

ANAGHLONE (1ST AND 2ND) PRESBYTERIAN
CHURCHES, CO. DOWN
[*see under* **ANNACLONE**]

ANAHILT PRESBYTERIAN CHURCH, CO. DOWN
[*see under* **HILLSBOROUGH**]

ANNACLONE PARISH, CO. DOWN

C.I. Annaclone (Dromore diocese)
[Earliest registers destroyed in Dublin]

Baptisms, 1878-; marriages, 1848-; burials, 1878-.   **In local custody**

Vestry minutes, 1860-1924; preachers' book, 1892-1943.   **D.2949/2**

P. 1st Anaghlone
Baptisms, 1868-1968; marriages, 1852-1925;
communicants' roll, 1868-90.   **MIC.1P/134;**
                                                             C.R.3/21-22

P. 2nd Anaghlone
Baptisms, 1839-99; communicants' roll, 1892; schedule
of investments, c.1900.   **MIC.1P/134;**
                                                             C.R.3/21-22

P. 1st and 2nd Anaghlone (United in 1890)
Baptisms, 1891-1979; communicants' roll, 1892-1953;
schedule of endowments, 1945.   **MIC.1P/134;**
                                                                 C.R.3/21-22

P. Katesbridge
[Katesbridge is in this vicinity but is actually an outlying
part of the parish of Newry]

R.C. Annaghlone (Tullyorier) (Dromore diocese)
[The head of a district which also comprises
Drumballyroney parish]

Baptisms, 1834-81; marriages, 1851-81;
burials, 1851-82.   **MIC.1D/24**

ANNAGELLIFF PARISH, CO. CAVAN

C.I. Derryheen (Kilmore diocese)
[Partly in Annagelliff parish]

Baptisms, 1879-1984; marriages, 1846-1917; burials,
1879-1983.   **MIC.1/237**

C.I. Annageliffe [*sic* Annagelliff] (Kilmore diocese)
[Held with Urney]

Baptisms, 1804-1940; marriages, 1804-1946; burials,
1804-1915; vestry minutes, 1737, 1741, 1753-99 and
1803-41.   **MIC.1/239**

R.C. Urney and Annagelliffe [*sic* Annagelliff]
(Kilmore diocese)

Baptisms, 1812-81; marriages, 1812-80.   **MIC.1D/75-76**

ANNAGH, CO. CAVAN

C.I. Annagh [or **Belturbet** or **Anna**] (Kilmore diocese)
Baptisms, 1803-1985; marriages, 1801-1916; burials,
1803-1985.   **MIC.1/240**

C.I. Cloverhill (St John's) (Kilmore diocese)
Baptisms, 1860-1985; marriages, 1860-1956.   **MIC.1/243**

C.I. Drumaloor (St Andrew's) (Kilmore diocese)
Baptisms, 1892-1983; burials, 1892-1985.   **MIC.1/241**

C.I. Killoghter [*sic* Killoughter] (Kilmore diocese)
Baptisms, 1827-1982; marriages, 1827-43; burials,
1827-1905.   **MIC.1/244**

M. Belturbet
   Baptisms, 1880-1974.   **MIC.1E/53**

P. Belturbet
   Baptisms, 1854-5 and 1894-1957; marriages, 1858-1924.   **MIC.1P/272**

R.C. Annagh (Kilmore diocese)
   Baptisms, 1875-81.   **MIC.1D/75**

ANNAGHMORE CHURCH OF IRELAND PARISH, CO. ARMAGH
   [*see under* **LOUGHGALL**]

ANNAHILT, CO. DOWN

C.I. Annahilt (Dromore diocese)
   [Earliest registers destroyed in Dublin]

   Baptisms, 1784-91; marriages, 1777; burials, 1784;
   vestry minutes, 1777-1819 and 1839-1901.   **MIC.1/101**

   Preachers' books, 1847 and 1865-72; Sunday School
   attendance books, 1869-1903; confirmations, 1871-89;
   accounts, 1850-51 and 1865-90; subscription lists,
   1875-87.   **D.2319**

   Baptisms, 1872-; marriages, 1845-; burials, 1877-.   **In local custody**

P. Cargycreevy
   Baptisms, 1887-1941; marriages, 1870-1923; communion
   roll, 1887-1925; marriage notices, 1889-1901.   **MIC.1P/358;**
                                                                MIC.1P/230/5

P. Loughaghery
   Baptisms, 1801-1939; marriages, 1801-1955; marriage
   notices, 1889-1901; burials, 1868-1917; session minutes,
   1801-96; committee minutes, 1909-35; weekly collection
   and other accounts, 1801-45; sacrament accounts, 1806-59;
   lists of communicants, 1824-60; transfer certificates,
   1808-42.   **MIC.1P/119;**
                                                                MIC.1P/230/5/2;
                                                                C.R.3/8

R.C. [Annahilt parish is part of Magheradroll or Ballynahinch
        or Dunmore Roman Catholic parish - *see under*
        MAGHERADROOL]

ANNAHILT PRESBYTERIAN CHURCH, CO. DOWN
   [*see under* **HILLSBOROUGH**]

ANNALONG CHURCH OF IRELAND PARISH, CO. DOWN
[*see under* **KILKEEL**]

ANNALONG PRESBYTERIAN CHURCH, CO. DOWN
[*see under* **KILKEEL**]

ANTRIM, CO. ANTRIM

C.I. Antrim (Connor diocese)
Baptisms, 1700-55 and 1785-1871; marriages, 1700-56,
1788-1845; burials, 1700-54 and 1786-1871.   **T.679/131-134**

Parish visiting book, 1915-16.   **D.1200/4**

M. Antrim [Wesleyan Methodists]
[Successively Ballymena Mission, Ballymena and Antrim
Mission/Circuit, Antrim and Glenavy Circuit and Antrim
Circuit]

Baptisms, 1819-1987 (circuit); marriages, 1836-60 and
1864-1915; circuit schedule books, 1860-94; minutes of
leaders' and stewards' meetings, 1855-87, with gaps;
register of members, 1826-91; seat rent ledger, 1887-1924;
collection journal, 1893-1918; annual report, 1899.   **MIC.1E/58**

Baptisms, 1829-45.   **MIC.429/1/490**

P. 1st Antrim (Millrow)
Baptisms, 1677-1733, 1753-85, 1791-2 and 1820-1960;
marriages, 1675-1736, 1820-39 and 1845-1913; deaths,
1820-35; indexes to baptisms, 1677-1733 and 1820-39,
and to marriages, 1675-1736 and 1820-39; family records
for the late 18th and 19th centuries; stipend account
books, 1837-64 and 1885-1924; communion roll, 1854-9;
Sabbath School library loan book, 1870 and 1879-81;
account books, 1821-61 and 1870-76; list of seatholders,
1838; session minutes, 1823-4; 1831-2, 1834-9 and
1842-54; a register of leaving certificates, 1842-50;
Sabbath School receipt and expenditure book, 1835-62,
with a weekly roll of teachers and salaries, 1840-41.   **MIC.1P/3; C.R.3/2**

P. 2nd Antrim (High Street)
Baptisms, 1850-1951.   **MIC.1P/346**

Marriages, 1863-92.   **In Presbyterian
                                                               Historical Society**

R.C. Antrim
Baptisms, 1873-81.   **MIC.1D/68**

[United with Drummaul up to 1873 - *see also under*
DRUMMAUL]

ARBOE, COS LONDONDERRY AND TYRONE

> **C.I. Arboe** (Armagh diocese)
> Baptisms, 1775-1813 and 1824-71; marriages, 1773-1812
> and 1824-45; burials, 1776-1813, 1827-1900 and
> 1905-06; vestry minutes, 1773-1833; list of the poor,
> 1789 and 1794; census, 1775; confirmation lists, 1775,
> 1828, 1833, 1837, 1840, 1843, 1870 and 1873; indexes
> to baptisms, 1775-1871, and marriages, 1773-1845.   **T.679/111, 115-119;**
> **D.1278**
>
> Baptisms, 1871-; marriages, 1845-; burials, 1907-; vestry
> minutes, 1834-; tithe applotment, 1826; register of
> vestrymen, 1870-; preachers' books, 1845-62 and 1869-.   **In local custody**

> **R.C. Arboe [or Ardboe]** (Archdiocese of Armagh)
> Baptisms, 1827-80; marriages, 1827-81.   **MIC.1D/34**

**ARDANGLIGGER CHURCH OF IRELAND PARISH,
CO. DONEGAL**
> [*see under* **TEMPLECRONE**]

ARDARA CHURCH OF IRELAND PARISH, CO. DONEGAL
> [*see under* **INISHKEEL**]

**ARDARA METHODIST CIRCUIT AND CHURCH,
CO. DONEGAL**
> [*see under* **INISHKEEL**]

ARDARA ROMAN CATHOLIC PARISH, CO. DONEGAL
> [*see under* **INISHKEEL**]

ARDCLINIS, CO. ANTRIM

> **C.I. Ardclinis** (Connor diocese)
> Baptisms, 1831-9 and 1877-; marriages, 1845-; burials,
> 1877-; vestry minutes, 1874-; register of vestrymen,
> 1888-.   **In local custody**

> **M. Carnlough** [Wesleyan Methodists]
> Baptisms, 1878-1915; marriages may be in with Larne
> marriages, 1863-1906; circuit schedule books, 1878-93
> and 1908-23.   **MIC.1E/39**

> **R.C.** [Ardclinis parish is in the Roman Catholic parish of Layd
> - *see under* **LAYD**].

> **R.C. Carnlough** (Down and Connor diocese)
> Baptisms, 1825-80; marriages, 1869-82.   **MIC.1D/70-71**

[Earlier marriages may be in the Glenarm registers -
see under **TICKMACREVAN**]

ARDEE, CO. LOUTH

C.I. Ardee (Armagh diocese)
Baptisms, 1732 and 1799-1868; marriages, 1744-52
and 1802-49; burials, 1742-55 and 1801-1985;
confirmations, 1824-66; vestry minutes, 1732-1802 and
1806-70; accounts, 1781-1802; list of inhabitants in
Ardee, 1760.   MIC.1/202

R.C. Ardee (Armagh diocese)
Baptisms, 1763-1810 and 1821-81; marriages, 1769-1810
and 1821-6; deaths, 1765-1810 and 1821-5.   MIC.1D/52

ARDGLASS, CO. DOWN

C.I. Ardglass (Down diocese)
[Earliest registers destroyed in Dublin]

Baptisms, 1871-; marriages, 1845-; burials, 1871-;
vestry minutes, 1897-; preachers' books, 1898-.   **In local custody**

R.C. Ardglass (Down diocese)
[Parishes of Ardglass and Dunsford form the Roman
Catholic parish of Dunsford - *see under* **DUNSFORT**]

ARDKEEN, CO. DOWN

C.I. Ardkeen (Down diocese)
Baptisms, 1745-1870; marriages, 1748-1848; burials,
1746-1875, with gaps; confirmations, 1745-1830; vestry
minutes, 1803-1930; lists of vestrymen, 1870 and
c.1912-c.1930; list of rectors, 1761-1830.   **T.679/121, 124, 247
                                                                   and 248; T.1065/28**

R.C. Ardkeen and Inishargy (Kircubbin)
(Down and Connor diocese)

[The Roman Catholic parish of Ardkeen includes most
of Ardkeen parish, Inishargy parish, St Andrew's parish
and Greyabbey parish]

Baptisms, 1828-38 and 1852-82; marriages, 1828-39
and 1852-89.   MIC.1D/74

R.C. Ballygalget
[The Roman Catholic parish of Ballygalget contains
part of Ardkeen parish - *see under* **ARDQUIN**]

ARDMORE CHURCH OF IRELAND PARISH, CO. ARMAGH
[*see under* MONTIAGHS]

ARDQUIN, CO. DOWN

C.I. Ardquin (Down diocese)
[Earliest registers destroyed in Dublin]

Baptisms, 1885-; marriages, 1846-; burials, 1887-;
vestry minutes, 1827-.   **In local custody**

R.C. Ballygalget (Down and Connor diocese)
[The Roman Catholic parish of Ballygalget contains
part of Ardquin parish, part of Ardkeen parish, and
the parishes of Castleboy and Slanes]

Baptisms, 1828-35, 1852-64 and 1866-81; marriages,
1852-82.   **MIC.1D/74**

R.C. Portaferry and Ballyphilip
[Most of Ardquin is in the Roman Catholic parish of
Portaferry and Ballyphilip - *see under* BALLYPHILIP]

ARDRAGH CHURCH OF IRELAND PARISH, CO. MONAGHAN
[*see under* MAGHEROSS]

ARDSTRAW, CO. TYRONE

C.I. Ardstraw (Derry diocese)
[Earliest registers destroyed in Dublin]

Sunday register, 1821-57, recording details of
collections, numbers attending services etc., with
occasional baptisms and publication of banns.   **T.2728**

Baptisms, 1882-; marriages, 1845-; burials, 1887-;
vestry minutes, 1872-; registers of vestrymen, 1870-;
preachers' books, 1821-.   **In local custody**

C.I. Baronscourt (Derry diocese)
[Earliest registers destroyed in Dublin]

Baptisms, 1877-; marriages, 1858-; burials, 1878;
register of vestrymen, 1870-.   **In local custody**

Sunday register, 1821-57, giving details of services.   **T.2728/1**

C.I. Drumclamph (Derry diocese)
[Earliest registers destroyed in Dublin]

Baptisms, 1877-1962; marriages, 1846-1928; burials,
1872-1943; vestry minutes, 1876-1921; register of
vestrymen, 1870-1985.   **MIC.1/304**

M. Cavandoragh [*sic* Cavandarragh][Wesleyan Methodists]
Baptisms, 1822-1961; marriages, 1874-1937.   **MIC.1E/62**

M. Coolnacrunaught [Wesleyan Methodists]
Baptisms may be included in Castlederg baptisms, 1822-.   **MIC.1E/62**

M. Lisleen [Wesleyan Methodists]
Baptisms, 1822-1961; marriages, 1883-1937.   **MIC.1E/62**

M. Newtownstewart
Baptisms, 1866-1978 [there may be baptisms for
Newtownstewart in the Omagh Circuit baptism register
from 1832 - *see* MIC1E/24]; marriages, 1890-1933;
membership register and quarterly class roll, 1863-1954;
circuit schedule book, 1866-79.   **MIC.1E/24, 26**

Baptisms, 1825-30.   **MIC.429/1/264**

P. Ardstraw
Baptisms, 1837-90; marriages, 1837-1939.   **MIC.1P/50**

P. 1st Castlederg (or Garvetagh)
Baptisms, 1823-1985; marriages, 1854-98.   **MIC.1P/73**

P. Clady
Marriages, 1845-71.   **MIC.1P/50**

P. Douglas
Baptisms, 1831-64 and 1868-1946; marriages, 1832-1936.   **MIC.1P/50, 59**

P. Drumlegagh (or 2nd Ardstraw)
Baptisms, 1865-1986; marriages, 1845-1930.   **MIC.1P/303**

P. 1st Newtownstewart
Baptisms, 1890-1903; marriages, 1845-1907.   **MIC.1P/59**

P. 2nd Newtownstewart
Baptisms, 1848 and 1861-1905; marriages, 1846-1910.   **MIC.1P/59**

P. 1st and 2nd Newtownstewart
Baptisms, 1903-85; session minutes, 1903-68.   **MIC.1P/59; T.2563**

R.C. Ardstraw East (Newstownstewart) (Derry diocese)
Baptisms, 1860-80; marriages, 1860-81.   **MIC.1D/60**

R.C. Ardstraw West (Derry diocese)
Baptisms, 1846-81; marriages, 1843-78 and 1880.   **MIC.1D/62**

R.P. Mulvin
Marriages, 1866-1905.   **MIC.1C/13**

ARDTREA ROMAN CATHOLIC PARISH, CO. TYRONE
[*see under* **ARTREA**]

ARMAGH, CO. ARMAGH

C.I. Armagh (Armagh diocese)
Baptisms, 1750-58 and 1775-1871; marriages, 1750-58
and 1776-1845; burials, 1750-58, 1770-75 and 1804-71,
with gaps; confirmations, 1824-70.   **T.679/135-156**

Baptisms, 1871-; marriages, 1845-; burials, 1872-;
vestry minutes, 1791-1872.   **In local custody**

C.I. Killylea
[*see under* **TYNAN**]

M. Armagh [Wesleyan Methodists]
Baptisms, 1872-1985 (circuit); marriages, 1863-1910. **MIC.1E/3**

Baptisms, 1845-6.   **MIC.429/1/433**

P. 1st Armagh
Baptisms, 1707-28, 1796-1803 and 1825-1949;
marriages, 1707-28, 1796-1823 and 1825-1910; lists of
seatholders, 1851, 1852 and 1857; indexes to baptisms,
1707-1803, and to marriages, 1707-1809; copies of
session accounts, 1707-32, with a list of session members,
1707.   **MIC.1P/4; D.1759/1B;
T.636/47-50**

Session accounts, 1707-32; stipend list, 1820; account
book, 1821-34.   **In Presbyterian
Historical Society**

P. 2nd Armagh
Baptisms, 1825-1915; marriages, 1825-1924.   **MIC.1P/281**

P. 3rd Armagh
Baptisms, 1837-1916; marriages, 1838-1907.   **MIC.1P/281**

P. The Mall (2nd and 3rd)
[United in 1916 and became known as 3rd and then as
the Mall]

Baptisms, 1916-86.   **MIC.1P/281**

R.C. Armagh (Armagh diocese)
Baptisms, 1796-1880; marriages, 1802-03, 1806-10 and
c.1816-1881.   **MIC.1D/41-42**

**ARMAGHBREAGUE CHURCH OF IRELAND PARISH,
CO. ARMAGH**
[*see under* **KEADY**]

ARMAGHBREAGUE PRESBYTERIAN CHURCH, CO. ARMAGH
[*see under* **KEADY**]

ARMOY, CO. ANTRIM

C.I. Armoy (Connor diocese)
[Earliest registers destroyed in Dublin]

Baptisms and burials, 1854-; marriages, 1845-; births,
marriages and burials, 1826-54; vestry minutes, 1758-.   **In local custody**

P. Armoy
Baptisms, 1842-1906; marriages, 1815-1920.   **MIC.1P/290**

R.C. Armoy (Connor diocese)
Baptisms , 1848-80; marriages, 1848-82.   **MIC.1D/69**

ARTREA, COS LONDONDERRY AND TYRONE

C.I. Artrea (Armagh diocese)
Baptisms, 1811-71, with gaps; marriages, 1811-45,
with gaps; burials, 1812-70, with gaps; confirmations,
1824, 1828, 1843, 1849, 1852, 1856, 1859 and 1863;
vestry minutes, 1812-1904; list of rectors, 1724-1914;
preachers' book, 1829-39.   **T.679/125-130**

Copy of vestry minutes, September 1730.   **T.500/3**

Baptisms, 1872-; marriages, 1845-; vestry minutes,
1773-1810; register of vestrymen, 1870-; preachers'
books, 1845-60 and 1882-.   **In local custody**

C.I. Ballyeglish (Armagh diocese)
[Formed out of Artrea and Tamlaght]

Baptisms, 1868-71; burials, 1868-77; confirmations,
1879, 1882 and 1888.   **T.679/174-175**

Baptisms, 1872-; marriages, 1868-; burials, 1878-;
vestry minutes, 1868-; confirmations, 1894; registers of
vestrymen, 1870-.   **In local custody**

C.I. Woods Chapel (Armagh diocese)
Baptisms, 1807 (or 1808)-97; marriages, 1808-45;
burials, 1808-89; vestry minutes, 1792-1895; poor
list, 1818; seat list, 1826; confirmations, 1809, 1816,
1824, 1837, 1840, 1843, 1846, 1849, 1856, 1859, 1866,
1870 and 1876.   **MIC.1/97**

Census of the parish, 1829.   **T.308**

Baptisms, 1897-; marriages, 1845-; burials, 1889-;
confirmations, 1876-; graveyard map and list, 1913.   **In local custody**

MOR. Gracefield
    Diaries, 1759-1902, with gaps; baptisms, 1750-1931;
    marriages, 1814-44, 1852 and 1869-1909; burials,
    1765-1930; register of members with an index,
    1759-1873, with gaps etc.   **MIC.1F/3**

P. 1st Moneymore
    Baptisms, 1827-1959; marriages, 1827-34 and 1845-1936;
    communion rolls, 1882 and 1902.   **MIC.1P/339**

P. 2nd Moneymore
    Baptisms, 1845-1949; marriages, 1868-1910.   **MIC.1P/340**

P. Salterstown
    Baptisms, 1847-; marriages, 1845-.   **In local custody**

R.C. Ardtrea and Desertlin (Moneymore) (Armagh diocese)
    Baptisms, 1832-4, 1838-43 and 1854-1939;
    marriages, 1830-43 and 1854-1937, with gaps.   **MIC.1D/35;
                                                              T.3050**

ARVAGH CHURCH OF IRELAND PARISH, CO. CAVAN
    [*see under* **KILLASHANDRA**]

ASHFIELD CHURCH OF IRELAND PARISH, CO. CAVAN
    [*see under* **KILDRUMSHERDAN**]

ATHLONE, CO. WESTMEATH

M. Athlone
    Baptisms, 1833-45.   **MIC.429/1/117**

AUGHENTAINE PRESBYTERIAN CHURCH, CO. TYRONE
    [*see under* **CLOGHER**]

**AUGHER (ST MARK'S) CHURCH OF IRELAND PARISH,
CO. TYRONE**
    [*see under* **CLOGHER**]

AUGHEYARREN METHODIST CHURCH, CO. TYRONE
    [*see under* **TERMONAMONGAN**]

AUGHINTAINE ROMAN CATHOLIC PARISH, CO. TYRONE
    [*see under* **CLOGHER**]

AUGHNACLOY METHODIST CHURCH, CO. TYRONE
[*see under* CARNTEEL]

AUGHNACLOY PRESBYTERIAN CHURCH, CO. TYRONE
[*see under* CARNTEEL]

**AUGHNACLOY ROMAN CATHOLIC CHAPEL,
CO. TYRONE**
[*see under* AGHALOO]

AUGHNAMULLEN, CO. MONAGHAN
[*see under* AGHNAMULLEN]

AUGHNISH, CO. DONEGAL

    C.I. Aughnish or Tullyaughnish (Raphoe diocese)
    [Includes Tullyfern]

    Baptisms, 1798-1820 and 1823-1983; marriages,
    1788-1818 and 1823-1935; burials, 1798-1818 and
    1823-1983; confirmations, 1886-1980; preachers'
    books, 1870-1920; account book, 1819-70;
    clergyman's visiting book, c.1860; register of members
    and minutes of the Diocesan Temperance Society and
    the Band of Hope in the parish, 1876-96.   **MIC.1/167**

    C.I. Glenalla (Raphoe diocese)
    Baptisms, 1871-1983; marriages, 1871-1951; burials,
    1906-81; vestry minutes, 1870-87 and 1923-52.   **MIC.1/195**

    C.I. Milford (Raphoe diocese)
    Baptisms, 1880-1981; marriages, 1860-1949; burials,
    1902-76; preachers' books, 1855-73.   **MIC.1/194**

    M. Ramelton [Wesleyan Methodists]
    Baptisms, 1829-1867 (Ramelton and Stranorlar Mission
    Station); circuit schedule books, 1865-81; circuit
    stewards' book, 1872-81.   **MIC.1E/46**

    Baptisms, 1830-41.   **MIC.429/1/504**

    P. 1st Ramelton
    Baptisms, 1806-1904; marriages, 1807-1944; session
    minutes, 1828-1907; committee minutes, 1862-1905;
    communicants' lists, 1807-57; stipend accounts,
    1806-37.   **MIC.1P/142**

    P. 2nd Ramelton
    Baptisms, 1808-11 and 1823-1911; marriages, 1808-10
    and 1824-1910; communicants' rolls, 1859-1911.   **MIC.1P/210**

P. 3rd Ramelton
  Baptisms, 1839-1902; marriages, 1839-44 and
  1846-1926; burials, 1839-40 and 1850-65; names of
  emigrants, 1839-42 and 1850-54; session minutes,
  1888-1962; committee minutes, 1902-62; communion
  rolls, 1858-1901. **MIC.1P/209**

R.C. Aughnish (Ramelton) (Raphoe diocese)
  Baptisms and marriages, 1873-81. **MIC.1D/85**

BADONY, CO. TYRONE
  [*see under* **BODONEY**]

BAILIEBOROUGH, CO. CAVAN

C.I. Bailieborough (Kilmore diocese)
  Baptisms, 1824-1985; marriages, 1809-1944; burials,
  1809-1915; list of preachers, 1825-7; map of Lisnalea
  and Greagharue, Co. Cavan, 1809. **MIC.1/252**

M. Bailieborough [Wesleyan Methodists]
  Baptisms, 1879-1970; marriages, 1887-1952; register of
  members, 1838-72; accounts, 1835-42. **MIC.1E/49, 54**

  [There are probably baptisms for Bailieborough in Cootehill
  Circuit records, 1835-6, 1843-6 and 1846-78]

  Baptisms, 1835-41. **MIC.429/1/95**

P. 1st Bailieborough or Corglass
  Baptisms, 1861-1983; marriages, 1845-1955. **MIC.1P/145**

P. 2nd Bailieborough or Trinity
  Baptisms, 1863-1983; marriages, 1845-1952. **MIC.1P/143**

R.C. Killann (Bailieborough) (Kilmore diocese)
  Baptisms, 1835-49 and 1868-80; marriages, 1835-50
  and 1868-80. **MIC.1D/82**

BALLAGHAMEEHAN CHURCH OF IRELAND
PARISH, CO. LEITRIM
  [*see under* **ROSSINVER**]

BALLEE, CO. DOWN

C.I. Ballee (Down diocese)
  Baptisms, 1792-1871; marriages, 1807, 1821 and
  1823-44; burials, 1816, 1823-42 and 1851-72; marriage
  notices, 1845-58. **T.679/157-159; D.2319**

N.S.P. Ballee
> Baptisms, 1811-1985; marriages, 1819-1936; marriage
> notice book, 1845-1910; committee minutes, 1860-83
> and 1936-63; stipend account book, 1872-87; file of
> accounts and memorabilia, c.1870-1982.   **MIC.1B/3**

R.C. Ballee and Ballyculter(Down and Connor diocese)
> [The Roman Catholic parish of Ballee and Ballyculter
> contains Ballee parish and part of Ballyculter parish]
>
> Baptisms, 1844-64 and 1870-81; marriages, 1843-82.   **MIC.1D/73**

BALLEEK CHURCH OF IRELAND PARISH, CO. ARMAGH
> [*see under* **LOUGHGILLY**]

BALLEEK ROMAN CATHOLIC PARISH, CO. ARMAGH
> [*see under* **LOUGHGILLY**]

BALLENON REFORMED PRESBYTERIAN CHURCH, CO. ARMAGH
> [*see under* **LOUGHGILLY**]

BALLINA METHODIST CHURCH, CO. MAYO
> [*see under* **KILMOREMOY**]

BALLINACOR METHODIST CHURCH, CO. ARMAGH
> [*see under* **SEAGOE**]

BALLINAMALLARD METHODIST CHURCH, CO. FERMANAGH
> [*see under* **MAGHERACROSS**]

BALLINAMORE ROMAN CATHOLIC CHURCH, CO. LEITRIM
> [*see under* **OUGHTERAGH**]

BALLINDERRY, CO. ANTRIM

C.I. Ballinderry (Connor diocese)
> Baptisms, 1806-71; marriages, 1805-45; burials,
> 1823-71; vestry minutes, 1790-1870 and 1929; extracts
> from baptisms relating to the Higgins family, 1806-37.   **T.679/160-170; T.1572**

MOR. Ballinderry
Baptisms, 1754-1817; marriages, 1784-1800; register of
members, 1755-1816; ministers' diaries, 1768, 1803-04,
1810-17 and 1842-90, which include baptisms, marriages
and deaths, and lists of members.   **MIC.1F/1**

P. Ballinderry
Copy of financial report showing the amount paid by each
seatholder to stipend and to the Sustentation fund, 1888-9.   **C.R.3/20**

R.C. Aghagallon (Down and Connor diocese)
[Part of Ballinderry parish is in the Roman Catholic
parish of Aghagallon - *see under* **AGHAGALLON**
and part is in the Roman Catholic parish of Glenavy -
see under **GLENAVY**]

BALLINDERRY, COS LONDONDERRY AND TYRONE

C.I. Ballinderry (Armagh diocese)
Baptisms, 1802-71; marriages, 1803-45; burials, 1802-71;
confirmation lists, 1824-1921; banns, 1813-92; list of
rectors, 1616-1951; notes on men who served in the
1st World War.   **T.679/171-172, 178**

Vestry minutes, 1773-; preachers' books, 1845-.   **In local custody**

R.C. Ballinderry (Armagh diocese)
Baptisms, 1826-39 and 1841-81; marriages, 1827-80.   **MIC.1D/32**

BALLINDRAIT PRESBYTERIAN CHURCH, CO. DONEGAL
[*see under* **CLONLEIGH**]

BALLINTEMPLE, CO. CAVAN

C.I. Ballintemple (Kilmore diocese)
Baptisms, 1880-1955; marriages, 1845-1952; burials,
1880-1925.   **MIC.1/256**

R.C. Ballintemple (Kilmore diocese)
Baptisms and marriages, 1862-81.   **MIC.1D/76**

BALLINTOY, CO. ANTRIM

C.I. Ballintoy (Connor diocese)
[Earliest registers destroyed in Dublin]

Marriages, 1845-59; burials, 1872-98; vestry minutes,
1712-1843; poor lists, 1790 and 1819-43; census,
1803.   **T.679/68-69;**
                                                                     MIC.1/111

C.I. Dunseverick (Connor diocese)
[Formed out of Billy and Ballintoy parishes]

Baptisms, 1832-95; marriages, 1833-45; burials,
1833-72; vestry minutes, 1830-76.   **T.679/71-72;
                                                      MIC.1/34/3**

Plans of the church, 1811.   **T.1124**

Baptisms, 1895-; marriages, 1845-; burials, 1872-;
preachers' books, 1861-.   **In local custody**

P. Toberkeigh
Baptisms, 1829-1944; marriages, 1830-1907;
communicants' rolls, 1830-74 and 1891-1945.   **MIC.1P/378**

R.C. Ballintoy (Down and Connor diocese)
[United with Armoy]

Baptisms and marriages, 1872-82.   **MIC.1D/69**

[Earlier baptisms and marriages may be in the
Armoy registers]

BALLINTRA METHODIST CHURCH, CO. DONEGAL
[*see under* **DRUMHOME**]

**BALLINTRA ROMAN CATHOLIC CHURCH,
CO. DONEGAL**
[*see under* **DRUMHOME**]

BALLYAGHRAN, CO. LONDONDERRY

C.I. Agherton (Connor diocese)
[Earliest registers destroyed in Dublin]

Baptisms, 1845-56, 1859 and 1873-95; marriages,
1845-1928; burials, 1874-1983; vestry minutes,
1875-1905.   **MIC.1/306**

Preachers' books, 1840-53 and 1889-; registers of
vestrymen, 1883-.   **In local custody**

Report and accounts, 1898.   **D.2800/14**

M. Portstewart
Baptisms, 1831-1987; marriages, 1864-1937(Coleraine)-
Portstewart marriages may be in with Coleraine.   **MIC.1E/63**

P. Portstewart
Baptisms, 1829-1927; marriages, 1846-1905; session
minutes, 1826-1923; committee minutes, 1871-1900.   **MIC.1P/83**

R.C. Coleraine
[Ballyaghran parish forms part of the Roman Catholic
parish of Coleraine - *see under* **COLERAINE** and
part of the Roman Catholic parish of Portrush -
see under **BALLYWILLIN**]

BALLYALBANY PRESBYTERIAN CHURCH, CO. MONAGHAN
[*see under* **TEDAVNET**]

BALLYARNET PRESBYTERIAN CHURCH, CO. LONDONDERRY
[*see under* **TEMPLEMORE**]

BALLYBAY, CO. MONAGHAN

C.I. Ballybay (Clogher diocese)
Baptisms, 1813-1981; marriages, 1822-1952;
burials, 1823-1983; vestry minutes, 1804-88;
confirmation list, 1831.   **MIC.1/150**

M. Ballybay
Baptisms, 1877-1910; marriages, 1877-1955; register of
members of Ballybay Band of Hope, 1894-1910.   **MIC.1E/54**

P. 1st Ballybay
Baptisms, 1834-1982; marriages, 1834-44 and 1849-1956.   **MIC.1P/171**

Baptisms, 1799-1837.   **In Presbyterian
Historical Society**

P. 2nd Ballybay
Baptisms, 1833-1918; marriages, 1845-1906.   **MIC.1P/197; C.R.3/28**

P. Derryvalley
Baptisms, 1816-1928; marriages, 1833-1953; lists of
communicants, 1839-1911.   **MIC.1P/173**

R.C. Tullycorbet (Ballybay) (Clogher diocese)
[Ballybay parish is part of the Roman Catholic
parish of Tullycorbet - *see under* **TULLYCORBET**]

BALLYBLACK PRESBYTERIAN CHURCH, CO. DOWN
[*see under* **NEWTOWNARDS**]

BALLYCAIRN PRESBYTERIAN CHURCH, CO. DOWN
[*see under* **DRUMBO**]

BALLYCARRY NON-SUBSCRIBING PRESBYTERIAN CHURCH, CO. ANTRIM
[*see under* **TEMPLECORRAN**]

BALLYCARRY PRESBYTERIAN CHURCH, CO. ANTRIM
[*see under* **TEMPLECORRAN**]

BALLYCASTLE METHODIST CHURCH, CO. ANTRIM
[*see under* **RAMOAN**]

BALLYCASTLE PRESBYTERIAN CHURCH, CO. ANTRIM
[*see under* **RAMOAN**]

BALLYCASTLE ROMAN CATHOLIC CHURCH, CO. ANTRIM
[*see under* **RAMOAN**]

BALLYCLABBER REFORMED PRESBYTERIAN CHURCH, CO. LONDONDERRY
[*see under* **COLERAINE**]

BALLYCLARE METHODIST CHURCHES, CO. ANTRIM
[Wesleyan Methodists and New Connexion]
[*see under* **DOAGH, GRANGE OF**]

BALLYCLARE NON-SUBSCRIBING PRESBYTERIAN CHURCH, CO. ANTRIM
[*see under* **DOAGH, GRANGE OF**]

BALLYCLARE PRESBYTERIAN CHURCH, CO. ANTRIM
[*see under* **DOAGH, GRANGE OF**]

BALLYCLARE REFORMED PRESBYTERIAN CHURCH, CO. ANTRIM
[*see under* **DOAGH, GRANGE OF**]

BALLYCLARE ROMAN CATHOLIC PARISH, CO. ANTRIM
[*see under* **DOAGH, GRANGE OF**]

BALLYCLOG, CO. TYRONE

C.I. Ballyclog (Armagh diocese)
Baptisms, 1818-1929; marriages, 1818-1932; burials,
1818-90; preachers' books, 1876-1966; vestry minutes,
1828-1926; Sustentation Fund account book, 1870-97.   **T.679/42, 182-183;
C.R.1/42**

Burials, 1891-.   **In local custody**

P. Albany
Baptisms, 1841-1925; committee minutes, 1842-1943;
session minutes, 1841-1917 and 1960; list of contributions
to the stipend of the church, 1860-61, and payments,
1861-2.   **MIC.1P/13; T.1736/2**

P. Brigh
Baptisms, 1837-1925; marriages, 1837-1920; burials,
1884-1912; session minutes, 1826-82; committee minutes,
1835-41 and 1885-1930; communicants' roll, 1842-1929
(from 1889 arranged by townland); family worship lists,
1854-81; collections, 1840-42.   **MIC.1P/13;
D.1759/1D/1**

R.C. [Ballyclog parish is part of the Roman Catholic parish of
Stewartstown - *see under* **DONAGHENRY**]

BALLYCLUG, CO. ANTRIM

C.I. Ballyclug (Connor diocese)
Baptisms, 1841-71; marriages, 1841-4; burials, 1841-71.   **T.679/179-180**

Baptisms, 1871-; marriages, 1845-; preachers' books,
1841-67, 1879-83 and 1899-.   **In local custody**

R.C. Crebilly
[Ballyclug parish is part of the Roman Catholic parish
of Kirkinriola and has a chapel at Crebilly - *see under*
KIRKINRIOLA]

BALLYCONNELL METHODIST CHURCH, CO. CAVAN
[*see under* **TOMREGAN**]

BALLYCOPELAND PRESBYTERIAN CHURCH, CO. DOWN
[*see under* **DONAGHADEE**]

BALLYCOR, CO. ANTRIM

C.I. Ballyeaston (Connor diocese)
[In Ballycor and Rashee parishes]

[Earliest records destroyed in Dublin]

Baptisms, 1866-; marriages, 1845-; burials, 1888-;   **In local custody**
preachers' books, 1888-.

P. 1st Ballyeaston
Baptisms, 1814-1924; marriages, 1813-90; indexes to
baptisms, 1814-1924.   **MIC.1P/24, 408, 420;
                                                             C.R.3/17, 51**

P. 2nd Ballyeaston
Baptisms, 1821-61, 1865-7 and 1883-1967; marriages,
1826-41 and 1845-1936; burials, 1842-9 and 1901-18;
committee minutes, 1869-1941; session minutes, 1862-1956;
communicants' lists, 1847-58; accounts, 1893-1903; seat
list, c.1870; list of stipend payers, 1873-91.   **MIC.1P/124**

R.C. [Ballycor parish was part of the Roman Catholic parish
of Larne and Carrickfergus - *see under* **LARNE** and
then became part of the Roman Catholic parish of
Ballyclare - *see under* **RALOO**]

BALLYCULTER, CO. DOWN

C.I. Ballyculter (Down diocese)
Baptisms, 1777-1870; marriages, 1812-45; burials,
1812-71; marriages notices, 1845-65.   **D.2319; T.679/49, 176-
                                                             177**

Baptisms, 1871-; marriages, 1846-; vestry minutes,
1814-; preachers' books, 1882-.   **In local custody**

P. Strangford
Baptisms, 1846-; marriages, 1848-.   **In local custody**

R.C. Ballee and Ballyculter (Down and Connor diocese)
[Part of Ballyculter parish is in the Roman Catholic
parish of Ballee and Ballyculter - *see under* **BALLEE**
and part is in the Roman Catholic parish of Saul -
see under **SAUL**]

BALLYDOWN PRESBYTERIAN CHURCH, CO. DOWN
[*see under* **SEAPATRICK**]

**BALLYEASTON CHURCH OF IRELAND PARISH,
CO. ANTRIM**
[*see under* **BALLYCOR**]

**BALLYEASTON (1ST AND 2ND) PRESBYTERIAN
CHURCHES, CO. ANTRIM**
[*see under* **BALLYCOR**]

**BALLYEDERLAND METHODIST CHURCH,
CO. DONEGAL**
    [*see under* **KILLAGHTEE**]

**BALLYEGLISH CHURCH OF IRELAND PARISH,
CO. TYRONE**
    [*see under* **ARTREA**]

BALLYFRENIS PRESBYTERIAN CHURCH, CO. DOWN
    [*see under* **DONAGHADEE**]

BALLYGALGET ROMAN CATHOLIC PARISH, CO. DOWN
    [*see under* **ARDQUIN**]

**BALLYGAWLEY CHURCH OF IRELAND PARISH,
CO. TYRONE**
    [*see under* **CARNTEEL**]

**BALLYGAWLEY PRESBYTERIAN CHURCH,
CO. TYRONE**
    [*see under* **ERRIGAL KEEROGUE**]

BALLYGILBERT PRESBYTERIAN CHURCH, CO. DOWN
    [*see under* **BANGOR**]

BALLYGONEY PRESBYTERIAN CHURCH, CO. TYRONE
    [*see under* **TAMLAGHT**]

BALLYGOWAN PRESBYTERIAN CHURCH, CO. DOWN
    [*see under* **KILLINCHY**]

**BALLYGOWAN ROMAN CATHOLIC CHURCH,
CO. ANTRIM**
    [*see under* **LARNE**]

BALLYGRAINEY PRESBYTERIAN CHURCH, CO. DOWN
    [*see under* **BANGOR**]

**BALLYHAGAN RELIGIOUS SOCIETY OF FRIENDS,
CO. ARMAGH**
    [*see under* **KILMORE, CO. ARMAGH**]

**BALLYHALBERT CHURCH OF IRELAND PARISH,
CO. DOWN**
   [*see under* ST ANDREW'S]

**BALLYHOBRIDGE PRESBYTERIAN CHURCH,
CO. MONAGHAN**
   [*see under* DRUMMULLY]

**BALLYHOLME CHURCH OF IRELAND PARISH,
CO. DOWN**
   [*see under* BANGOR]

BALLYHOLME METHODIST CHURCH, CO. DOWN
   [*see under* BANGOR]

**BALLYJAMESDUFF CHURCH OF IRELAND PARISH,
CO. CAVAN**
   [*see under* CASTLERAHAN]

BALLYJAMESDUFF METHODIST CHURCH, CO. CAVAN
   [*see under* CASTLERAHAN]

**BALLYJAMESDUFF PRESBYTERIAN CHURCH,
CO. CAVAN**
   [*see under* CASTLERAHAN]

BALLYKEEL BAPTIST CHURCH, CO. DOWN
   [*see under* DROMORE]

**BALLYKELLY PRESBYTERIAN CHURCH,
CO. LONDONDERRY**
   [*see under* TAMLAGHT FINLAGAN]

BALLYKINLER, CO. DOWN

   C.I. Ballykinler (Down diocese)
      [An impropriate rectory linked to Christ Church,
      Dublin.]

   R.C. Tyrella and Ballykinlar (Down and Connor diocese)
      [*see under* TYRELLA]

**BALLYLENNON (1ST, 2ND AND 3RD) PRESBYTERIAN
CHURCHES, CO. DONEGAL**
   [*see under* TAUGHBOYNE]

BALLYLINNY, CO. ANTRIM

    C.I. Ballylinny (Connor diocese)
        [United to Carnmoney - *see under* **CARNMONEY**]

    P. Ballylinny
        Baptisms, 1837-1922; marriages, 1837-1900.   MIC.1P/327; C.R.3/16

    R.C. [This parish was part of the Roman Catholic district of
        Larne and Carrickfergus - *see under* **LARNE AND**
        CARRICKFERGUS and later of the Roman Catholic
        parish of Ballyclare - *see under* **RALOO**]

**BALLYLINTAGH PRESBYTERIAN CHURCH,
CO. LONDONDERRY**
    [*see under* **AGHADOWEY**]

**BALLYMACALENY CHURCH OF IRELAND PARISH,
CO. CAVAN**
    [*see under* **SCRABBY**]

**BALLYMACARRETT CHURCH OF IRELAND PARISH,
CO. DOWN**
    [*see under* **KNOCKBREDA**]

**BALLYMACARRETT (1ST) PRESBYTERIAN CHURCH,
CO. DOWN**
    [*see under* **KNOCKBREDA**]

**BALLYMACARRETT ROMAN CATHOLIC PARISH,
CO. DOWN**
    [*see under* **KNOCKBREDA**]

BALLYMACHUGH, CO. CAVAN

    C.I. Ballymachugh (Kilmore diocese)
        Baptisms, 1816-1932; marriages, 1815-1901; burials,
        1816-1986.   MIC.1/271

**BALLYMACNAB ROMAN CATHOLIC PARISH,
CO. ARMAGH**
    [*see under* **KILCLOONEY**]

**BALLYMAGRANE PRESBYTERIAN CHURCH,
CO. TYRONE**
    [*see under* **AGHALOO**]

BALLYMARTIN, CO. ANTRIM

    C.I. Ballymartin (Connor diocese)
        [Part of the union of Carnmoney - *see under*
        CARNMONEY]

BALLYMASCANLON, CO. LOUTH

    R.C. Lordship and Ballymascanlon (Ravensdale)
    (Armagh diocese)

        Baptisms, 1838-81; marriages, 1838-80.   MIC.1D/46-47

        [Part of Ballymascanlon parish is in the Roman Catholic
        parish of Faughart - *see also under* **FAUGHART**]

BALLYMENA BAPTIST CHURCH, CO. ANTRIM
    [*see under* **KIRKINRIOLA**]

**BALLYMENA CONGREGATIONAL CHURCH,
CO. ANTRIM**
    [*see under* **KIRKINRIOLA**]

**BALLYMENA METHODIST CIRCUIT AND CHURCH,
CO. ANTRIM**
    [*see under* **KIRKINRIOLA**]

**BALLYMENA NON-SUBSCRIBING PRESBYTERIAN
CHURCH, CO. ANTRIM**
    [*see under* **KIRKINRIOLA**]

**BALLYMENA (1ST, 2ND, WELLINGTON STREET
AND WEST CHURCH) PRESBYTERIAN CHURCHES,
CO. ANTRIM**
    [*see under* **KIRKINRIOLA**]

**BALLYMENA ROMAN CATHOLIC CHURCH,
CO. ANTRIM**
    [*see under* **KIRKINRIOLA**]

BALLYMODAN, CO. CORK

    M. Bandon Circuit
        Baptisms, 1824-44.   MIC.429/1/29

BALLYMONEY, CO. ANTRIM

C.I. Ballymoney (Connor diocese)
Baptisms, 1807-98; marriages, 1807-45; burials,
1807-88; vestry minutes, 1821-1932.   **T.679/195-201**

M. Ballymoney [in Coleraine Circuit]
Baptisms, 1831-1987; marriages, 1864-1929.   **MIC.1E/63**

P. 1st Ballymoney
Baptisms, 1751-71, with gaps, and 1817-1926;
marriages, 1817-1926; session minutes, c.1733-1734,
1827-66 and 1890-1900; committee minutes, 1824-1919;
register of families, 1817; communicants' roll, 1881-6
and 1890-97; poor accounts, 1751-9; account book
containing details of subscriptions for a memorial to the
Rev. Robert Park, minister of 1st Ballymoney, 1876.   **MIC.1P/363; C.R.3/1**

Marriage notices, 1862-1911.   **MIC.1P/117**

P. St James' or 2nd Ballymoney
[After 1840 known as **3rd Ballymoney**]

Baptisms, 1835-1940; marriages, 1835-1903.   **MIC.1P/266**

Marriage notices, 1862-1911.   **MIC.1P/117**

P. Trinity, Ballymoney
Marriages, 1845-1921.   **MIC.1P/35**

P. Drumreagh
Baptisms, 1864-1906; marriages, 1845-1912; session
minutes, 1878-1944; communicants' lists, 1864-1906.   **MIC.1P/374**

Marriage notices, 1862-1911.   **MIC.1P/117**

P. Garryduff
Baptisms, 1885-1985; marriages, 1851-1936.   **MIC.1P/265**

P. Roseyards
Marriages, 1845-.   **In local custody**

R.C. Ballymoney (Down and Connor diocese)
[United with Dunluce]

Baptisms, 1853-82; marriages, 1853-79.   **MIC.1D/69A**

BALLYMORE, CO. ARMAGH

B. Poyntzpass
Roll book, 1894.   **In local custody**

B. Tandragee [*sic* Tanderagee] **and Fivemilehill**
    Marriages, 1872-; burials, 1874-; minutes, 1864-.   **In local custody**

C.I. Acton (Armagh diocese)
    [Earliest registers destroyed in Dublin]

    Baptisms, 1877-; marriages, 1845-; burials, 1877-;
    vestry minutes, 1793-; preachers' books, 1858-.   **In local custody**

C.I. Ballymore (Armagh diocese)
    Baptisms, 1783-1871, which include a list of
    Presbyterians baptised, 1822-31; marriages, 1783-1850;
    burials, 1783-1871; vestry minutes, 1771-1810; vestry
    account book, 1821-7; confirmations, 1843, 1846, 1849,
    1852 and 1856; estate rental for the manors of
    Ballymore, Acton, Clare etc., possibly used for tithe or
    cess purposes, 1812-27; history of the church from
    the 17th century.   **T.679/52, 203-205,**
                                                         270-271; T.2706/8

    Baptisms, 1871-; marriages, 1846-; burials, 1871-;
    vestry minutes, 1820-.   **In local custody**

C.I. Clare (Armagh diocese)
    [Partly in Ballymore parish]

    [Earliest records destroyed in Dublin]

    Baptisms, 1880-; marriages, 1845-; burials, 1880-.   **In local custody**

M. Tandragee [*sic* Tanderagee] **and Fivemilehill**
    [Wesleyan Methodists]

    Baptisms, 1836-1981; marriages, 1838-45 and
    1863-1937.   **MIC.1E/5**

    Baptisms, 1819-42.   **MIC.429/1/477**

P. Clare
    Baptisms, 1824-1945; marriages, 1825-1936.   **MIC.1P/329**

P. Cromore
    Baptisms, 1831-; marriages, 1832-.   **In local custody**

P. Poyntzpass
    Baptisms, 1850-; marriages, 1846-.   **In local custody**

P. Tandragee [*sic* Tanderagee]
    Baptisms, 1835-1913; marriages, 1835-1916.   **MIC.1P/258**

P. Tyrone's Ditches
    Registers from 1864.   **In local custody**

R.C. Ballymore and Mullabrack (Tandragee)
(Armagh diocese)

Baptisms, and marriages, 1843-56 and 1859-80.   **MIC.1D/37**

BALLYMOYER CHURCH OF IRELAND PARISH, CO. ARMAGH
[*see under* **BALLYMYRE**]

BALLYMYRE, CO. ARMAGH

C.I. Ballymoyer (Armagh diocese)
Baptisms, 1820-73 and 1926-7; marriages, 1820-45;
burials, 1820-70; vestry minutes, 1821-99;
confirmations, 1824, 1828, 1833, 1837, 1840 and 1843.   **T.679/202, 231;**
                                                                  MIC.1/113

Baptisms, 1927-; marriages, 1846-; burials, 1871-.   **In local custody**

C.I. Balleek
[Linked to Ballymoyer Parish Church but formed out
of Loughgilly parish - *see under* **LOUGHGILLY**]

R.C. [*see under* **LOUGHGILLY**]

BALLYNAHATTY, (1ST AND 2ND) PRESBYTERIAN CHURCHES, CO. MONAGHAN
[*see under* **DRUMRAGH**]

BALLYNAHINCH (1ST, 2ND AND 3RD) PRESBYTERIAN CHURCHES, CO. DOWN
[*see under* **MAGHERADROOL**]

BALLYNAHINCH ROMAN CATHOLIC CHURCH, CO. DOWN
[*see under* **MAGHERADROOL**]

BALLYNASCREEN, CO. LONDONDERRY

C.I. Ballynascreen (or Ballinascreen) (Derry diocese)
Baptisms, 1808-19 and 1824-71; marriages, 1825-6 and
1828-45; burials, 1824-73; census, 1842 and 1888; list
of rectors, 1622-1952; list of preachers, 1825-42.   **T.679/45, 206-208, 227**

Parish reports, 1870; lists of subscribers to the building
fund, 1887.   **T.1713/2-3**

Baptisms, 1872-; marriages, 1845-; burials, 1874-; vestry minutes, 1808-.   **In local custody**

C.I. St Anne's, Sixtowns (Derry Diocese)
[Originally a chapel of ease in Ballinascreen]

[Earliest records destroyed in Dublin]

Visitation report, 1867 and 1870.   **T.1713/1**

Baptisms, 1877-; marriages, 1881-; burials, 1878-.   **In local custody**

P. Draperstown
Baptisms,1837-1947; marriages, 1837-44 and 1878-1923;
session minutes, 1845-86; communicants' lists, 1871,
1875-9 and 1883.   **MIC.1P/343**

R.C. Ballinascreen (Draperstown) (Derry diocese)
Baptisms, 1836 and 1846-81; marriages, 1834-85;
funerals, 1831-2 and 1848-51.   **MIC.1D/59**

BALLYNURE, CO. ANTRIM

C.I. Ballynure (Connor diocese)
Baptisms, 1812-72; marriages, 1803-45; burials, 1840
and 1852-80.   **T.679/209-213**

Baptisms, 1873-; marriages, 1845-; burials, 1881-;
vestry minutes, 1818-; preachers' books, 1854-.   **In local custody**

C. Straid
Baptisms, 1837-1915; marriages, 1839-65; deaths, 1839;
lists of members with details of emigration, 1837-50.   **C.R. 7/9**

M. Ballynure
Baptisms, 1843-; marriages, 1864-76.   **In local custody**

P. Ballynure
Baptisms, 1819-1918; marriages, 1819-99.   **MIC.1P/103**

R.C. Ballyclare
[*see under* **LARNE and CARRICKFERGUS**
and *also under* **RALOO**]

BALLYPHILIP, CO. DOWN

C.I. Ballyphilip (Down diocese)
Baptisms, 1745-1871; marriages, 1746-1844; marriage
notices, 1851-65; burials, 1745-1883; poor lists, 1808-13.   **T.679/218-221, 226;
D.2319**

Baptisms, 1872-; marriages, 1845-; vestry minutes,
1751-; register of vestrymen, 1870-; preachers' books,
1886-. **In local custody**

M. Portaferry (Newtownards Circuit)
Baptisms, 1870-c.1880; circuit schedule book, 1870-78. **D.2687**

P. Portaferry
Baptisms, 1699-1786 and 1822-1953; marriages,
1750-84 and 1822-1936; marriage notice books,
1879-1906; burials, 1836-1989; list of members who
emigrated, 1852-72; communicants' roll, 1870; receipts
and accounts, 1841-1916; title deeds and legal papers,
1778-1893; testamentary papers, 1812-69.

**MIC.1P/137;
MIC.1P/230/6; T.1634;
D.2709/2; C.R.3/24**

R.C. Ballyphilip and Portaferry (Down and Connor diocese)
[Contains most of the civil parishes of Ardquin,
Ballyphilip and Ballytrustan]

Baptisms, marriages and some funerals, 1843-81. **MIC.1D/74**

BALLYRASHANE, COS ANTRIM AND LONDONDERRY

C.I. Ballyrashane (Connor diocese)
[Earliest registers destroyed in Dublin]

Baptisms, 1877-; marriages, 1846-; burials, 1877-;
vestry minutes, 1827-; churchwardens' account books,
1828-; preachers' books, 1827-. **In local custody**

P. Ballyrashane
Baptisms, 1863-1928; marriages, 1846-1936. **MIC.1P/70**

P. Ballywatt
(Known as 2nd Ballyrashane before 1871)

Baptisms, 1867-1927; marriages, 1845-1914. **MIC.1P/379**

R.C. [*see under* COLERAINE and *also under* BALLYWILLIN]

BALLYREAGH PRESBYTERIAN CHURCH, CO. TYRONE
[*see under* CARNTEEL]

BALLYRONEY PRESBYTERIAN CHURCH, CO. DOWN
[*see under* DRUMBALLYRONEY]

BALLYSCULLION, COS ANTRIM AND LONDONDERRY

C.I. Ballyscullion (Derry and Connor dioceses)
[Earliest registers destroyed in Dublin]

Baptisms, 1863-; marriages, 1845-; burials, 1891-;
vestry minutes, 1876-; register of vestrymen, 1870-;
preachers' books, 1894-.   **In local custody**

C.I. Castledawson (Derry diocese)
[Partly in Magherafelt parish]

Baptisms, 1846-85; burials, 1846-77; vestry minutes,
1870-89.   **T.679/2, 381-382**

Baptisms, 1886-; marriages, 1846-; registers of
vestrymen, 1874-; preachers' books, 1876-; church
wardens' account books, 1875-.   **In local custody**

P. Bellaghy (1st and 2nd)
Baptisms, 1862-1987; marriages 1845-50 (1st); marriages,
1845-1919 (2nd).   **MIC.1P/377**

R.C. Ballyscullion (Bellaghy) (Derry diocese)
Baptisms, 1844-81; marriages, 1844-83.   **MIC.1D/58**

BALLYSCULLION, GRANGE OF, CO. ANTRIM

P. Grange
Baptisms, 1824-1913; marriages, 1824-1926.   **MIC.1P/375**

BALLYSHANNON METHODIST CIRCUIT AND CHURCH, CO. DONEGAL
[*see under* **KILBARRON**]

BALLYSHANNON PRESBYTERIAN CHURCH, CO. DONEGAL
[*see under* **KILBARRON**]

BALLYSHANNNON ROMAN CATHOLIC CHURCH, CO. DONEGAL
[*see under* **KILBARRON**]

BALLYTRUSTAN, CO. DOWN

C.I. Ballytrustan
[United with Ballyphilip - *see under* **BALLYPHILIP**]

R.C. Ballytrustan
[Ballytrustan is in the Roman Catholic parish
of Portaferry - *see under* **BALLYPHILIP**]

BALLYWALTER, CO. DOWN

C.I. Ballywalter (Down diocese)
Baptisms, 1845-74; burials, 1844-78; vestry minutes,
1856-78; communicants' list, 1883.   T.679/222-223

Baptisms, 1874-; marriages, 1845-; burials, 1878-;
vestry minutes, 1879-; preachers' books, 1878-.   **In local custody**

P. 1st Ballywalter
Baptisms, 1824-1923; marriages, 1803-18 and 1824-1922;
communion roll, 1873 and 1875; session minutes, 1864-73.   **MIC.1P/104**

P. 2nd Ballywalter
Baptisms, 1820-1942; marriages, 1845-1901; communion
rolls, 1883-1949; stipend and other accounts, 1829-95;
receipt and expenditure books, 1818-73, including
collections for the poor, and a list of new communicants,
1852.   **MIC.1P/104**

BALLYWATT PRESBYTERIAN CHURCH, CO. ANTRIM
[*see under* **BALLYRASHANE**]

BALLYWEANEY PRESBYTERIAN CHURCH, CO. ANTRIM
[*see under* **LOUGHGUILE**]

BALLYWILLIN, COS ANTRIM AND LONDONDERRY

C.I. Ballywillin (Connor diocese)
Baptisms, 1826-71; marriages, 1825-44; burials,
1827-71; vestry minutes, 1710-55 and 1811-91;
preachers' book, 1847-1901; account book, 1827-31,
which contains mostly household and farm accounts of
the incumbent.   T.679/18; C.R.1/34;
                                                              MIC.1/287

M. Portrush (Coleraine Circuit)
Baptisms, 1831-1987; marriages, 1890-1935.   **MIC.1E/63**

P. Ballywillin
Baptisms, 1862-1939; marriages, 1846-1909; session
minutes, 1886-1947.   **MIC.1P/368**

P. Portrush
Baptisms, 1843-1953; marriages, 1846-1907; accounts, 1841-94; committee minutes, 1866-1906; session book containing details about new communicants, deaths, preaching etc., 1841-1906; membership register of Portrush Total Abstinence Society, 1845-94.   **MIC.1P/415**

R.C. Portrush and Bushmills (Down and Connor diocese)   **MIC.1D/72**
Baptisms, 1844-81; marriages, 1848-89.

R.P. Portrush or Glenmanus
Session minutes, 1900-51; treasurers' accounts, 1899-1924 and 1934-60.   **C.R.5/7**

BALTEAGH, CO. LONDONDERRY

C.I. Balteagh (Derry diocese)
[Earliest registers destroyed in Dublin]

Baptisms, 1896-; marriages, 1845-; burials, 1896-; vestry minutes, 1895-; register of vestrymen, 1870-; preachers' books, 1896-.   **In local custody**

P. Balteagh
Marriages, 1845-1936; communicants' register, 1890-1957; treasurers' notebook and receipts, 1832-46.   **MIC.1P/228; D.2383**

R.C. Balteagh
[This parish is part of the district of Newtownlimavady and is linked to chapels at Drumachose and Tamlaghtfinlagan - *see under* **DRUMACHOSE** and also part of Errigal Roman Catholic parish - *see under* **ERRIGAL**]

BANAGHER, CO. LONDONDERRY

C.I. Banagher (Derry diocese)
Baptisms, 1821-70; marriages, 1827-46; burials, 1837-72.   **T.679/228-229**

Baptisms, 1870-; marriages, 1845-; burials, 1873-; vestry minutes, 1877-; registers of vestrymen, 1870-.   **In local custody**

C.I. Feeny (Derry diocese)
Baptisms, 1821-; marriages, 1839-; burials, 1839-; vestry minutes, 1870-.   **In local custody**

C.I. Learmount
[Originally formed out of part of Banager - *see under* **LEARMOUNT**]

P. Banagher
> Baptisms, 1834-1984; marriages, 1845-1920; membership
> register of Banagher Temperance Association, 1857-1900.   **MIC.1P/227**

R.C. Banagher (Derry diocese)
> Baptisms, 1848-78 [incomplete]; marriages, 1857-78
> [incomplete].   **MIC.1D/59**

BANBRIDGE BAPTIST CHURCH, CO. DOWN
> [*see under* **SEAPATRICK**]

BANBRIDGE NON-SUBSCRBING PRESBYTERIAN CHURCH, CO. DOWN
> [*see under* **SEAPATRICK**]

BANDON METHODIST CIRCUIT, CO. CORK
> [*see under* **BALLYMODAN**]

BANGOR, CO. DOWN

C.I. Ballyholme (Down diocese)
> Baptisms, 1940-; marriages, 1940-; vestry minutes,
> 1928-; registers of vestrymen, 1954-.   **In local custody**

C.I. Bangor (St Comgall's) (Down diocese)
> Baptisms, 1803-77; marriages, 1805-44; burials,
> 1815-76; confirmations, 1851, 1855, 1858, 1861, 1863,
> 1865, 1868 and 1873.   **T.679/230, 234-236**
>
> Baptisms, 1878-; marriages, 1845-; burials, 1877-; vestry
> minutes, 1788-; preachers' books, 1828-; registers of
> vestrymen, 1871-.   **In local custody**

C.I. Bangor Abbey (Down diocese)
> [Earliest registers destroyed in Dublin]
>
> Baptisms, 1920-; marriages, 1923-; burials, 1941-;
> preachers' books, 1901-.   **In local custody**

C.I. Glencraig (Down diocese)
> [Partly in Bangor parish and partly in Holywood
> parish - *see under* **HOLYWOOD**]

C.I. Groomsport (Down diocese)
> [Earliest registers destroyed in Dublin]
>
> Baptisms, 1876-; marriages, 1869-; vestry minutes,
> 1871-; preachers' books, 1852-.   **In local custody**

M. Ballyholme
   Baptisms, 1937-; marriages, 1938-.   **In local custody**

M. Queen's Parade, Bangor
   Baptisms, 1893-; marriages, 1867-.   **In local custody**

M. Wesley Centenary Church, Bangor
   Baptisms, 1893-; marriages, 1894-.   **In local custody**

P. 1st Bangor
   Baptisms, 1852-88 and 1895-1923; marriages, 1808-1932;
   index to marriages, 1808-45; title deeds and leases,
   1696-1868.   **MIC.1P/23; C.R.3/4**

P. 2nd Bangor or Trinity
   Baptisms, 1829-1984; marriages, 1829-44.   **MIC.1P/256**

P. Ballygilbert
   Baptisms, 1841-1901; marriages, 1843-1905; new
   communicants, 1845-55; autobiographical details on
   families in the congregation compiled in 1846.   **MIC.1P/392;
                                                         T.2653/1**

P. Ballygrainey
   Baptisms, 1830-1940; marriages, 1838-1912; deaths,
   1861-4, 1877-1951 and 1962-74; marriage notices,
   1879-1906.   **MIC.1P/230/6;
                                                         MIC.1P/407**

   Session minutes, 1862-1972.   **In Presbyterian
                                                         Historical Society**

P. Conlig
   Baptisms, 1845-1919; marriages, 1850-1935; committee
   minutes, 1848-1937; session and committee minutes,
   with lists of communicants, 1848-1956.   **MIC.1P/94**

   Marriage notices, 1845-1941.   **MIC.1P/230/6**

P. Groomsport
   Baptisms, 1841-1903; marriages, 1841-1936.   **MIC.1P/262**

R.C. Bangor
   [This parish forms part of the district of Newtownards -
   see under **NEWTOWNARDS**]

R.P. Bangor (Hamilton Road)
   Account books, 1952-75; minutes, 1930-60.   **C.R.5/8**

BANNFOOT METHODIST CHURCH, CO. ARMAGH
   [*see under* **MONTIAGHS**]

**BANNSIDE PRESBYTERIAN CHURCH, BANBRIDGE,
CO. DOWN**
　　　[*see under* **SEAPATRICK**]

**BARONSCOURT CHURCH OF IRELAND PARISH,
CO. TYRONE**
　　　[*see under* **ARDSTRAW**]

BARONSTOWN, CO. LOUTH

　　C.I.　Baronstown　(Armagh diocese)
　　　　[Later amalgamated with Dundalk Parish Church]

　　　　Baptisms, 1878-1962; marriages, 1846-1951; burials,
　　　　1878-1958.　　　　　　　　　　　　　　　　MIC.1/206

　　R.C.　Dunbin, Haggardstown (Kilkerley) (Armagh diocese)
　　　　[Chapel at Kilcurly]
　　　　[*see under* **DUNBIN**]

BARR CHURCH OF IRELAND PARISH, CO. TYRONE
　　　[*see under* **KILSKEERY**]

BELFAST

　　B. Antrim Road
　　　　Marriages, 1897-1924.　　　　　　　　　　T.2788/3-6

　　B. Regent Street
　　　　Marriages, 1878-96.　　　　　　　　　　　T.2788/1-2

　　B. Great Victoria Street
　　　　Marriages, 1869; minutes, 1863-.　　　　　**In local custody**

　　C. Albertbridge Road
　　　　Baptisms, 1867-; marriages, 1868-.　　　　**In local custody**

　　C. Cliftonpark
　　　　Baptisms, 1876-; marriages, 1878-.　　　　**In local custody**

　　C. Donegal Street
　　　　Minutes and accounts of Hanna Street Mission Sabbath
　　　　School, 1894-1926, and minutes and newspaper cuttings
　　　　about a sale of work for the Mission, 1907-08.　　D.2021

　　C. Spamount
　　　　Baptisms, 1880-; marriages, 1874-.　　　　**In local custody**

C.I. All Saints (University Street) (Connor diocese)
Baptisms, 1888-; marriages, 1893-; burials, 1952-;
vestry minutes, 1887-.   **In local custody**

C.I. Christ Church (Connor diocese)
Baptisms, 1835-92; marriages, 1837-45 and
1856-1930; marriage banns, 1856-1930; burials,
1838-1902 (no entries 1859-63 or 1872-81); census,
1852.   **T.679/262,272-274,**
                                                                   279-285, 287-288,
                                                                   295-301; C.R.1/13

Vestry minutes, 1879-.   **In local custody**

C.I. Columbkille, Knock (Down diocese)
Baptisms, 1890-; marriages, 1896-; vestry minutes,
1894-.   **In local custody**

C.I. Dundela, St Mark's (Down diocese)
Baptisms, 1864-89.   **MIC.1/53**

Plans and elevations for alterations to the church, 1890,
and printed programmes for laying the foundation
stone, 1876.   **C.R.1/52**

Baptisms, 1889-; marriages, 1879-; vestry minutes,
1882-.   **In local custody**

C.I. Holy Trinity
[*see under* **Trinity**]

C.I. Mariners' Chapel (with St Anne's, Shankill)
(Connor diocese)

Baptisms, 1868-1922.   **T.679/253A-B**

C.I. St Aidan's (Connor diocese)
Baptisms, 1893-; marriages, 1895-; vestry minutes, 1893-.   **In local custody**

C.I. St Andrew's (Connor diocese)
Baptisms, 1881-; marriages, 1870-.   **In local custody**

C.I. St Anne's, Shankill (Connor diocese)
Baptisms, 1745-1871; marriages, 1745-1845; burials,
1745-69, 1784-1809 and 1824-83; index to baptisms,
marriages and burials, 1745-1823; index to baptisms,
1824-66.   **T.679/224, 225,**
                                                                 237-246, 249-252,
                                                                 254-256, 259-261

Baptisms, 1872-1901; indexes to baptisms, 1872-84;
marriages, 1845-1900.   **MIC.1/178**

Burials, 1884-; vestry minutes, 1808-1934; registers of
vestrymen, 1870-. **In local custody**

[There is a printed volume containing transcripts of
marriage entries, 1745-99]

C.I. St Barnabas' (Connor diocese)
Baptisms, 1892-; marriages, 1893-; vestry minutes,
1893-. **In local custody**

C.I. St Clement's (Down diocese)
Baptisms, 1897-; marriages, 1902-; vestry minutes,
1897-. **In local custody**

C.I. St Columba's
Baptisms, 1890-; marriages, 1896-; vestry minutes,
1894-. **In local custody**

C.I. St Donard's (Down diocese)
Baptisms, 1900-; marriages, 1903-; preachers' books,
1900-. **In local custody**

C.I. St Finnian's, Cregagh (Down diocese)
Baptisms, 1928-; marriages, 1934-. **In local custody**

C.I. St George's (Connor diocese)
Baptisms, 1817-70; marriages, 1817-33 and 1836; list
of parishioners and journal, 1837-43. **T.679/263-266;
MIC.1/116**

Burials, 1847-; vestry minutes, 1867-. **In local custody**

Index to baptisms, 1817-70, and to marriages, 1817-33. **In Public Search
Room**

C.I. St James' (Connor diocese)
Baptisms, marriages and vestry minutes, 1871-. **In local custody**

C.I. St John's, Malone (Connor diocese)
Baptisms, 1842-87; marriages, 1842-4. **D.231**

Index to baptisms, 1842-87, and marriages, 1842-4. **In Public Search
Room**

Baptisms, 1887-; marriages, 1846-; vestry minutes,
1893-. **In local custody**

C.I. St John's, Orangefield (Down diocese)
Baptisms, 1853-70. **T.679/30**

Baptisms, 1871-; marriages, 1855-. **In local custody**

C.I. St Jude's, Ballynafeigh (Down diocese)
Baptisms, 1873-; marriages, 1874-; burials, 1874-;
vestry minutes, 1873-.   **In local custody**

C.I. St Luke's, Lower Falls (Connor diocese)
[Earliest registers destroyed in Dublin)

C.I. St Mark's, Ballysillan (Connor diocese)
Baptisms, 1856-71.   **T.679/113-114**

Baptisms, 1871-; marriages, 1860-.   **In local custody**

C.I. St Mark's, Dundela
[*see under* **DUNDELA**]

C.I. St Mary's (Connor diocese)
Baptisms, 1867-72; burials, 1867-70.   **T.679/269, 275**

Baptisms, 1872-; marriages, 1869-; burials, 1870-;
vestry minutes, 1870-.   **In local custody**

C.I. St Mary Magdalene's (Connor diocese)
Private baptisms, 1847-77; baptisms, 1855-72.   **T.679/232-233**

Baptisms, 1872-; marriages, 1862-; vestry minutes,
1870-.   **In local custody**

C.I. St Matthias' (Connor diocese)
Correspondence about the building of the church and
plans, 1891-2.   **C.R.1/11**

C.I. St Matthew's (Connor diocese)
[Earliest registers destroyed in Dublin]

Baptisms, 1846-71.   **T.679/12**

Baptisms, 1871-; marriages, 1856-; burials, 1887-;
vestry minutes, 1858-.   **In local custody**

C.I. St Michael's (Connor diocese)
Baptisms, 1893-; marriages, 1900-; vestry minutes,
1893-.   **In local custody**

C.I. St Nicholas' (Lisburn Road) (Connor diocese)
Baptisms, 1901-; marriages, 1902; vestry minutes,
1902-; preachers' books, 1901-.   **In local custody**

C.I. St Patrick's, Ballymacarrett (Down diocese)
Baptisms, 1827-71; marriages, 1827-57.   **T.679/29, 29A, 214-217**

Vestry minutes, 1827-.   **In local custody**

C.I. St Paul's (Connor diocese)
[Earliest registers destroyed in Dublin]

C.I. St Peter's (Connor diocese)
Baptisms, 1896-. **In local custody**

C.I. St Philip's, Drew Memorial (Connor diocese)
Baptisms, 1871-; marriages, 1872-; vestry minutes,
1869-. **In local custody**

C.I. St Silas' (Connor diocese)
Baptisms, 1899-. **In local custody**

C.I. St Stephen's (Connor diocese)
Baptisms, 1868-; marriages, 1869-; burials, 1869-;
vestry minutes, 1871. **In local custody**

C.I. St Thomas' (Eglantine Avenue) (Connor diocese)
Baptisms, 1871-1925; marriages, 1871-1929; vestry
minutes, 1870-1957; preachers' books, 1870-1969;
register of vestrymen, 1871-1921; account books,
1870-1965; parish magazines, 1953-65; minutes of
St Thomas' Literary and Debating Society, 1885-91
and 1909-12, of its Society of Bell Ringers, 1893-1955,
and of the trustees of the church, 1865-1960. **C.R.1/36**

C.I. Trinity (Connor diocese)
Baptisms, 1844-85. **T.679/28; D.523/A-C**

Plan of the church by John Fraser, 1843. **C.R.1/3**

Index to baptisms, 1844-77. **In Public Search
Room**

Baptisms, 1885-; marriages, 1855-. **In local custody**

C.I. Upper Falls (Connor diocese)
Baptisms, 1855-72; vestry minutes, 1860-86, with a list
of vestrymen, 1896, and a list of subscribers to the
building fund, 1855-61. **T.679/315-317**

Baptisms, 1872-; marriages, 1863-. **In local custody**

C.I. Whiterock (Luther Church) (Connor diocese)
Baptisms and marriages, 1931-; vestry minutes,
1879-1924. **In local custody**

C.I. Willowfield (Down diocese)
Baptisms, marriages and vestry minutes, 1872-. **In local custody**

M. Agnes Street
Baptisms, 1864-; marriages, 1868-. **In local custody**

M. Ballymacarrett
[*see under* **Mountpottinger**]

M. Carlisle Memorial or Carlisle Circus
    Circuit schedule book, 1908-23; trustees' minute book,
    1876-1916; deeds registers, 1875-88.   **MIC.1E/59**

    Baptisms and marriages, 1877-.   **In local custody**

M. Castlereagh Road
    Baptisms, 1895-7.   **MIC.1E/56**

M. Crumlin Road
    Baptisms, 1878-; marriages, 1886-.   **In local custody**

M. Donegall Place [Primitive Wesleyan Methodists]
    Baptisms, 1871-85; marriages, 1872-95.   **MIC.1E/2**

M. Donegall Square East [Wesleyan Methodists]
    Baptisms, 1815-1928; marriages, 1835-42 and 1863-1911. **MIC.1E/1**

    Baptisms, 1815-43.   **MIC.429/1/267, 465**

M. Duncairn Gardens
    Baptisms, 1890-; marriages, 1895-.
    [Records in Carlisle Memorial Church]   **In local custody**

M. Falls Road
    Baptisms, 1882-; marriages, 1863-.
    [Marriages and baptisms before 1863 at Donegall Square
    Church; baptisms, 1904-06, at Grosvenor Hall].   **In local custody**

M. Frederick Street
    Baptisms, 1841-2 [may relate to Frederick Street].   MIC.429/1/518

    Baptisms, 1841-1904; marriages, 1841-1904.
    [Registers at North Belfast Mission]   **In local custody**

M. Grosvenor Hall, Belfast, Central Methodist Mission
    Baptisms, 1895-; marriages, 1896-.   **In local custody**

M. Hydepark (North Belfast Mission)
    Baptisms, 1834-; marriages, 1868-. [At Ballyclare]   **In local custody**

M. Jennymount
    Baptisms, 1873-; marriages, 1913-.   **In local custody**

M. Knock
    Baptisms, 1874-1912; marriages, 1872-1906; circuit
    schedule book, 1879-94; membership register and
    quarterly class roll, 1899-1921; pew register, 1871-1912;
    library register, 1887-1914.   **MIC.1E/40**

M. Ligoniel
    Baptisms, 1870-; marriages, 1893-.   **In local custody**

M. Melbourne Street [Primitive Methodists]
    Baptisms, 1834-1907; marriages, 1875-1908.   **MIC.1E/19; C.R.6/1**

M. Mountpottinger [Ballymacarret until 1891]
    Baptisms, 1885-1901; marriages, 1888-1900; membership
    register and quarterly class roll, 1911-22; congregational
    register, c.1920.   **MIC.1E/56**

M. Newtownards Road
    Baptisms and marriages, 1864-.   **In local custody**

M. Ormeau Road
    Baptisms, 1870-; marriages, 1884-.   **In local custody**

M. Osborne Park
    Baptisms, 1894-; marriages, 1895-.   **In local custody**

M. Primitive Street
    Baptisms, 1885-; marriages, 1878-.
    [At Sandy Row Church]   **In local custody**

M. Salem New Connexion
    Baptisms, 1829-; marriages, 1904-.
    [At North Belfast Mission]   **In local custody**

M. Sandy Row
    Baptisms, 1885-; marriages, 1878-.
    [Earlier baptisms at University Road Church]   **In local custody**

M. Shankill Road
    Baptisms, 1874-; marriages, 1915-.   **In local custody**

M. University Road
    Baptisms, 1865-1947; marriages, 1866-1969; minutes of
    leaders' and quarterly meetings, 1861-85; minutes of
    quarterly meetings, 1884-1962; minutes of leaders'
    meetings, 1925-65; trustees' minutes, 1879-1970; annual
    reports, 1889-1986, with gaps; circuit schedule books,
    1865-78, 1895-1906 and 1928-83; registers of members,
    1865-91 and 1900-54; minutes of the Band of Hope
    Committee, 1896-9.   **C.R.6/5**

N.S.P. All Souls (2nd)
    Baptisms, 1782-92 and 1816-28; marriages, 1771-87 and
    1817-27; committee minutes, 1808-28; poor accounts,
    1792-1816.   **C.R.4/9**

N.S.P. Domestic Mission, Stanhope Street
    Marriages, 1881-1937; visitors' book, 1945-54.   **C.R.4/13**

N.S.P. Mountpottinger
    Album of newspaper cuttings, annual reports, statements
    of accounts etc., 1874-1962.   **MIC.1B/8**

N.S.P. Rosemary Street (1st)
　　Baptisms, 1757-1977; marriages, 1790-1930; burials,
　　1712-36, with funeral accounts; lists of members, 1760,
　　1775, 1781, 1783, 1790, 1812 and 1830.　　　　　　　**C.R.4/5; MIC.1B/2;**
　　　　　　　　　　　　　　　　　　　　　　　　　　　　　　　　　T.1763/6; T.1964

　　Committee minutes, 1760-.　　　　　　　　　　　　　　**In local custody**

N.S.P. York Street
　　Records from c.1840.　　　　　　　　　　　　　　　　**In local custody**

P. Academy Street
　　[*see under* **Ekenhead**]

P. Agnes Street
　　Baptisms, 1869-81.　　　　　　　　　　　　　　　　　**MIC.1P/47**

P. Albert Street
　　Baptisms, 1852-1921; marriages, 1854-1933; session
　　minutes, 1857-1920; committee minutes, 1852-1920;
　　communicants' rolls, 1853-1926.　　　　　　　　　　**MIC.1P/16**

P. Alexandra
　　[*see under* **York Street**]

P. Alfred Street
　　[Church registers are with Fitzroy Presbyterian Church]

P. Argyle Place
　　Baptisms and marriages, 1853-.　　　　　　　　　　　**In local custody**

P. Ballymacarrett
　　Baptisms, 1837-1921; marriages, 1845-1928.　　　　　**MIC.1P/15**

P. Ballysillan
　　Baptisms, 1839-1960; marriages, 1845-1902; committee
　　minutes, 1836-93; session minutes, 1869-1951.　　　　**MIC.1P/22**

P. Belmont
　　Baptisms, 1862-1920.　　　　　　　　　　　　　　　　**C.R.3/39**

　　Marriages, 1862-1901.　　　　　　　　　　　　　　　**MIC.1P/118**

P. Berry Street
　　Baptisms, 1869-1984; marriages, 1869-1912, with
　　indexes, 1869-1974.　　　　　　　　　　　　　　　　**MIC.1P/356**

　　Printed history, 1769-1969.　　　　　　　　　　　　　**C.R.3/34**
　　[*see also* **St Enoch's**]

P. Clifton Street
　　Baptisms, 1861-1949; marriages, 1862-1941;
　　communicants' rolls, 1869-.　　　　　　　　　　　　　**In Presbyterian**
　　　　　　　　　　　　　　　　　　　　　　　　　　　　　　　　　Historical Society

P. Cliftonville
[*see under* **Donegall Street**]

P. College Square North
Marriages, 1845-1906; session minutes, 1849-1906;
committee minutes, 1840-1906.   **MIC.1P/107**

Baptisms, 1840-1967; marriages, 1840-45.   **In Presbyterian
                                                                 Historical Society**

P. Crescent
[Known as Linenhall before 1887]

Baptisms, 1831-1974; marriages, 1831-1908; committee
minutes, 1844-87.   **MIC.1P/57**

P. Donegall Pass
Baptisms, 1868-1973; marriages, 1873-1922.   **MIC.1P/116**

P. Donegall Street
[Cliftonville from 1886]

Baptisms, 1880-1972; marriages, 1863-1912.   **MIC.1P/394**

Baptisms, 1825-42; marriages, 1826-43; stipend books,
1833-53; communicants' roll, 1886-1915.   **In Presbyterian
                                                                 Historical Society**

P. Duncairn
Baptisms, 1861-1985; marriages, 1862-1904; church
reports, 1863-92; session minutes, 1861-1925; committee
minutes, 1859-92.   **MIC.1P/41**

Fragments of a plan of the church by Young & MacKenzie,
1880.   **C.R.3/56**

P. Eglinton
Baptisms, 1840-1937; marriages, 1840-44 and 1853-1933;
accounts, 1849-60.   **MIC.1P/40**

P. Ekenhead, (Academy Street)
Baptisms, 1864-1929; marriages, 1866-1926; session
minutes, 1871-1950; committee minutes, 1866-1927;
membership register of the Band of Hope, 1874-96;
annual reports, 1920, 1921 and 1928-41; history of the
church from 1866 to c.1920.   **MIC.1P/8**

P. Elmwood
Baptisms, 1880-1967; marriages, 1862-1974;
communicants' roll, 1876-1975; committee minutes,
1858-1960; session minutes, 1867-1926; stipend book,
1878-1915.   **In Presbyterian
                                                                 Historical Society**

P. Fisherwick
Baptisms, 1810-1965; marriages, 1828-1915; session
minutes, 1833-77; list of communicants, 1833-9; deacons'
court minutes, 1877-1915.   **MIC.1P/92**

P. Fitzroy
Baptisms, 1820-1963; marriages, 1821-1905; session
minutes, 1824-76; communicants' list, 1857-75;
appointments, 1862-71; list of church members,
1853-66.   **MIC.1P/14**

[Alfred Street church registers are with Fitzroy]

P. Great Victoria Street
Baptisms, 1860-1940; marriages, 1861-1901; committee
minutes, 1858-97.   **MIC.1P/74**

P. Linenhall
[*see under* **Crescent**]

P. McQuiston Memorial
Baptisms, 1893-1941; marriages, 1893-1901.   **MIC.1P/100**

P. Malone
Baptisms, 1837-75; marriages, 1838-1920; committee
minutes, 1834-1920; session minutes, 1883-1921.   **MIC.1P/2**

P. May Street
Baptisms, 1835-1931; marriages, 1835-1926; session
minutes, 1834-8, 1855 and 1871-1947; committee minutes,
1831-1919; alphabetical congregational list, c.1855.   **MIC.1P/9**

Copies of the church magazine, *Greeting*, recording
baptisms, marriages and deaths, 1908-88, with gaps.   **C.R.3/55**

P. Newtownbreda
[*see under* **KNOCKBREDA**]

P. Rosemary
Annual reports, 1942-84; session minutes, 1941-50.   **C.R.3/32; MIC.1P/8**

P. Rosemary Street
[Baptisms from 1868-1941 destroyed during the 2nd World
War]

Baptisms, c.1723-1867, with an index; marriages,
c.1741-1846, with an index; annual reports, 1872-1941; pew
rent books, 1726-73, 1788-96, 1816-56 and 1866-73; lists
of communicants, 1728-42 and 1850-67; lists of catechisable
persons, 1725-6; session minutes, 1827-1940; committee
minutes, 1774-1929; accounts, 1721-70 and 1828-47;
stipend book, 1789-1846.   **MIC.1P/7; T.654**

P. St Enoch's
Baptisms, 1853-1904 [up to 1876 this congregation was in
Berry Street]; marriages, 1852-1907.   **MIC.1P/21**

P. Sinclair Seamen's
Baptisms, 1854-1958; marriages, 1855-1907. **MIC.1P/55**

P. Townsend Street
Baptisms, 1835-1901; marriages, 1836-1907. **MIC.1P/336**

Published history of church, 1833-1983. **C.R.3/27**

Account books relating to congregational endowments
and charities, 1878-1988. **C.R.3/52**

P. Westbourne
Baptisms, 1880-1920; marriages, 1881-1924. **MIC.1P/11**

P. York Street, now **Alexandra**
Baptisms, 1840-1908; marriages, 1840-1933; session
book, 1839-1923; committee minutes, 1840-1939; cash
book, 1888-1910. **MIC.1P/112**

R.C. Ballymacarrett (Down and Connor diocese)
Baptisms and marriages, 1841-80. **MIC.1D/65**

R.C. Holy Cross (Ardoyne) (Down and Connor diocese)
Baptisms and marriages, 1868-81; record of converts,
1868-80. **MIC.1D/65**

R.C. St Joseph's (Prince's Dock) (Down and Connor diocese)
Baptisms and marriages, 1872-81. **MIC.1D/67**

R.C. St Malachy's (Alfred Street) (Down and Connor diocese)
Baptisms and marriages, 1858-81. **MIC.1D/64**

R.C. St Mary's (Chapel Lane) (Down and Connor diocese)
Baptisms and marriages, 1867-81. **MIC.1D/67**

R.C. St Patrick's (Donegall Street) (Down and Connor diocese)
Baptisms, 1798-1811, 1814-67 and 1875-80; marriages,
1798-1812 and 1814-67. **MIC.1D/66-67**

R.C. St Paul's (Falls Road) (Down and Connor diocese)
Baptisms and marriages, 1887-. **In local custody**

R.C. St Peter's (Derby Street) (Down and Connor diocese)
Baptisms and marriages, 1866-81. **MIC.1D/64-65**

R.P. Botanic Avenue [later became **Linenhall Street**]
Marriages, 1881-1933; congregational minutes, 1825-50
and 1875-1903; session minutes, 1833-62. **MIC.1C/5; C.R.5/4**

**R.P. College Street South or Chancellor Memorial or
Grosvenor Road**
[Grosvenor Road amalgamated with College Street
South]

Marriages, 1863-1971; minutes, 1866-1967. **MIC.1C/2, 4; C.R.5/2**

R.P. Dublin Road
 Marriages, 1891-1976.   MIC.1C/3

R.P. Grosvenor Road
 [*see under* **College Street South**]

R.P. Linenhall Street
 [*see under* **Botanic Avenue**]

BELLAGHY (1ST AND 2ND) PRESBYTERIAN CHURCHES, CO. LONDONDERRY
 [*see under* **BALLYSCULLION**)

BELLASIS PRESBYTERIAN CHURCH, CO. CAVAN
 [*see under* **LURGAN**]

BELLEEK, CO. FERMANAGH

C.I. Belleek (Clogher diocese)
 Baptisms, 1820-1918; marriages, 1823-1912; burials,
 1822-86 (with gaps); list of rectors, 1791-1945, and list
 of curates, 1824-1946; vestry minutes, 1822-1934.   T.679/65, 257-258;
                                                                         MIC.1/270; C.R.1/59

M. Belleek
 Baptisms, 1832-77 [possibly in Ballyshannnon Circuit];
 1878-1910 [Pettigo Circuit]; post-1910 baptisms may be
 in with Churchill Circuit baptisms; marriages, 1877-1937.   MIC.1E/17, 35, 38

R.C. Belleek
 [It is part of the district of Templecarn (Carn) or
 Pettigo - *see under* **TEMPLECARN**]

BELLEVILLE PRESBYTERIAN CHURCH, CO. ARMAGH
 [*see under* **MONTIAGHS**]

BELTURBET CHURCH OF IRELAND PARISH, CO. CAVAN
 [*see under* **ANNAGH**]

BELTURBET METHODIST CHURCH, CO. CAVAN
 [*see under* **ANNAGH**]

BELTURBET PRESBYTERIAN CHURCH, CO. CAVAN
 [*see under* **ANNAGH**]

BENBURB PRESBYTERIAN CHURCH, CO. TYRONE
[*see under* **CLONFEACLE**]

BENVARDEN PRESBYTERIAN CHURCH, CO. ANTRIM
[*see under* **DERRYKEIGHAN**]

BERAGH METHODIST CHURCH, CO. TYRONE
[*see under* **CLOGHERNEY**]

BERAGH ROMAN CATHOLIC PARISH, CO. TYRONE
[*see under* **CLOGHERNEY**]

BESSBROOK METHODIST CHURCH, CO. ARMAGH
[*see under* **KILLEVY**]

BESSBROOK PRESBYTERIAN CHURCH, CO. ARMAGH
[*see under* **KILLEVY**]

BILLIS CHURCH OF IRELAND PARISH, CO. CAVAN
[*see under* **KILLINKERE**]

BILLY PARISH, CO. ANTRIM

> **C.I. Billy** (Connor diocese)
> > [Earliest registers destroyed in Dublin]
>
> > Marriages, 1845-1914; vestry minutes, 1787-1849.   **C.R.1/29**
>
> > Baptisms, 1882-; burials, 1882-; confirmation registers,
> > 1865-; preachers' books, 1870-; registers of vestrymen,
> > 1870-.   **In local custody**
>
> **C.I. Dunseverick**
> > [Partly in Billy parish and partly in Ballintoy parish -
> > *see under* **BALLINTOY**]
>
> **M. Billy**
> > Baptisms, 1831-1987; marriages, 1871-1931.   **MIC.1E/63**
>
> **P. Bushmills**
> > Baptisms, 1820-1966; marriages, 1821-1936.   **MIC.1P/113**
>
> **P. Mosside**
> > Baptisms, 1842-1930; marriages, 1842-1936; burials,
> > 1855-78; communicants' roll, 1891-1921; census of
> > membership, 1922-3.   **MIC.1P/91**

P. Toberdoney
  No pre-1900 baptisms exist; marriages, 1864-1913.   **MIC.1P/371**

R.P. Bushmills
  Lease of site for church, 1836 and memoranda about
  appointment of trustees, 1882 and 1885.   **C.R.5/14**

R.C. Bushmills
  [*see under* **BALLYWILLIN**]

**BLACKBOG ROMAN CATHOLIC PARISH,
CO. FERMANAGH**
  [*see under* **TEMPLECARN**]

BLACKLION METHODIST CHURCH, CO. CAVAN
  [*see under* **KILLINAGH**]

BLACKSCULL METHODIST CHURCH, CO. DOWN
  [*see under* **TULLYLISH**]

**BLACKWATERTOWN METHODIST CHURCH,
CO. ARMAGH**
  [*see under* **CLONFEACLE**]

BLARIS (or LISBURN), COS ANTRIM AND DOWN

  C.I. Eglantine (All Saints) (Connor diocese)
      Baptisms, 1875-; marriages, 1881-; burials, 1920-;
      vestry minutes, 1876-.   **In local custody**

  C.I. Lisburn (Christ Church Cathedral) (Connor diocese)
      Baptisms, 1637, 1639-41, 1643-6 and 1655-1933;
      baptisms of Huguenot children, 1707-36; marriages,
      1639-41, 1643-6 and 1664-1967; burials, 1639-41 and
      1661-1929; burials in Lisburn Cathedral churchyard,
      1670-1951; vestry minutes, 1675-1970; confirmations,
      1667, 1675 and 1678; cess books, c.1800 and 1847;
      preachers' books, 1819-1961; account book, 1870-1909;
      register of vestrymen, 1870-1904; abstract of schools
      and Sunday Schools in the parish, 1824; letters patent
      constituting the parish church of Blaris or Lisburn as a
      cathedral church, 1674; notebook of the
      Rev. Thomas Haslam, c.1675-1695, which contains a
      contemporary account of the Battle of the Boyne, 1690;
      abstract of the population of Lisburn parish, 1820.   **T.679/107, 112;
                                                                      T.1602; MIC.1/3-5;
                                                                      C.R.1/35; D.1823**

C.I. Christ Church, Lisburn (Connor diocese)
Baptisms, 1849-73.   MIC.1/5

Marriages, 1874-; vestry minutes, 1902-16 and 1924-;
register of vestrymen, 1887-; preachers' books, 1843-57,
1865-94 and 1911-.   **In local custody**

C.I. Broomhedge (Connor diocese)
[Earliest registers destroyed in Dublin]

Baptisms, 1855-; marriages, 1889-; burials, 1858-;
vestry minutes, 1870-; preachers' books, 1842-.   **In local custody**

M. Broomhedge [Methodist New Connexion until 1905]
Marriages, 1869-1931
[*see also under* **Lisburn** (Wesleyan Methodists)]   **MIC.1E/42**

M. Broomhedge [Wesleyan Methodists]
[*see under* **M. Lisburn (Seymour Street)** below]

M. Lisburn (Seymour Street) [Wesleyan Methodists]
[Meetings at Lisburn, Magheragall, Priesthill and
Broomhedge]

Baptisms, 1827-1975; marriages, 1864-1911; circuit
schedule book, 1923-36; accounts, 1825-47; membership
lists, 1833-95.   **MIC.1E/61**

Baptisms, 1827-46.   **MIC.429/1/387**

M. Lisburn [Primitive Methodists]
Baptisms, 1850-74.   **MIC.1E/61**

M. Lisburn [Methodist New Connexion]
[Churches at Lisburn, Priesthill and Broomhedge]

Baptisms, 1840-54; minutes of quarterly meetings,
1838-98; lists of members, 1840-55 and 1862-94.   **MIC.1E/44**

M. Priesthill [Methodist New Connexion until 1905]
Baptisms, 1847-1908; marriages, 1864-1928; minutes of
leaders' quarterly meetings, 1864-1914; list of members,
1865-6, 1868, 1889-90 and 1893.   **MIC.1E/41**

M. Priesthill [Wesleyan Methodists]
[*see under* **Lisburn, Seymour Street** above]

P. 1st Lisburn
Baptisms, 1692-1732, 1736-64 and 1779-1927; marriages,
1688-96, 1711-1718/19 and 1782-1895; communion roll,
c.1863; statistics about families in the congregation, 1863;
session minutes, 1688-1709 and 1711-63, which include
discipline cases, 1805-24 and 1854-87; subscription list

for the new meeting house, 1764-5; seat lists and pew rents,
1764-1824; accounts, 1775-1817.   **MIC.1P/159; C.R.3/11;**
                                                                    T.808/14892

P. Railway Street, Lisburn
Baptisms, 1860-1930; marriages, 1861-72 and 1882-1905;
committee minutes, 1860-1906; session minutes,
1868-1905; Elise Milne Barbour Memorial Hall
committee minutes, 1912-52; building committee minutes,
1861-6.   **MIC.1P/75**

P. Sloan Street, Lisburn
Baptisms, 1861-1921; marriages, 1868-87 (no marriages
extant from 1889-1900); marriage notices, 1889-1901;
communicants' roll book, 1861-1915.   **MIC.1P/356;**
                                                                    MIC.1P/230/5

P. Maze
Baptisms, 1856-1957; marriages, 1856-1918; communion
roll, 1856-1939.   **MIC.1P/399**

R.C. Blaris (Connor diocese)
List of subscriptions in Holy Trinity cemetery,
1875-1955.   **T.1602**

Registers from 1840.   **In local custody**

R.S.F. Lisburn Monthly Meeting
Men's monthly meeting minutes,1675-1967; women's
monthly meeting minutes, 1793-1800 and 1813-57;
ministers' and elders' minutes, 1791-1935; births,
1781-1981; marriages, 1766-1808 and 1817-1971;
removal certificates, 1766-1904; register of members,
1794-1980; disownment records, 1703-1903; record
book of sufferings, 1811-61; account book, 1789-1834;
minutes of the poor committee, 1806-32; testimonies
acknowledging misconduct, 1801-41 etc.   **MIC.16/7-23**

BLUESTONE METHODIST CHURCH, CO. ARMAGH
[*see under* **SEAGOE**]

**BOARDMILLS (1ST) PRESBYTERIAN CHURCH,
CO. DOWN**
[*see under* **KILLANEY**]

**BOARDMILLS (2ND) PRESBYTERIAN CHURCH,
CO. DOWN**
[*see under* **SAINTFIELD**]

BODONY LOWER, CO. TYRONE

C.I. Badony Lower [*sic* Bodony Lower] (Derry diocese)
Baptisms, 1812-75; marriages, 1817-45; burials, 1820-73.   **T.679/76-77, 79**

Baptisms, 1875-; marriages, 1845-; burials, 1874-; vestry
minutes, 1816-; registers of vestrymen, 1870-; account
books, 1870-1905; preachers' books, 1892-.   **In local custody**

Indexes to baptisms, marriages and burials, 1828-37.   **In Public Search Room**

C.I. Greenan (Derry diocese)
Marriages, 1879-; preachers' books, 1887-.   **In local custody**
[For baptisms and burials *see* Badony Lower]

P. Badoney
Marriages, 1845-1912.   **MIC.1P/278**

P. Crockatanty
Marriages, 1876-1924.   **MIC.1P/254**

P. Gortin
Baptisms, 1843-1985; marriages, 1844-1935; session
minutes, 1842-81; census of congregation, 1843; lists of
emigrants, 1854-84; communion attendances, 1843-66.   **MIC.1P/253; T.1629**

R.C. Badoney Lower and Greencastle (Gortin)
(Derry diocese)

Baptisms, 1865-81; marriages, 1865-80.   **MIC.1D/60**

BODONEY UPPER, CO. TYRONE

C.I. Badony Upper [*sic* Bodony] (Derry diocese)
[Earliest registers destroyed in Dublin]

Copy baptisms, 1806-10; copy burials, 1809-27.   **T.808/6124-6127**

Baptisms, 1886-; marriages, 1846-; burials, 1886-
(in with Badoney Lower records); registers of vestrymen,
1870-; preachers' books, 1907-.   **In local custody**

P. Corrick
Marriages, 1851-83 and 1890-1935.   **MIC.1P/279**

P. Glenelly
Baptisms, 1828-63; marriages, 1828-1915.   **MIC.1P/280; C.R. 3/60**

R.C. Badoney Upper (Cranagh) (Derry diocese)
Baptisms, 1866-81.   **MIC.1D/60**

BOHO, CO. FERMANAGH

C.I. Boho (Clogher diocese)
[Earliest original registers destroyed in Dublin]

Copy baptisms, 1840-78; marriages, 1847-76; burials,
1840-79.   **T.941/1**

Vestry minutes, 1870-.   **In local custody**

C.I. Kiltyclogher
[Partly in Boho parish - *see under* **CLOONCLARE**]

R.C. Devenish (Botha, Derrygonnelly) (Clogher diocese)
[Boho parish forms part of the Roman Catholic district
of Devenish or Derrygonnelly which also includes
Inishmacsaint - *see under* **DEVENISH** and
INISHMACSAINT]

BOVEEDY PRESBYTERIAN CHURCH, CO. LONDONDERRY
[*see under* **TAMLAGHT O'CRILLY**]

BOVEVAGH, CO. LONDONDERRY

C.I. Bovevagh (Derry diocese)
[Earliest registers destroyed in Dublin]

Baptisms, 1878-; marriages, 1845-; burials, 1878-; vestry
minutes, 1777-; registers of vestrymen, 1871-; preachers'
books, 1890-.   **In local custody**

P. Bovevagh
Baptisms, 1818-38 and 1843-1934; marriages, 1818-30,
1834-8, 1843-5 and 1858-1927; deaths, 1870-73; session
minutes, 1826-37, 1861-94 and 1896-1956; minutes of
session and committee, 1857-91; committee minutes,
1897-1939; accounts, 1857-79; lists of communicants,
1829-59, 1863, 1868-9, 1872, 1879-94 and c.1901-c.1933;
seat list, c.1870; list of stipend payers and amount paid,
1871-1915, and other accounts, 1870-96.   **MIC.1P/229**

R.C. Banagher (Derry diocese)
[Bovevagh parish forms part of Banagher and
Dungiven Roman Catholic district - *see under*
BANAGHER and **DUNGIVEN**]

BRACKAVILLE CHURCH OF IRELAND PARISH, CO. TYRONE
[*see under* **DONAGHENRY**]

BRAID ROMAN CATHOLIC PARISH, CO. ANTRIM
[*see under* **RACAVAN**]

BRANTRY CHURCH OF IRELAND PARISH, CO. TYRONE
[*see under* **AGHALOO**]

**BREADY REFORMED PRESBYTERIAN CHURCH,
CO. TYRONE**
[*see under* **DONAGHEDY**]

BRIGH PRESBYTERIAN CHURCH, CO. TYRONE
[*see under* **BALLYCLOG**]

BRIGHT, CO. DOWN

    C.I. Bright (Down diocese)
        [Earliest registers destroyed in Dublin]

        Vestry minutes, 1770-1923, with lists of the poor,
        1791-1842.   **MIC.1/115**

        Baptisms, 1880-; marriages, 1845-; burials, 1880-;
        registers of vestrymen, 1870-; churchwardens' account
        books, 1870-.   **In local custody**

    R.C. Bright, Rossglass and Killough (Down diocese)
        Baptisms and marriages, 1856-81.   **MIC.1D/74**

**BROADLANE REFORMED PRESBYTERIAN CHURCH,
CO. LONDONDERRY**
[*see under* **DRUMACHOSE**]

**BROOKEBOROUGH METHODIST CHURCH,
CO. FERMANAGH**
[*see under* **AGHAVEA**]

**BROOKSIDE (3RD) PRESBYTERIAN CHURCH,
CO. ANTRIM**
[see under **AHOGHILL**]

BROOKVALE PRESBYTERIAN CHURCH, CO. DOWN
[*see under* **DRUMBALLYRONEY**]

**BROOMFIELD CHURCH OF IRELAND PARISH,
CO. MONAGHAN**
[*see under* **CLONTIBRET**]

**BROOMHEDGE CHURCH OF IRELAND PARISH,
CO. DOWN**
  [*see under* **BLARIS**]

**BROOMHEDGE METHODIST NEW CONNEXION
CHURCH, CO. DOWN**
  [*see under* **BLARIS**]

**BROUGHSHANE (1ST AND 2ND) PRESBYTERIAN
CHURCHES, CO. ANTRIM**
  [*see under* **RACAVAN**]

**BRYANSFORD CHURCH OF IRELAND PARISH,
CO. DOWN**
  [*see under* **KILCOO**]

BRYANSFORD ROMAN CATHOLIC PARISH, CO. DOWN
  [*see under* **MAGHERA**]

BUCKNA PRESBYTERIAN CHURCH, CO. ANTRIM
  [*see under* **RACAVAN**]

BUNCRANA PRESBYTERIAN CHURCH, CO. DONEGAL
  [*see under* **FAHAN LOWER**]

BUNDORAN METHODIST CHURCH, CO. DONEGAL
  [*see under* **INISHMACSAINT**)

BURT, CO. DONEGAL

  C.I. Burt (Raphoe diocese)
    Baptisms, 1829-1913; marriages, 1829-1929; burials,   **MIC.1/183**
    1829-1941.

    Baptisms, 1802-28; vestry minutes, 1809-.   **In local custody**

  P. Burt
    Baptisms, 1833-78; marriages, 1837-1907; session
    minutes, 1833-69.   **MIC.1P/33; T.2725**

  R.C. Burt and Inch (Fahan) (Derry diocese)
    Baptisms, 1859-80; marriages, 1856-80; deaths, 1860-66.   **MIC.1D/55**

  R.C. Iskaheen (Derry diocese)
    [*see under* **MUFF**]

BUSHMILLS PRESBYTERIAN CHURCH, CO. ANTRIM
[*see under* **BILLY**]

BUSHMILLS REFORMED PRESBYTERIAN CHURCH, CO. ANTRIM
[*see under* **BILLY**]

BUSHMILLS ROMAN CATHOLIC PARISH, CO. ANTRIM
[*see under* **BALLYWILLIN**]

BUSHVALE PRESBYTERIAN CHURCH, CO. ANTRIM
[*see under* **KILRAGHTS**]

CAHANS PRESBYTERIAN CHURCH, CO. MONAGHAN
[*see under* **TULLYCORBET**]

CAIRNALBANA [*sic* CARNALBANAGH] **PRESBYTERIAN CHURCH, CO. ANTRIM**
[*see under* **TICKMACREVAN**]

CAIRNCASTLE NON-SUBSCRIBING PRESBYTERIAN CHURCH, CO. ANTRIM
[*see under* **CARNCASTLE**]

CAIRNCASTLE PRESBYTERIAN CHURCH, CO. ANTRIM
[*see under* **CARNCASTLE**]

CALEDON CHURCH OF IRELAND PARISH, CO. TYRONE
[*see under* **AGHALOO**]

CALEDON METHODIST CHURCH, CO. TYRONE
[*see under* **AGHALOO**]

CALEDON PRESBYTERIAN CHURCH, CO. TYRONE
[*see under* **AGHALOO**]

CAMLIN, CO. ANTRIM

C.I. [Camlin parish is part of the benefice of Glenavy -
see under **GLENAVY**]

M. Crumlin (Ballymena and Antrim Circuit)
Baptisms, 1829-c.1880; membership register, 1826-c.1880;
minutes of leaders' and stewards' meetings, 1855-c.1880;
circuit schedule book, 1860-79. [Crumlin may be
included in all or some of these circuit records]   **MIC.1E/58**

P. Crumlin
Baptisms, 1838-1913; marriages, 1846-1936;
communicants' roll, 1889-1928; minutes and accounts of
session and committee, 1840-67; committee minutes,
1883-1964; session minutes, 1904-51.   **MIC.1P/125**

R.C. Glenavy and Killead
[Camlin parish forms part of the Roman Catholic district
of Glenavy - *see under* **GLENAVY**]

CAMLOUGH CHURCH OF IRELAND PARISH, CO. ARMAGH
[*see under* **KILLEVY**]

CAMUS, CO. TYRONE

C.I. Camus-Juxta-Mourne (Derry diocese)
Baptisms, 1803-1908; marriages, 1804-1907 (apart from
1806-12); burials, 1826-1922; banns, 1849-62;
confirmation list, 1824; register of vestrymen,
1871-1920; account book, 1889-1901; vestry minutes,
1838-1937.   **T.679/306-310;
MIC.1/307**

Preachers' books, 1842-51 and 1860-; accounts, 1889-.   **In local custody**

M. Strabane (Strabane and Castlederg Circuit, Strabane and
Ramelton Circuit and Strabane Circuit)

Baptisms, 1822-64; marriages, 1865-1935; circuit schedule
books, 1869-1909; membership register, 1897-1947;
minutes of quarterly leaders' meetings, 1880-1910;
circuit steward's book, 1872-86.   **MIC.1E/46, 62**

Baptisms, 1867-.   **In local custody**

P. 1st Strabane
Baptisms, 1828-1937; marriages, 1845-1919.   **MIC.1P/10**

R.C. Clonleigh and Camus (Strabane) (Derry diocese)
[*see under* **CLONLEIGH**]

CAMUS-JUXTA-BANN CHURCH OF IRELAND PARISH, CO. LONDONDERRY
[*see under* **MACOSQUIN**]

CAPPAGH, CO. TYRONE

C.I. Cappagh (Derry Diocese)
Baptisms, 1753-1871; marriages, 1752-1850; burials, 1758-1809 and 1834-92; vestry minutes, 1755-1851, with lists of applotters, 1805-17 and 1839-50; poor lists, 1802-11.
T.679/289, 303-305, 333-334, 338

Baptisms, 1872-; marriages, 1851-; churchwardens' account books, 1832-; vestry minutes, 1753-90 and 1852-; register of vestrymen, 1870-; preachers' books, 1871-.
In local custody

C.I. Edenderry (Derry diocese)
Baptisms, 1841-92; burials, 1849-1923.
MIC.1/45

Baptisms, 1890-; burials, 1924-; marriages, 1851-; vestry minutes, 1871-; registers of vestrymen, 1870-; churchwardens' account books, 1871-.
In local custody

C.I. Lislimnaghan (Derry diocese)
Baptisms, 1862-; marriages, 1865-; burials, 1864-; vestry minutes, 1863-; churchwardens' accounts, 1862-; register of vestrymen, 1870-; preachers' book, 1862-; church accounts, 1870-99.
In local custody

C.I. Mountfield
[Established as a district curacy out of Cappagh]

[Earliest registers destroyed in Dublin]

Baptisms, 1877-; marriages, 1845-; vestry minutes, 1918-; registers of vestrymen, 1870-; preachers' books, 1923-.
In local custody

M. Aghagallon
Baptisms, c.1832-1892, circuit schedule books, 1866-92; membership register, 1863-92.
MIC.1E/24

M. Mayne [*sic* Maine]
Baptisms, 1831-; marriages, 1922-.
In local custody

P. Edenderry
Baptisms, 1845-1945; marriages, 1845-1935; committee minutes, 1875-1966; session minutes, 1875 and 1882-1951.
MIC.1P/108

P. Mountjoy
[Known as Crossroads up to 1878]

Baptisms, 1821-1979; marriages, 1821-1924; list of seat holders, 1832; pew rents, 1829.
MIC.1P/242; CR.3/29

R.C. **Cappagh** (**Ardstraw**) (Derry diocese)
Baptisms and marriages, 1843-83; deaths, 1843-65.   **MIC.1D/60-61**

**CARGINAGH CHURCH OF IRELAND CHURCH,
CO. DOWN**
[*see under* **KILKEEL**]

CARGYCREEVY PRESBYTERIAN CHURCH, CO. DOWN
[*see under* **ANNAHILT**]

CARLAND PRESBYTERIAN CHURCH, CO. TYRONE
[*see under* **DONAGHMORE**]

CARLINGFORD, CO. LOUTH

C.I. **Carlingford** (Armagh diocese)
[Earliest registers destroyed in Dublin]

Marriages, 1845-; vestry minutes, 1822-; register of
vestrymen, 1870-; preachers' books, 1881-.   **In local custody**

C.I. **Omeath** (Armagh diocese)
Baptisms, 1883-1936, with an index; marriages,
1845-1930, with an index; burials, 1883-1936, with an
index; preachers' book, 1841-1922.   **MIC.1/285**

R.C. **Carlingford** (Armagh diocese)
Baptisms, 1835-81, marriages, 1835-82; deaths, 1835-48
and 1869-82.   **MIC.1D/45**

R.C. **South Carlingford** (**Grange Cooley**) (Armagh diocese)
Baptisms, 1811-81; marriages, 1811-82.   **MIC.1D/44**

**CARLISLE ROAD METHODIST CHURCH,
LONDONDERRY, CO. LONDONDERRY**
[*see under* **TEMPLEMORE**]

**CARLISLE ROAD (OR 4TH DERRY) PRESBYTERIAN
CHURCH, CO. LONDONDERRY**
[*see under* **TEMPLEMORE**]

CARLOW, CO. CARLOW

M. **Carlow circuit**
Baptisms, 1844-50.   **MIC.429/1/109**

CARN ROMAN CATHOLIC PARISH, CO. DONEGAL
[*see under* **TEMPLECARN**]

CARNALBANAGH PRESBYTERIAN CHURCH, CO. ANTRIM
[*see under* **CAIRNALBANA**]

CARNCASTLE [or CAIRNCASTLE], CO. ANTRIM

C.I. **Carncastle** (Connor diocese)
[Linked to Kilwaughter - *see under* **KILWAUGHTER**]

N.S.P. **Cairncastle**
Baptisms, 1881-1957; marriages, 1845-1935.   MIC.1B/5

P. **Cairncastle**
Baptisms, 1832-52 and 1891-1944; marriages, 1832-43
and 1845-1936; session minutes, 1871-1907; stipend
accounts, 1840-41; stipend collection books, 1872-1908;
Sustentation Fund payments and stipend list, 1876-84;
index to baptisms, 1832-52, and to marriages, 1832-1935.   MIC.1P/328; T.3054

R.C. [Carncastle forms part of the Roman Catholic district of
Larne and Carrickfergus - *see under* **LARNE**]

CARNDAISY BAPTIST CHURCH, CO. LONDONDERRY
[*see under* **KILCRONAGHAN**]

CARNDONAGH PRESBYTERIAN CHURCH, CO. DONEGAL
[*see under* **DONAGH**]

CARNDONAGH ROMAN CATHOLIC CHURCH, CO. DONEGAL
[*see under* **DONAGH, CO. DONEGAL**]

CARNLOUGH METHODIST CHURCH, CO. ANTRIM
[*see under* **ARDCLINIS**]

CARNLOUGH ROMAN CATHOLIC PARISH, CO. ANTRIM
[*see under* **ARDCLINIS**]

CARNMONEY, CO. ANTRIM

C. **Whiteabbey**
Baptisms, 1884-; marriages, 1888-.   **In local custody**

C.I. Carnmoney (Connor diocese)
[United with Ballylinagh and Ballymartin]

Baptisms, 1788-1871; marriages, 1791-1845; burials,
1845-79; confirmation lists, 1850-91; list of parishioners,
1870; preachers' books, 1823-80 and 1914-40;
committee minutes, 1903; list of vestrymen, 1888.   **T.679/325-329, 332;
D.852/8, 48, 85, 91,
105, 122, 125**

Baptisms, 1871-; marriages, 1845-; burials, 1879-; vestry
minutes, 1808-; registers of vestrymen, 1881-; preachers'
books, 1880-.   **In local custody**

C.I. Jordanstown (St Patrick's) (Connor diocese)
Baptisms, 1868-82 and 1891-1974; marriages,
1869-1904.   **MIC.1/215**

Burials, 1951-; vestry minutes, 1884-; registers of
vestrymen, 1884-.   **In local custody**

C.I. Whitehouse (Connor diocese)
Baptisms, 1850-77.   **MIC.1/81**

Baptisms, 1878-; marriages, 1851-; burials, 1934-; vestry
minutes, 1870-; preachers' books, 1840-; registers of
vestrymen, 1848-.   **In local custody**

P. Carnmoney
Baptisms, 1708-1800 and 1819-1968; marriages,
1708-1807, 1819-27 and 1829-41; notebook giving
marriages, births and deaths of various families, with an
index, 1708-1917; session and committee minutes, 1833
and 1847-1933; session minutes, 1859-1933; names of
those who transferred from other congregations, 1708-25
and 1859-60.   **MIC.1P/37; T.1013;
C.R.3/15**

P. Whiteabbey
[Baptisms before 1921 destroyed in a fire]

A few baptisms, 1895-1921; marriages, 1897-1911;
session minutes, 1850-1949; building committee minutes,
1833-52.   **MIC.1P/84**

R.C. Greencastle (Whitehouse) (Down and Connor diocese)
[Part of Carnmoney parish is in the Roman Catholic
parish of Whitehouse and part is in the district of
Belfast - *see under* **BELFAST**]

Baptisms and marriages, 1854-81.   **MIC.1D/71**

Parish magazine, 1976.   **C.R.2/7**

CARNONE PRESBYTERIAN CHURCH, CO. DONEGAL
[*see under* **DONAGHMORE, CO. DONEGAL**]

**CARNTALL OR CLOGHER PRESBYTERIAN CHURCH,
CO. TYRONE**
   [*see under* **CLOGHER**]

CARNTEEL, CO. TYRONE

   C.I. Carnteel (Armagh diocese)
      Baptisms, 1805-70; marriages, 1805-54; burials,
      1805-71; vestry minutes, 1712-1807; confirmation lists,
      1824-40, with gaps.   **T.679/302, 330, 337,
                                                             355-358, 364**

      Baptisms, 1871-; marriages, 1855-; burials, 1872-; vestry
      minutes, 1807-.   **In local custody**

   C.I. Ballygawley (Armagh diocese)
      [Formed out of parts of Carnteel and Errigal Keerogue
      parishes]

      [Earliest registers destroyed in Dublin]

      Baptisms, 1879-; marriages, 1849-; burials, 1879-.   **In local custody**

   C.I. Brantry (Armagh diocese)
      [Formed out of part of Carnteel, Aghaloo and
      Clonfeacle parishes - *see under* **AGHALOO**]

   M. Aughnacloy [For some time in Blacklion Circuit]
      Baptisms, 1877-c.1950.   **MIC.1E/12**

      Baptisms, 1823-43.   **MIC.429/1/186**

      Marriages, 1866-.   **In local custody**

   P. Aughnacloy
      Baptisms, 1812-1977; indexes to baptisms, 1812-42;
      marriages, 1812-24, 1830-41and 1845-1911; indexes
      to marriages, 1812-41; committee minutes, 1825-70;
      session minutes, 1842-70.   **MIC.1P/38**

   P. Ballyreagh
      Baptisms, 1823-1943; marriages, 1843-1936; session
      minutes, 1845-77; lists of communicants, 1846-1929.   **MIC.1P/424**

   R.C. Aughnacloy (Armagh diocese)
      [United with Aghaloo - *see under* **AGHALOO**]

CARRICK, CO. LONDONDERRY

C.I. Carrick (Derry diocese)
[Earliest registers destroyed in Dublin]

Baptisms, 1877-; marriages, 1848-; vestry minutes,
1848-; preachers' books, 1839-.   **In local custody**

CARRICKERGUS, CO. ANTRIM

B. Carrickfergus
Baptisms, marriages and minutes, 1864-.   **In local custody**

C.I. Carrickfergus (St Nicholas's) (Connor diocese)
Baptisms, 1740-99 and 1822-75; marriages, 1740-1845;
burials, 1740-1800 and 1825-70; confirmation lists,
1828-54.   **T.679/323-324, 339-343**

Plans of the church, 1931; accounts of building church
spire, 1778.   **C.R.1/25**

C. Carrickfergus
Baptisms, 1819-1969; marriages, 1824-43; list of members,
1824, 1847 and 1862; minutes, 1823-36 and 1862-3;
collections for the poor, 1860s.   **C.R.7/8**

M. Carrickfergus
Baptisms, 1815-58.   **MIC.429/1/352**

Baptisms, 1826-43; marriages, 1864-.   **In local custody**

P. 1st Carrickfergus
Baptisms, 1823-1901; marriages, 1823-1905; committee
minutes, 1824-1946; session minutes, 1860-1935; building
committee minutes, 1826-9 and 1879-81; account books,
1815-89; pew book, 1914-34; Sustentation Fund minutes,
1876-88.   **MIC.1P/157**

P. Carrickfergus (Joymount or 2nd)
Baptisms, 1852-1907; marriages, 1853-1908; session
minutes, 1852-78 and 1885-1925; committee minutes,
1852-94; building committee minutes, 1853-6;
communicants' lists, 1852-80 and 1890-99; lists of seats and
stipend payers, 1856-67, and stipend accounts, 1865-6;
Sabbath collection and expenditure accounts, 1853-1979.   **MIC.1P/332**

P. Loughmorne
[Up until 1892 it was part of the Eastern Reformed
Presbyterian Church]

Baptisms, 1848-53 and 1892-1952; marriages, 1863-1930.   **MIC.1P/160; C.R.3/43**

P. Woodburn
   Baptisms, 1863/5-1952; marriages, 1866-1932.   MIC.1P/160; C.R.3/43

R.C. Carrickfergus [Linked to Larne and Ballygowan up to
   c.1852 - *see also under* **LARNE**]

   Baptisms, 1852-72; marriages, 1852-72; indexes to
   baptisms and marriages, 1828-1852.   MIC.1D/68, 90

CARRICKFIN CHAPEL OF EASE (CHURCH OF IRELAND), CO. DONEGAL
   [*see under* **TEMPLECRONE**]

CARRICKMACLIN PRESBYTERIAN CHURCH, CO. MONAGHAN
   [*see under* **MAGHEROSS**]

CARRICKMACROSS CHURCH OF IRELAND PARISH, CO. MONAGHAN
   [*see under* **MAGHEROSS**]

CARRICKMACROSS ROMAN CATHOLIC PARISH, CO. MONAGHAN
   [*see under* **MAGHEROSS**]

CARRICKMANNON [*sic* CARRICKMANNAN] ROMAN CATHOLIC CHURCH, CO. DOWN
   [*see under* **SAINTFIELD**]

CARRICKMORE ROMAN CATHOLIC CHURCH, CO. TYRONE
   [*see under* **TERMONMAGUIRK**]

CARRIGALLEN, CO. LEITRIM

C.I. Carrigallen (Kilmore diocese)
   Baptisms, 1883-1986; marriages, 1845-1941; burials,
   1874-1936.   MIC.1/290

C.I. Killegar (Kilmore diocese)
   Baptisms, 1877-1985; marriages, 1845-1917; burials,
   1878-1986.   MIC.1/122

C.I. Newtowngore
   Baptisms, 1877-1921; marriages, 1847-1927; burials,
   1877-1981.   MIC.1/258

M. Newtowngore
Baptisms, 1882-1961; marriages, 1897-1949; quarterly
meeting minute books, 1897-1936.   **MIC.1E/55**

P. Carrigallen
Visitation book with details of each family by townland
and dates of baptisms of children, 1837-92; marriages,
1845-1909.   **MIC.1P/163**

R.C. Carrigallen (Mullanadaragh and'Aughal')
(Kilmore diocese)

Baptisms, 1829-91, with gaps; marriages, 1841-90, with
gaps; deaths, 1841-60.   **MIC.1D/7, 83**

**CARRIGART (HOLY TRINITY) CHURCH OF IRELAND
PARISH, CO. DONEGAL**
[*see under* **MEVAGH**]

CARRIGART PRESBYTERIAN CHURCH, CO. DONEGAL
[*see under* **MEVAGH**]

**CARRIGART ROMAN CATHOLIC CHURCH,
CO. DONEGAL**
[*see under* **MEVAGH**]

**CARROWDORE CHURCH OF IRELAND PARISH,
CO. DOWN**
[*see under* **DONAGHADEE**]

CARROWDORE PRESBYTERIAN CHURCH, CO. DOWN
[*see under* **DONAGHADEE**]

CARRYDUFF PRESBYTERIAN CHURCH, CO. DOWN
[*see under* **DRUMBO**]

**CASTLE ARCHDALE CHURCH OF IRELAND PARISH,
CO. FERMANAGH**
[*see under* **DERRYVULLAN**]

CASTLEBAR METHODIST CIRCUIT, CO. MAYO
[*see under* **AGLISH**]

**CASTLEBLAYNEY METHODIST CHURCH,
CO. MONAGHAN**
[*see under* **MUCKNO**]

**CASTLEBLAYNEY (1ST AND 2ND) PRESBYTERIAN
CHURCHES, CO. MONAGHAN**
    [*see under* **MUCKNO**]

**CASTLEBLAYNEY ROMAN CATHOLIC PARISH,
CO. MONAGHAN**
    [*see under* **MUCKNO**]

CASTLEBOY, CO. DOWN

    P. Cloughey
        Baptisms, 1841-1946; marriages, 1845-1907.   **MIC.1P/314**

        Transcript of graveyard inscriptions, 1865-1954.   **T.1602/4**

    R.C. [The Roman Catholic parish of Ballygalget contains
        Castleboy parish - *see under* **ARDQUIN**]

**CASTLECAULFIELD METHODIST CHURCH,
CO. TYRONE**
    [*see under* **DONAGHMORE**]

**CASTLECAULFIELD PRESBYTERIAN CHURCH,
CO. TYRONE**
    [*see under* **DONAGHMORE**]

**CASTLEDAWSON CHURCH OF IRELAND PARISH,
CO. LONDONDERRY**
    [*see under* **BALLYSCULLION**]

**CASTLEDAWSON METHODIST CHURCH,
CO. LONDONDERRY**
    [*see under* **MAGHERAFELT**]

**CASTLEDAWSON PRESBYTERIAN CHURCH,
CO. LONDONDERRY**
    [*see under* **MAGHERAFELT**]

**CASTLEDERG CHURCH OF IRELAND PARISH,
CO. TYRONE**
    [*see under* **URNEY, COS TYRONE AND DONEGAL**]

CASTLEDERG METHODIST CHURCH, CO. TYRONE
    [*see under* **URNEY, COS TYRONE AND DONEGAL**]

CASTLEDERG (1ST) PRESBYTERIAN CHURCH, CO. TYRONE
[*see under* ARDSTRAW]

CASTLEDERG (2ND) PRESBYTERIAN CHURCH, CO. TYRONE
[*see under* URNEY, COS TYRONE AND DONEGAL]

CASTLEFIN METHODIST CHURCH, CO. DONEGAL
[*see under* DONAGHMORE, CO. DONEGAL]

CASTLERAHAN CHURCH OF IRELAND PARISH, CO. CAVAN

C.I. Castlerahan (Kilmore diocese)
Baptisms, 1879-1986; marriages, 1846-1956; burials, 1879-1982.　　　　　　　　　　　　　　　　　　**MIC.1/273**

C.I. Ballyjamesduff (Kilmore diocese)
[Partly in Castlerahan, Denn, Lurgan and Crosserlough parishes]

Baptisms, 1877-1986; marriages, 1845-1955; burials, 1879-1985.　　　　　　　　　　　　　　　　　　**MIC.1/273**

M. Ballyjamesduff
Baptisms, c.1839-1928; marriages, 1886-1917.　　　　**MIC.1E/50-51**

P. Ballyjamesduff
Baptisms and session minutes, 1834-7.　　　　**In Presbyterian Historical Society**

R.C Castlerahan and Munterconnaght (Kilmore diocese)
Baptisms, 1752-71, 1773-6, 1814-20, 1828-41 and
1854-79; marriages, 1751-71, 1773-5, 1814-20, 1832-41
and 1855-78; deaths, 1751-8, 1761-9, 1773-5, 1814-20
and 1832-41.　　　　　　　　　　　　　　　　　　**MIC.1D/81**

CASTLEREAGH PRESBYTERIAN CHURCH, CO. DOWN
[*see under* KNOCKBREDA]

CASTLEROCK CHURCH OF IRELAND PARISH, CO. LONDONDERRY
[*see under* DUNBOE]

CASTLETERRA, CO. CAVAN

C.I. Castleterra (or Ballyhaise) (Kilmore diocese)
Baptisms, 1877-1983; marriages, 1845-1910; burials,
1878-1986; membership register, 1870-1966.   **MIC.1/294**

R.C. Castletara (Kilmore diocese)
Baptisms, 1763-1809 and 1862-81; marriages, 1763-93
and 1808-09.   **MIC.1D/83-84**

CASTLEWELLAN CHURCH OF IRELAND PARISH, CO. DOWN
[*see under* KILMEGAN]

CASTLEWELLAN METHODIST CHURCH, CO. DOWN
[*see under* KILMEGAN]

CASTLEWELLAN PRESBYTERIAN CHURCH, CO. DOWN
[*see under* KILMEGAN]

CASTLEWELLAN ROMAN CATHOLIC CHURCH, CO. DOWN
[*see under* KILMEGAN]

CAVAN METHODIST CIRCUIT AND CHURCH, CO. CAVAN
[*see under* URNEY, CO. CAVAN]

CAVAN METHODIST CHURCH, CO. TYRONE
[*see under* DONACAVEY]

CAVANALECK PRESBYTERIAN CHURCH, CO. FERMANAGH
[*see under* AGHALURCHER]

CAVANDORAGH METHODIST CHURCH, CO. TYRONE
[*see under* ARDSTRAW]

CHARLEMONT CHURCH OF IRELAND PARISH, CO. ARMAGH
[*see under* LOUGHGALL]

CHARLESTOWN, CO. LOUTH

    C.I. Charlestown (Armagh diocese)
        Baptisms, 1822-36; marriages, 1824-45; burials,
        1823-80; confirmations, 1824-82, with gaps.   **MIC.1/200**

        Vestry minutes, 1840-.   **In local custody**

    R.C. [Charlestown parish is in the Roman Catholic parish of
        Tallanstown - *see under* **TALLANSTOWN**]

**CHRIST CHURCH, CHURCH OF IRELAND PARISH,
LISBURN, CO. ANTRIM**
    [*see under* **BLARIS**]

**CHRIST CHURCH CATHEDRAL (CHURCH OF IRELAND),
LISBURN, CO. ANTRIM**
    [*see under* **BLARIS**]

CHURCHILL METHODIST CHURCH, CO. FERMANAGH
    [*see under* **INISHMACSAINT**]

**CHURCHTOWN PRESBYTERIAN CHURCH,
CO. LONDONDERRY**
    [*see under* **TAMLAGHT O'CRILLY**]

**CLABBY CHURCH OF IRELAND PARISH,
CO. FERMANAGH**
    [*see under* **ENNISKILLEN**]

CLABBY METHODIST CHURCH, CO. FERMANAGH
    [*see under* **ENNISKILLEN**]

CLADY PRESBYTERIAN CHURCH, CO. TYRONE
    [*see under* **ARDSTRAW**]

CLADYMORE PRESBYTERIAN CHURCH, CO. ARMAGH
    [*see under* **KILCLOONEY**]

CLAGGAN PRESBYTERIAN CHURCH, CO. TYRONE
    [*see under* **LISSAN**]

**CLANABOGAN CHURCH OF IRELAND PARISH,
CO. TYRONE**
    [*see under* **DRUMRAGH**]

**CLANVARAGHAN ROMAN CATHOLIC CHURCH,
CO. DOWN**
    [*see under* **LOUGHINISLAND**]

CLARE CHURCH OF IRELAND PARISH, CO. ARMAGH
    [*see under* **BALLYMORE**]

CLARE PRESBYTERIAN CHURCH, CO. ARMAGH
    [*see under* **BALLYMORE**]

**CLARENDON STREET REFORMED PRESBYTERIAN
CHURCH, LONDONDERRY, CO. LONDONDERRY**
    [*see under* **TEMPLEMORE**]

**CLARKESBRIDGE PRESBYTERIAN CHURCH,
CO. ARMAGH**
    [*see under* **NEWTOWNHAMILTON**]

**CLAUDY ROMAN CATHOLIC CHURCH,
CO. LONDONDERRY**
    [*see under* **CUMBER UPPER**]

CLEENISH, CO. FERMANAGH

    C.I. Cleenish (Clogher diocese)
    [Earliest registers destroyed in Dublin]

        Baptisms, 1886-1947; marriages, 1845-1934; burials,
        1886-1922.   **MIC.1/224**

        Vestry minutes, 1823-; registers of vestrymen, 1886.   **In local custody**

    C.I. Kiltyclogher [Partly in Cleenish parish - *see under*
        CLOONCLARE]

    C.I. Lisbellaw (Clogher diocese)
    [Earliest registers destroyed in Dublin]

        Baptisms, 1877-; marriages, 1845-; burials, 1877-;
        vestry minutes, 1827-; registers of vestrymen, 1870-1930.   **In local custody**

    C.I. Mullaghdun (Clogher diocese)
    [Earliest registers destroyed in Dublin]

        Baptisms, 1819-36 and 1878-99; marriages, 1819-34 and
        1845-1921; burials, 1819-35 and 1878-1927.   **MIC.1/245**

        Vestry minutes, 1871-; registers of vestrymen, 1918-34.   **In local custody**

M. Letterbreen
Enniskillen Circuit records may include baptisms,
1823-1953, and marriages, 1864-1906, for Letterbreen;
circuit schedule book, 1866-80; minutes of quarterly
meetings, 1877-93.   **MIC.1E/15**

M. Lisbellaw [Primitive Wesleyan Methodists]
Baptisms, 1872-8.   **MIC.1E/9**

M. Lisbellaw [Wesleyan Methodists]
Baptisms, 1823-78; marriages, 1866-70; circuit schedule
book, 1866-80.   **MIC.1E/15**

M. Lisbellaw (post 1878)
Baptisms, 1879-1953; marriages, 1891-1937; circuit
schedule book, 1880-93.   **MIC.1E/10, 15**

P. Lisbellaw
Baptisms, 1851-1984; marriages, 1846-1936.   **MIC.1P/284**

R.C. Cleenish (Clogher diocese)
Baptisms, 1835-9 and 1859-81; marriages, 1866-81.   **MIC.1D/14**

[*See also under* **ENNISKILLEN** as part of the parish
forms part of the Roman Catholic parish of Enniskillen]

CLOGH CHURCH OF IRELAND PARISH,
CO. MONAGHAN
[*see under* **CLONES**]

CLOGHAN ROMAN CATHOLIC CHURCH, CO. DONEGAL
[*see under* **KILTEEVOGUE**]

CLOGHER, CO. LOUTH

R.C. Clogher or Clogherhead or Walshestown
(Armagh diocese)

Baptisms, 1744-77, 1780-99 and 1833-81; marriages,
1742-71, 1780-99 and 1833-81; deaths, 1744-72 and
1780-99, with gaps.   **MIC.1D/53**

CLOGHER, CO. TYRONE

C.I. Augher, St Mark's (Clogher diocese)
Baptisms, 1866-1985; marriages, 1869-1935.   **MIC.1/23, 230**

[Burials may be in with Clogher records]

C.I. Clogher (Clogher diocese)
Baptisms, 1763-1935; marriages, 1777-8 and 1796-1845; burials, 1783 and 1798-1882; list of churchwardens, 1713-1900; vestry minutes, 1713-95 and 1815-1901; confirmation list, 1866.

MIC.1/22-23; T.2655/4/1

Marriages, 1845-; burials, 1882-.

In local custody

C.I. Fivemiletown (Clogher diocese)
[Formed out of Aghalurcher and Clogher parishes]

Baptisms, 1804-77; marriages, 1804-45; burials, 1808-1909.

MIC.1/5-6

Baptisms, 1877-; marriages, 1845-; burials, 1910-; vestry minutes, 1870-; register of vestrymen, 1870-; preachers' books, 1890-.

In local custody

C.I. Newtownsaville (Clogher diocese)
Baptisms, 1877-1901; marriages, 1860-1935; burials, 1877-1933.

MIC.1/228

Register of vestrymen, 1924-.

In local custody

M. Fivemiletown [Wesleyan Methodists]
Baptisms, 1841-1933; marriages, 1873-9 and 1883-1933; circuit schedule books, 1865-79 and 1881-1910; circuit quarterly meeting minutes, 1900-37; lists of members, 1879, 1884, 1887, 1889 and c.1890; Sunday School roll book used as a Temperance Pledge book, 1879-82.

MIC.1E/28, 47

M. Fivemiletown [Primitive Wesleyan Methodists]
Marriages, 1873-8.

MIC.1E/47

P. Aughentaine [*sic* Aughintain]
Baptisms, 1836-1953; marriages, 1845-1909; marriage notices, 1846-1906; committee minutes, 1887-9.

MIC.1P/80; MIC.1P/230/4

P. Carntall or Clogher
Baptisms, 1819-45 and 1858-1985; marriages, 1829-1934; marriage notices, 1860-1906; lists of communicants, 1829-38, 1860-97 and 1903-13; session minutes, 1825-43 and 1862-1954; committee minutes, 1831-1929; account book, 1814-62; stipend and other accounts, 1874-1924.

MIC.1P/96; MIC.1P/230/4B

P. Glenhoy
Baptisms, 1852 and 1864-1984; marriages, 1869-1907; marriage notices, 1860-1906.

MIC.1P/255; MIC.1P/230/4B

R.C. Aughintaine [*sic* Aghintain] **(Fivemiletown)**
(Clogher diocese)

Baptisms, 1870-81; marriages, 1870-83.   **MIC.1D/12**

R.C. Clogher (Clogher diocese)
Baptisms, 1856-81; marriages, 1825-35 and 1840-81.   **MIC.1D/10; C.R.2/14**

CLOGHERNEY, CO. TYRONE

C.I. Clogherney (Armagh diocese)
[Earliest registers destroyed in Dublin]

Baptisms, 1859-1951; marriages, 1845-1935; burials,
1886-1933.   **MIC.1/119; C.R.1/5**

Vestry minutes, 1824-; register of vestrymen, 1870-;
preachers' books, 1845-.   **In local custody**

M. Beragh
Baptisms, 1832-1953; circuit schedule books, 1866-1909;
membership registers, 1863-1907; quarterly meeting
minute book, 1859-1902; circuit stewards' book, 1829-85.

P. Clogherney
Baptisms, 1865-1984; marriages, 1845-1930; printed
history of the church.   **MIC.1P/246;**
                                                          D.3000/T/631

P. Seskinore (formerly **Newtownparry**)
Baptisms, 1863-1937; marriages, 1845-1928.   **MIC.1P/245**

R.C. Beragh (**Ballintacker**) (Armagh diocese)
Baptisms, 1832-81; marriages, 1834-82.   **MIC.1D/35**

CLOGHJORDAN, CO. TIPPERARY

M. Cloughjordan
Baptisms, 1834-43.   **MIC.429/1/89**

CLONALLAN, CO. DOWN

C.I. Clonallan (Dromore diocese)
[United to Warrenpoint in 1922]

[Earliest registers destroyed in Dublin]

Baptisms, 1884-; marriages, 1845-; burials, 1884-; vestry
minutes, 1806-; churchwardens' accounts, 1806-45 and
1862-1909; registers of vestrymen, 1873-; preachers'
books, 1862-75 and 1917-.   **In local custody**

Index to names on gravestones in Clonallan, compiled in
1901 by Dr P Crosslé. **C.R.1/9**

R.C. Clonallon (Dromore diocese)
[Partly in Warrenpoint parish]

Baptisms, 1826-69; marriages, 1826-82. **MIC.1D/22**

CLONANEESE LOWER AND UPPER PRESBYTERIAN CHURCHES, CO. TYRONE
[*see under* **KILLEESHIL**]

CLONCA, CO. DONEGAL

C.I. Cloncha (Raphoe diocese)
[Earliest registers destroyed in Dublin]

Vestry minutes, 1693-1707. **D.803**

Baptisms, 1877-, but there are imperfect copies of
baptisms from 1829; marriages, 1845-; burials, 1877-,
but there are imperfect copies of burials from 1858;
vestry minutes, 1828-; registers of vestrymen, 1870-;
preachers' books, 1835-64, 1886-91 and 1900-. **In local custody**

P. Malin
Baptisms, 1866-1983; marriages, 1845-1948;
communicants' roll, 1863-1937. **MIC.1P/236; C.R.3/44**

R.C. Clonca (Malin) (Derry diocese)
[Partly in Clonca parish]

Baptisms, 1856-81; marriages, 1870-85. **MIC.1D/54**

R.C. Culdaff (Derry diocese)
[Partly in Clonca parish - *see under* **CULDAFF**]

CLONDAHORKY, CO. DONEGAL

C.I. Clondehorkey (Raphoe diocese)
Baptisms, 1871-1906; marriages, 1845-1915; burials,
1884-1926; vestry minutes, 1818-1951. **MIC.1/199**

Register of vestrymen, 1870-; preachers' books, 1879-. **In local custody**

C.I. Dunfanaghy (Raphoe diocese)
Baptisms, 1873-1983; marriages, 1875-1910; burials,
1873-1983; vestry minutes, 1873-1909. **MIC.1/160**

P. Dunfanaghy
Baptisms, 1830-91 and 1895; marriages, 1830-45; session
minutes, 1830-98; communicants' roll, 1863-71. **MIC.1P/152**

R.C. Clondahorkey (Raphoe diocese)
  Baptisms, 1877-81; marriages, 1877-82.   **MIC.1D/86**

CLONDAVADDOG, CO. DONEGAL

C.I. Clondevaddock (Raphoe diocese)
  Baptisms, 1794-1931; marriages, 1794-1919; burials,
  1794-1933; vestry minutes, 1843-1950; confirmation
  rolls, 1876-1961, with gaps; account books, 1853-94
  and 1899-1919; census, 1796; details about schools in the
  area, 1876-9.   **MIC.1/164**

R.C. Clondavadoc (Fanad) (Raphoe diocese)
  Baptisms, 1847-71; marriages and deaths, 1847-69.   **MIC.1D/87**

CLONDERMOT, CO. LONDONDERRY

C.I. Clooney (Derry diocese)
  Baptisms, 1867-1900; burials, 1867-98.   **MIC.1/6**

  Marriages, 1868-; vestry minutes, 1867-; registers of
  vestrymen, 1872-; preachers' books, 1867-.   **In local custody**

C.I. Glendermott (Derry diocese)
  Baptisms, 1810-70; marriages, 1808-45; burials, 1828-70. **MIC.1/108**

  Baptisms, 1871-; marriages, 1846-; burials, 1871-; vestry
  minutes, 1899-; register of vestrymen, 1870-; preachers'
  books, 1856-.   **In local custody**

P. Glendermott
  Baptisms, 1855-.   **In local custody**

P. Gortnessy
  Baptisms, 1839-1983; marriages, 1845-1977.   **MIC.1P/189**

P. Waterside
  Baptisms, 1866-1935; marriages, 1866-1911.   **MIC.1P/427**

R.C. Glendermott (Waterside) (Derry diocese)
  Baptisms, 1864-81; marriages, 1864-80.   **MIC.1D/56**

  Printed history of St Columb's, 1841-1991.   **C.R.2/18**

R.P. Faughan
  Marriages, 1864-1932; session minutes, 1848-1947;
  committee minutes, 1888-1938, with accounts, 1881-92.   **MIC.1C/10**

CLONDUFF, CO. DOWN

C.I. Clonduff (Down diocese)
Baptisms, 1782-1871; marriages, 1786-1850; burials,
1787-1849 and 1864-73; accounts, 1871-1913; vestry
minutes, 1811-70.   **T.679/17, 344-349**

Vestry minutes, 1870-; churchwardens' accounts,
1811-1903.   **In local custody**

P. Clonduff
Baptisms, 1842-1968; marriages, 1864-1936.   **MIC.1P/126**

P. Hilltown
Baptisms, 1845-1968; marriages, 1864-1914.   **MIC.1P/127**

R.C. Clonduff (Dromore diocese)
Baptisms, 1850-80; marriages, 1850-80; funerals,
1850-81.   **MIC.1D/29**

Printed history of Clonduff parish from the 17th century
to 1940.   **C.R.2/4**

CLONENAGH AND CLONAGHEEN

M. Mountrath
Baptisms, 1834-46.   **MIC.429/1/124**

CLONES, COS FERMANAGH AND MONAGHAN

C.I. Aghadrumsee (Clogher diocese)
Baptisms, marriages and burials, 1829-1935.   **MIC.1/236**

Vestry minute books, 1871-.   **In local custody**

C.I. Clogh (Clogher diocese)
Baptisms, 1811-91; marriages, 1792-1910; burials,
1810-1986.   **MIC.1/288**

Baptisms, 1891-; marriages, 1910-; vestry minutes,
1831-; preachers' books, 1866-.   **In local custody**

C.I. Clones (Clogher diocese)
Baptisms, 1682-1873; marriages, 1682-1788 and
1792-1912; burials, 1682-1704, 1709, 1722-5, 1733-4
and 1808-1901; vestry minutes, 1688-1885, which
include list of seatholders, 1735-83, details of visitations,
1803-08, and list of the poor, c.1741; preachers' book,
1841-63; list of clergy, 1609-1873.   **MIC.1/147; C.R.1/58**

M. Clones [Primitive Wesleyan Methodists]
   Baptisms, 1872-80.   **MIC.1E/27**

M. Clones [Wesleyan Methodists]
   Baptisms, 1839-1970; marriages, 1872-1946.   **MIC.1E/27, 51A**

   Baptisms, 1839-43.   **MIC.429/1/169**

P. Clones
   Baptisms, 1856-1984; marriages, 1859-1956.   **MIC.1P/273**

P. Smithborough
   Baptisms, 1868-1983; marriages, 1845-1927; burials,
   1883-1982; session minutes, 1873-4 and 1883-1983;
   communicants, 1889-1913 and 1932-55.   **MIC.1P/200**

P. Stonebridge
   Baptisms, 1819-1980; marriages, 1819-1956; visitation
   book giving details of families in each townland, 1834.   **MIC.1P/165**

R.C. Clones (Clogher diocese)
   Baptisms, 1848-81; marriages, 1821-81.   **MIC.1D/1, 20-21**

R.C. Roslea (Clogher diocese)
   Baptisms and marriages, 1862-81.   **MIC.1D/20**

CLONFEACLE, COS ARMAGH AND TYRONE

C.I. Annaghmore (Armagh diocese)
   [*see under* **LOUGHGALL**]

C.I. Brantry (Armagh diocese)
   [Partly in Clonfeacle parish - *see under* **AGHALOO**]

C.I. Clonfeacle (Armagh diocese)
   [Earliest registers destroyed in Dublin]

   Extracts from vestry minutes, 1763-1831.   **T.679/43**

   Baptisms, 1869-; marriages, 1845-; burials, 1870-; vestry
   minutes, c.1870.   **In local custody**

C.I. Derrygortreavy (Armagh diocese)
   [Earliest registers destroyed in Dublin]

   Baptisms, 1875-; marriages, 1845-; burials, 1878-.   **In local custody**

C.I. Moy (Armagh diocese)
   [Earliest registers destroyed in Dublin]

   Baptisms, 1880-; marriages, 1845-; burials, 1881-; vestry
   minutes, 1873-; preachers' books, 1845-.   **In local custody**

M. Blackwatertown
  Baptisms, 1874-; marriages, 1899-.   **In local custody**

M. Moy
  Baptisms, 1874-; marriages, 1863-; circuit schedule books,
  1879-; minutes of quarterly meetings, 1879-.   **In local custody**

P. Benburb
  Baptisms, 1874-1985; marriages, 1845-1936; committee
  minutes, 1858-1923.   **MIC.1P/60**

P. Eglish
  Baptisms, 1856-1963; marriages, 1846-1936; deaths,
  1858-1927; session minutes, 1858-1963; communion roll,
  1858-1961.   **MIC.1P/122**

P. Moy
  Baptisms, 1851-1986; marriages, 1852-1917; committee
  minutes, 1853-69 and 1871-99; communion roll, 1933-44;
  lease of land in Moy for the erection of the church, 1854.   **MIC.1P/36; C.R.3/36**

R.C. Clonfeacle (Moy) (Armagh diocese)
  Baptisms and marriages, 1814-81.   **MIC.1D/31**

CLONKEEN, CO. LOUTH

C.I. Clonkeen (Armagh diocese)
  [United with Charlestown in 1886]

  Vestry minutes, 1795-1886.   **MIC.1/201**

  Vestry minutes, 1745-94.   **In local custody**

R.C. [Clonkeen parish is in the Roman Catholic parish of
  Tallanstown - *see under* **TALLANSTOWN**]

CLONLEIGH, CO. DONEGAL

C.I. Clonleigh (Raphoe diocese)
  Baptisms, 1872-1983; marriages, 1845-1956; burials,
  1877-1984; vestry minutes, 1788-1828; confirmation
  register, 1863-1983; Sustentation Fund account book,
  1870-73.   **MIC.1/179**

  Vestry minutes, 1870-; preachers' books, 1870-.   **In local custody**

P. Ballindrait
  Baptisms, 1819-61 and 1873-1923; marriages, 1827-8 and
  1845-1901.   **MIC.1P/185**

R.C. Clonleigh and Camus (Derry diocese)
   [Partly in Camus parish]

   Baptisms, 1773-95, 1836-7 and 1853-80; marriages,
   1778-81 and 1843-81.   **MIC.1D/61**

CLONMAIN METHODIST CHURCH, CO. ARMAGH
   [*see under* **LOUGHGALL**]

CLONMANY, CO. DONEGAL

   C.I. Clonmany (Derry diocese)
      Baptisms, 1891-; marriages, 1845-; burials, 1893-;
      register of vestrymen, 1870-.   **In local custody**

   R.C. Clonmany (Derry diocese)
      Baptisms, 1852-81.   **MIC.1D/54**

CLONMORE, CO. LOUTH

   R.C. Togher (Armagh diocese)
      Baptisms, 1791-1828 and 1869-81; marriages,
      1791-1828 and 1873-81; deaths, 1791-1817.   **MIC.1D/48**

CLONOE, CO. TYRONE

   C.I. Brackaville (Armagh diocese)
      [Partly in Clonoe parish - *see under* **DONAGHENRY**]

   C.I. Clonoe (Armagh diocese)
      Baptisms, 1824-1957; marriages, 1812-13, 1818 and
      1824-45; burials, 1824-1957; vestry minutes, 1783-1852;
      confirmations, 1824, 1828, 1833, 1837, 1849, 1852, 1856
      and 1859; list of rectors, 1791-1957; gravestone
      inscriptions, c.1671-1830; preachers' books, 1887-1902;
      treasurers' books, 1926-35.   **MIC.1/11; T.2831**

      Marriages, 1845-; preachers' books, 1872-.   **In local custody**

   R.C. Clonoe
      Baptisms, 1810-16 and 1822-81; marriages, 1806-16 and
      1823-81; deaths, 1806-16.   **MIC.1D/30**

CLONTARF PRESBYTERIAN CHURCH, DUBLIN
   [*see under* **DUBLIN**]

CLONTIBRET, CO. MONAGHAN

C.I. Clontibret (Clogher diocese)
Baptisms, 1864-5 and 1876-1983; marriages, 1845-1940;
burials, 1864-5 and 1876-1951; vestry minutes, 1711 and
1749-1876; preachers' book, 1846-1926; lists of the poor,
1834-46 and 1858-60; Clontibret National School roll
book, 1873-83.   **MIC.1/149; D.2365**

C.I. Broomfield (Clogher diocese)
[Partly in Clontibret parish and partly in Donaghmoyne
parish]

Baptisms, 1877-1959; marriages, 1857-1953; burials,
1878-1957; vestry minutes, 1844-1963; accounts,
1845-60; list of churchwardens, 1844-57.   **MIC.1/152**

R.C. Clontibret (Clogher diocese)
Baptisms, 1860-81; marriages, 1861-81.   **MIC.1D/16**

R.C. Muckno (Clogher diocese)
[Partly in Clontibret - *see under* **MUCKNO**]

CLONTIBRET (1ST) PRESBYTERIAN CHURCH,
CO. MONAGHAN
[*see under* **MONAGHAN**]

CLONTIBRET (2ND) PRESBYTERIAN CHURCH,
CO. MONAGHAN
[*see under* **TULLYCORBET**]

CLOONCLARE, CO. LEITRIM

C.I. Cloonclare or Manorhamilton (Kilmore diocese)

Baptisms, 1816-1972; marriages, 1816-1921; burials,
1816-1972.   **MIC.1/268**

C.I. Kiltyclogher (Kilmore diocese)
[Partly in Cloonclare parish]

Baptisms, 1898-1985; burials, 1877-1982.   **MIC.1/232**

M. Manorhamilton
Baptisms, 1836-43.   **MIC.429/1/214**

CLOONEY CHURCH OF IRELAND PARISH,
CO. LONDONDERRY
[*see under* **CLONDERMOT**]

CLOUGH PRESBYTERIAN CHURCH, CO. ANTRIM
[*see under* **DUNAGHY**]

**CLOUGH NON-SUBSCRIBING PRESBYTERIAN
CHURCH, CO. DOWN**
[*see under* **LOUGHINISLAND**]

CLOUGH PRESBYTERIAN CHURCH, CO. DOWN
[*see under* **LOUGHINISLAND**]

CLOUGHEY PRESBYTERIAN CHURCH, CO. DOWN
[*see under* **CASTLEBOY**]

**CLOUGHMILLS ROMAN CATHOLIC PARISH,
CO. ANTRIM**
[*see under* **FINVOY**]

**CLOUGHWATER PRESBYTERIAN CHURCH,
CO. ANTRIM**
[*see under* **SKERRY**]

**CLOUGHWATER REFORMED PRESBYTERIAN CHURCH,
CO. ANTRIM**
[*see under* **KILRAGHTS**]

CLOVENEDEN PRESBYTERIAN CHURCH, CO. ARMAGH
[*see under* **LOUGHGALL**]

**CLOVERHILL CHURCH OF IRELAND PARISH,
CO. CAVAN**
[*see under* **ANNAGH**]

COAGH PRESBYTERIAN CHURCH, CO. TYRONE
[*see under* **TAMLAGHT**]

COAGH ROMAN CATHOLIC PARISH, CO. TYRONE
[*see under* **TAMLAGHT**]

**COALISLAND ROMAN CATHOLIC CHURCH,
CO. TYRONE**
[*see under* **DONAGHENRY**]

COLAGHTY [*sic* COOLAGHTY] CHURCH OF IRELAND PARISH, CO. FERMANAGH
[*see under* MAGHERACULMONEY]

COLERAINE, CO. LONDONDERRY

C. Coleraine
Baptisms, 1837-50, 1859-81 and 1938-; marriages, 1847-8, 1855 and 1938-; burials, 1844-9; minutes, 1844-50 and 1854-98.   **In local custody**

C.I. Coleraine (Connor diocese)
Baptisms, 1769-1873; baptisms in Coleraine workhouse, 1842-78; marriages, 1769-1845; burials, 1769-1882; vestry minutes, 1769-1816; communicants, 1818-37; preachers' books, 1823-37 and 1852-66.   **MIC.1/7A**

M. Coleraine
Baptisms, 1831-1987; marriages, 1864-1937.   **MIC.1E/63**

Baptisms, 1831-41.   **MIC.429/1/373**

P. 1st Coleraine
Baptisms, 1845-1901; marriages, 1845-1901; marriage notices, 1951-71; session minutes, 1836-44 and 1853-1926; committee minutes, 1827-30 and 1916-35.   **MIC.1P/54; C.R.3/10**

P. 2nd Coleraine (New Row)
Baptisms, 1834 (1 entry) and 1842-1986; marriages, 1809-40 and 1845-1928; index to marriages, 1809-40; marriage notices, 1863-1951; register of families, 1831; Sunday School register, 1837-51; list of seatholders, 1834; communion roll, 1848-96; extract from treasurers' book, 1774-1834; account book, 1836-66; collection books, 1830-65; stipend and other accounts, 1828-34; session minutes, 1850-1932.   **MIC.1P/31; T.1069; D.1642**

P. 3rd Coleraine (Terrace Row)
Baptisms, 1862-1939; marriages, 1845-1903; marriage notices, 1863-1951; communion roll, 1862-3.   **MIC.1P/101; D.1642**

R.C. Coleraine (Down and Connor diocese)
Baptisms and marriages, 1848-81.   **MIC.1D/70**

R.C. Killowen (St John's, Coleraine) (Down and Connor diocese)
[Partly in Coleraine parish but also includes parishes of Aghadowey, Ballyrashane, Dunboe, Killowen, Macosquin and part of Ballyaghran]

Baptisms, 1843-80.   **MIC.1D/62**

R.P. Ballyclabber
Baptisms, 1862-1932; marriages, 1863-91; session
minutes, 1847-1947; committee minutes, 1877-1910,
with accounts and lists of members, 1863-1926.   **MIC.1C/22**

COLLON, CO. LOUTH

C.I. Collon, Mosstown and Dromin (Armagh diocese)
Baptisms, 1790-1969; marriages, 1790-1845; burials,
1791-1950; vestry minutes, 1771-1872, which include a
list of those exempt from payment of hearth tax, 1793,
poor lists, 1766-1817, and cess applotment lists, 1772-87;
confirmation lists, 1824-70.   **MIC.1/163**

R.C. Collon (Armagh diocese)
Baptisms, 1789-1807 and 1819-81; marriages, 1789-1807,
1817-45 and 1848-81.   **MIC.1D/48**

COLUMBKILLE, CO. LONGFORD

C.I. Columbkille [Formerly Ardagh diocese but now in Kilmore
diocese]

Baptisms, 1894-1985; marriages, 1845-1934; burials,
1896-1985.   **MIC.1/292**

COMBER, CO. DOWN

C.I. Comber (Down diocese)
Baptisms, 1683-1877; marriages, 1683-1845; burials,
1683-1881; vestry minutes, 1700-1914, which include
a list of churchwardens, 1797-1834, and poor lists, c.1799-
c.1834.   **T.679/407, 409,
                                                                 411-415B**

Extracts from Comber parish registers, 1712-1840.   **T.921**

Lists of burials in the churchyard, 1918-21; and plan of
churchyard, c.1920.   **C.R.1/40**

M. Comber
Baptisms, 1884-1945; marriages, 1894-1937; circuit
schedule books, 1884-1936; membership registers and
quarterly class rolls, 1899-1943; treasurers' account book,
1912-19.   **D.2687**

Baptisms, 1842-43.   **MIC.429/1/535**

N.S.P Comber
Baptisms, 1838-1904; marriages, 1838-45, 1848 and
1850-1971; notes on deaths, 1920-66; committee

minutes, 1863-1911 and 1915-64; brief sketch of the
history of the congregation, written c.1880; annual
reports, 1866-1913.   **MIC.1B/1**

N.S.P. Moneyrea
   Marriage notice book, 1845-58.   **C.R.4/15A/1**

   Trust deeds relating to the church, 1719-1875.   **T.1627**

P. 1st Comber
   Baptisms, 1847-70; marriages, 1845-71.   **MIC.1P/58**

   Marriage notices, 1883-1918.   **D.2643**

P. 2nd Comber
   Baptisms, 1852, 1862-71 and 1873-1921; marriages,
   1845-1908.   **MIC.1P/395**

   Marriage notices, 1882-1900.   **D.2643/1**

   Baptisms, 1827-74; marriages, 1834-45.   **In Presbyterian
                                                                 Historical Society**

R.C. [Comber parish forms part of the Roman Catholic parish
         of Newtownards - *see under* **NEWTOWNARDS**]

CONLIG PRESBYTERIAN CHURCH, CO. DOWN
   [*see under* **BANGOR**]

CONNOR, CO. ANTRIM

C.I. Connor (Connor diocese)
      [Earliest records destroyed in Dublin]

      Baptisms, 1871-; marriages, 1845-; burials, 1879-.   **In local custody**

P. Connor
   Baptisms, 1819-1963; marriages, 1845-1900.   **MIC.1P/162**

P. Kells
   Baptisms, 1873-97; marriages, 1889-1921.   **MIC.1P/310**

R.C. Drummaul (Down and Connor diocese)
      [Connor parish is united with Drummaul and Antrim -
      see under **DRUMMAUL**]

R.P. Kellswater
   Minutes, c.1789-1802 and 1806-09.   **C.R.5/9**

CONVOY, CO. DONEGAL

C.I. Convoy (Raphoe diocese)
Baptisms, 1871-1981; marriages, 1845-1902; burials, 1881-1980; register of vestrymen, 1870-1917; register of members, 1870.   **MIC.1/208**

P. Convoy
Baptisms, 1822-1914; marriages, 1846-1938.   **MIC.1P/220**

R.C. Raphoe (Raphoe diocese)
[Convoy parish forms part of the Roman Catholic parish of Raphoe - *see under* **RAPHOE**]

R.P. Convoy
Marriages, 1868-1940.   **MIC.1C/6**

CONWAL, CO. DONEGAL

C.I. Conwall (Raphoe diocese)
Baptisms, 1876-1951; marriages, 1845-1950; burials, 1878-1904; vestry minutes, 1823-70, with accounts, 1822-34.   **MIC.1/211**

Vestry minutes, 1871-2.   **In local custody**

M. Letterkenny
Baptisms, 1830-41.   **MIC.429/1/504**

P. 1st Letterkenny
Baptisms, 1821-9 and 1848-1900; marriages, 1845-1929; deaths, 1864-1901.   **MIC.1P/223**

P. 2nd Letterkenny
Baptisms, 1821-58; marriages, 1821-43; session minutes, 1821-58, recording names of those admitted to the congregation; history of the congregation, 1820-57.   **MIC.1P/225**

P. 3rd Letterkenny
Baptisms, 1841-1907 and 1922-4; marriages, 1845-1928.   **MIC.1P/222**

P. Trenta
Baptisms, 1836-86; marriages, 1838-1938; deaths, 1843-87.   **MIC.1P/224**

R.C. Conwall and Glenswilly (Letterkenny)
(Raphoe diocese)

Baptisms, 1874-81; marriages, 1877-81.   **MIC.1D/85**

R.C. Conwall and Leck (Letterkenny) (Raphoe diocese)
Baptisms, 1853-62 and 1868-81; marriages, 1857-63.   **MIC.1D/85**

R.P. Gortlee
    Baptisms, 1872-1922.   **MIC.1P/226**

COOKSTOWN BAPTIST CHURCH, CO. TYRONE
    [*see under* **DERRYLORAN**]

COOKSTOWN METHODIST CHURCH, CO. TYRONE
    [*see under* **DERRYLORAN**]

COOKSTOWN (1ST, 2ND and 3RD) PRESBYTERIAN CHURCHES, CO. TYRONE
    [*see under* **DERRYLORAN**]

COOLNACRUNAUGHT METHODIST CHURCH, CO. TYRONE
    [*see under* **ARDSTRAW**]

COOLEY CHURCH OF IRELAND PARISH, CO. TYRONE
    [*see under* **TERMONMAGUIRK**]

COOLOCK, CO. DUBLIN

    C.I. Coolock (Dublin diocese)
      Baptisms and marriages, 1794-9.   **D.1503/3/8/1**

COONEEN CHURCH OF IRELAND PARISH, CO. FERMANAGH
    [*see under* **AGHALURCHER**]

COOTEHILL (1ST and 2ND) PRESBYTERIAN CHURCHES, CO. CAVAN
    [*see under* **DRUMGOON**]

COOTEHILL PRIMITIVE WESLEYAN METHODIST CHURCH, CO. CAVAN
    [*see under* **DRUMGOON**]

COOTEHILL WESLEYAN METHODIST CIRCUIT AND CHURCH, COS CAVAN AND MONAGHAN
    [*see under* **DRUMGOON**]

COOTEHILL ROMAN CATHOLIC CHURCH, CO. CAVAN
    [*see under* **DRUMGOON**]

CORGLASS PRESBYTERIAN CHURCH, CO. CAVAN
    [*see under* **BAILIEBOROUGH**]

CORK, CO. CORK

  M. Cork and Cove Circuit
    Baptisms, 1842-4.   **MIC.429/1/530-531**

CORLEA PRESBYTERIAN CHURCH, CO. MONAGHAN
    [*see under* **AGHNAMULLEN**]

CORLESPRATTEN [*sic* CORLISBRATTAN] **METHODIST CHURCH, CO. CAVAN**
    [*see under* **KILLASHANDRA**]

CORLOUGH ROMAN CATHOLIC PARISH, CO. CAVAN
    [*see under* **TEMPLEPORT**]

CORONARY [*sic* CORRANEARY] **PRESBYTERIAN CHURCH, CO. CAVAN**
    [*see under* **KNOCKBRIDE**]

CORRANEARY PRESBYTERIAN CHURCH, CO. CAVAN
    [*see under* **CORONARY**]

CORRAWALLEN CHURCH OF IRELAND PARISH, CO. LEITRIM
    [*see under* **DRUMREILLY**]

CORRICK PRESBYTERIAN CHURCH, CO. TYRONE
    [*see under* **BODONY UPPER**]

CORTUBBER [*sic* CORTOBER] **METHODIST CHURCH, CO. MONAGHAN**
    [*see under* **KILDRUMSHERDAN**]

CORVALLEY [*sic* CORVALLY] **PRESBYTERIAN CHURCH, CO. MONAGHAN**
    [Formerly known as **CARRICKMACLIN** and sometimes
    referred to as **CARRICKMACROSS** - *see under*
    MAGHEROSS]

COVE METHODIST CHURCH, CO. CORK
[*see under* CORK]

CRAIGADOOISH CHAPEL OF EASE (CHURCH OF IRELAND), CO. DONEGAL
[*see under* TAUGHBOYNE]

CRAIGMORE METHODIST CHURCH, CO. ANTRIM
[*see under* AGHAGALLON]

CRAIGS, CO. ANTRIM

C.I. Craigs (Connor diocese)
Baptisms, 1839-1925; marriages, 1841-1925; burials, 1841-1944; register of vestrymen, 1870-1910.　　**MIC.1/34**

Sunday School roll books, 1842-6 and 1866; Sustentation Fund account book, 1871-7; register of marriage banns published, 1850-1962; communicants, 1893-1901; confirmations, 1833-1900; lists of families, 1893-1901; minutes of Craigs Church Society, 1860-81, with a list of members, 1860-61.　　**C.R.1/55**

Vestry minutes, 1840-.　　**In local custody**

M. Cullybackey (Originally a United Free Presbyterian Church)

Baptisms, 1839-; marriages, 1869-.　　**In local custody**

P. Cullybackey (Cunningham Memorial)
Baptisms, 1812-43 and 1848-1925; marriages, 1818-38 and 1845-1919; list of communicants, 1800-36; list of seatholders and stipend payers, 1821-36.　　**MIC.1P/88; C.R.3/7**

Baptisms, 1726-1815; marriages, 1727-92.　　**In Presbyterian Historical Society**

R.C. [*see under* AHOGHILL]

R.P. Cullybackey
Baptisms, 1836-1940; marriages, 1822-52 and 1863-1908; communicants' roll books, 1843-1931; session minutes, 1818-1938; committee minutes, 1926-83; register of members, c.1900.　　**MIC.1C/19**

R.P. Kellswater and Cullybackey
Minutes, c.1789-1802 and 1806-07.　　**C.R.5/9**

CRANAGILL METHODIST CHURCH, CO. ARMAGH
[*see under* **TARTARAGHAN**]

CRANFIELD, CO. ANTRIM

   C.I. Cranfield
        [*see under* **DUNEANE**]

   R.C. [*see under* **DRUMMAUL**]

**CREEVAGH REFORMED PRESBYTERIAN CHURCH,
CO. MONAGHAN**
        [*see under* **TULLYCORBET**]

**CREEVAN OR 2ND BALLYNAHATTY PRESBYTERIAN
CHURCH, CO. MONAGHAN**
        [*see under* **DRUMRAGH**]

CREGGAN, COS ARMAGH AND LOUTH

   C.I. Creggan (Armagh diocese)
        Baptisms, 1808-1925; marriages, 1808-39; marriage
        banns, 1816-28; burials, 1808-1917; vestry minutes,
        1793-1887; confirmation lists, 1824-66.   **MIC.1/11, 112;
                                                                   T.679/47**

        Baptisms, 1925-; marriages, 1845-; burials, 1917-; vestry
        minutes, 1888-; register of vestrymen, 1870-; preachers'
        books, 1845-.   **In local custody**

   P. Creggan or Freeduff
        Baptisms, 1835-; marriages, 1837-.   **In local custody**

   R.C. Lower Creggan (Armagh diocese)
        Baptisms, 1845-80; marriages, 1845-81.   **MIC.1D/40**

   R.C. Upper Creggan (Crossmaglen) (Armagh diocese)
        Baptisms and marriages, 1796-1803, 1812-29 and
        1845-81.   **MIC.1D/43**

CRIEVE PRESBYTERIAN CHURCH, CO. MONAGHAN
        [*see under* **AGHNAMULLEN**]

**CROCKATANTY PRESBYTERIAN CHURCH,
CO. TYRONE**
        [*see under* **BODONY LOWER**]

**CROGHAN, LATER KILLESHANDRA, PRESBYTERIAN
CHURCH, CO. CAVAN**
[*see under* **KILLASHANDRA**]

**CROM, HOLY TRINITY, CHURCH OF IRELAND PARISH,
CO. FERMANAGH**
[*see under* **KINAWLEY**]

CROMORE PRESBYTERIAN CHURCH, CO. ARMAGH
[*see under* **BALLYMORE**]

**CROSSDUFF CHURCH OF IRELAND PARISH,
CO. MONAGHAN**
[*see under* **AGHNAMULLEN**]

**CROSSGAR PRESBYTERIAN CHURCH,
CO. LONDONDERRY**
[*see under* **MACOSQUIN**]

CROSSERLOUGH, CO. CAVAN

    C.I. Kildrumferton or Crosserlough or Kilnaleck
        (Kilmore diocese)
        Baptisms, 1801-78; marriages, 1801-1949; burials,
        1803-1938.   **MIC.1/267**

    C.I. Ballyjamesduff (Kilmore diocese)
        [Partly in Crosserlough - *see under* **CASTLERAHAN**]

    R.C. Crosserlough (Kilmore diocese)
        Baptisms, 1843-81; marriages, 1843-81; funerals,
        1843-76.   **MIC.1D/77**

CROSSROADS PRESBYTERIAN CHURCH, CO. DONEGAL
[*see under* **ALL SAINTS**]

**CROSSROADS (OR CAPPAGH OR MOUNTJOY)
PRESBYTERIAN CHURCH, CO. TYRONE**
[*see under* **CAPPAGH**]

CRUMLIN METHODIST CHURCH, CO. ANTRIM
[*see under* **CAMLIN**]

CRUMLIN PRESBYTERIAN CHURCH, CO. ANTRIM
[*see under* **CAMLIN**]

CULDAFF, CO. DONEGAL

C.I. Culdaff (Formerly Derry diocese but now in
    Raphoe diocese)

Vestry minutes, 1693-1804; baptisms, 1668-c.1790, with
gaps; marriages, 1713-21 and 1770-82; burials, 1714-18.   **D.803**

Baptisms, 1875-1987; marriages, 1845-1921; burials,
1876-1980; vestry minutes, 1858-73 and 1877-1988;
register of vestrymen, 1870-1987; preachers' books,
1879-1941; plan of church, c.1885; account book,
1897-98; notes about the history of the church, 1869-87.   **MIC.1/278**

C.I. Gleneely (formerly Derry diocese but now in
    Raphoe diocese)

Baptisms, 1872-1981; marriages, 1859-1954.   **MIC.1/185**

Burials, 1910-; vestry minutes, 1913-; preachers' books,
1856-; registers of vestrymen, 1870-.   **In local custody**

R.C. Culdaff (Derry diocese)
Baptisms, 1838-41 and 1847-80; marriages, 1849-80.   **MIC.1D/55**

R.C. Clonca (Derry diocese)
[Partly in Culdaff parish - *see under* **CLONCA**]

CULFEIGHTRIN, CO. ANTRIM

C.I. Culfeightrin (Connor diocese)
[Earliest registers destroyed in Dublin]

Burials, 1805-31.   **MIC.1/109**

Baptisms, 1878-; marriages, 1845-; burials, 1879-; vestry
minutes, 1870-.   **In local custody**

C.I. Cushendun (Connor diocese)
[Earliest registers destroyed in Dublin]

Baptisms, 1877-; marriages, 1875-; burials, 1909-; vestry
minutes, 1875-; preachers' books, 1875-; churchwardens'
accounts, 1871-.   **In local custody**

R.C. Culfeightrin (Down and Connor diocese)
Baptisms, 1825-81; marriages, 1834-80.   **MIC.1D/68, 69A**

R.C. Culfeightrin (with Cushendun and Ennispollan)
    (Down and Connor diocese)

[Also Craigs and Cushleak (Cushendun)]

Baptisms and marriages, 1848-52 and 1862-81; funerals,
1845-52.   **MIC.1D/69 A-B**

CULLYBACKEY METHODIST CHURCH, CO. ANTRIM
[*see under* **CRAIGS**]

**CULLYBACKEY (CUNNINGHAM MEMORIAL)
PRESBYTERIAN CHURCH, CO. ANTRIM**
[*see under* **CRAIGS**]

**CULLYBACKEY REFORMED PRESBYTERIAN CHURCH,
CO. ANTRIM**
[*see under* **CRAIGS**]

**CULMAINE ROMAN CATHOLIC CHURCH,
CO. FERMANAGH**
[*see under* **MAGHERACULMONEY**]

**CULMORE CHURCH OF IRELAND PARISH,
CO. LONDONDERRY**
[*see under* **TEMPLEMORE**]

CUMBER LOWER, CO. LONDONDERRY

> **C.I. Cumber Lower** (Derry diocese)
> Baptisms, 1804-77; marriages, 1806-45; burials, 1828 and
> 1855-70; vestry minutes, 1801-70, with baptism and
> marriage entries.   **T.679/377-379**
>
> Baptisms, 1877-; marriages, 1845-; burials, 1871-; vestry
> minutes, 1871-; registers of vestrymen, 1870-.   **In local custody**

> **C.I. Learmount**
> [Originally formed out of part of Cumber Lower -
> *see under* **LEARMOUNT**]

> **P. Cumber Lower**
> Baptisms, 1827-67; marriages, 1843-1906.   **MIC.1P/147**

> **R.C. Faughanvale and Cumber Lower**
> [*see under* **FAUGHANVALE**]

> **R.C. Glendermott**
> [Part of Cumber Lower parish is in the Roman Catholic
> parish of Glendermott - *see under* **CLONDERMOT**]

CUMBER UPPER, CO. LONDONDERRY

   C.I. Cumber Upper (Derry diocese)
      Baptisms, 1811-18 and 1826-72; marriages, 1811-14 and
      1826-45; burials, 1837-1900; vestry minutes, 1807-95;
      list of vestrymen, 1870 and 1877.   **MIC.1/15/2; MIC.1/16**

      Baptisms, 1872-; marriages, 1845-.   **In local custody**

   C.I. Learmount
      [Originally formed out of part of Cumber Upper -
      see under **LEARMOUNT**]

   P. Cumber Upper
      Baptisms, 1874-1983; marriages, 1845-1936.   **MIC.1P/148**

   R.C. Cumber Upper and Learmount (Claudy)
      (Derry diocese)

      Baptisms, 1863-81; marriages, 1863-82.   **MIC.1D/57**

   R.C. Banager
      [Part of Cumber Upper is in the Roman Catholic parish
      of Banagher - *see under* **BANAGHER**]

CUNNINGHAM MEMORIAL PRESBYTERIAN CHURCH,
CULLYBACKEY, CO. ANTRIM
      [*see under* **CRAIGS**]

CURRAN PRESBYTERIAN CHURCH,
CO. LONDONDERRY
      [*see under* **MAGHERA**]

CURRIN, COS FERMANAGH AND MONAGHAN

   C.I. Currin (Clogher diocese)
      Baptisms, 1835-1904; marriages, 1812-1956; burials,
      1816-1922; confirmations, 1897, 1900 and 1906.   **MIC.1/133**

      Baptisms, 1810-34; burials, 1810-12; vestry minutes,
      1870.   **In local custody**

   M. Drum
      Baptisms, 1877-1910; marriages (may be in with
      Cootehill), 1871-1955.   **MIC.1E/54**

   P. 1st Drum
      Baptisms, 1867-1931; marriages, 1845-1936.   **MIC.1P/201**

   P. 2nd Drum
      Baptisms, 1868-1983; marriages, 1845-1904.   **MIC.1P/202**

R.C. Currin
[*see under* **DRUMMULLY**]

CUSHENDALL PRESBYTERIAN CHURCH, CO. ANTRIM
[*see under* **LAYD**]

**CUSHENDALL ROMAN CATHOLIC PARISH,
CO. ANTRIM**
[*see under* **LAYD**]

**CUSHENDUN CHURCH OF IRELAND PARISH,
CO. ANTRIM**
[*see under* **CULFEIGHTRIN**]

CUSHENDUN PRESBYTERIAN CHURCH, CO. ANTRIM
[*see under* **LAYD**]

DARVER, CO. LOUTH

    C.I. Derver or Darver (Armagh diocese)
        Marriages, 1870-75.   **MIC.1/277**

    R.C. Darver (Armagh diocese)
        Baptisms, 1787-1880; marriages, 1837-83; deaths,
        1871-9.   **MIC.1D/47**

DEER PARK METHODIST CHURCH, CO. LONGFORD
[*see under* **KILGLASS**]

DENN, CO. CAVAN

    C.I. Denn (Kilmore diocese)
        Baptisms, 1879-1982; marriages, 1845-1954;
        burials, 1879-1986.   **MIC.1/238**

    C.I. Ballyjamesduff (Kilmore diocese)
        [Partly in Denn Parish - *see under* **CASTLERAHAN**]

    R.C. Denn (Kilmore diocese)
        Baptisms, 1856-74, with gaps; marriages, 1856-8.   **MIC.1D/83**

DERG CHURCH OF IRELAND PARISH, CO. TYRONE
[*see under* **URNEY, COS TYRONE and DONEGAL**]

**DERNAKESH CHAPEL OF EASE (CHURCH OF
IRELAND), CO. CAVAN**
    [*see under* **DRUMGOON**]

**DERRAMORE PRESBYTERIAN CHURCH,
CO. LONDONDERRY**
    [*see under* **DRUMACHOSE**]

**DERRY (1ST) PRESBYTERIAN CHURCH,
CO. LONDONDERRY**
    [*see under* **TEMPLEMORE**]

**DERRY (2ND) PRESBYTERIAN CHURCH,
CO. LONDONDERRY**
    [*see under* **TEMPLEMORE**]

DERRYAGHY, CO. ANTRIM

    C.I. Derriaghy (Connor diocese)

Baptisms, 1696-1763, 1771-1806, 1810-12 and 1821-1932; marriages, 1696-1746, 1772, 1818-1907; burials, 1696-1738, 1772-3, 1823-4, 1827-34 and 1836-1927; vestry minutes, 1709-58 and 1794-1871, including confirmation list, 1705, and seatholders' list, 1812; preachers' books, 1834-78; account book of payments relating to Miss Fletcher's bequest to the poor of Derriaghy, 1839-1920; membership register, accounts, book catalogue and minutes of Derriaghy Parochial Young Men's Christian Society's Library, 1847-62; sexton's day books recording details of deaths, 1863-1927.	**MIC.1/32-33; C.R.1/1; T.679/35; T.2527**
Registers of vestrymen, 1831-; vestry minutes, 1872-.	**In local custody**

    C.I. Stoneyford (Connor diocese)

Baptisms, 1839-1925; preachers' books, 1834-87.	**MIC.1/32; C.R.1/1**
Vestry minutes, 1887-; marriages, 1887-.	**In local custody**

    R.C. Hannahstown, Rock and Derriaghy
        (Down and Connor diocese)

Baptisms and marriages, 1877-80.	**MIC.1D/63**

DERRYALL METHODIST CHURCH, CO. ARMAGH
    [*see under* **DRUMCREE**]

DERRYANVIL METHODIST CHURCH, CO. ARMAGH
[*see under* DRUMCREE]

DERRYBRUSK, CO. FERMANAGH

C.I. Derrybrusk (Clogher diocese)
[Earliest registers destroyed in Dublin]

Baptisms, 1877-; marriages, 1870-; burials, 1911-;
vestrymen's lists, 1870-.   **In local custody**

C.I. Garvary (Clogher diocese)
[Partly in Derrybrusk parish - *see under*
ENNISKILLEN]

M. Inishmore or Innishmore [Primitive Wesleyan and
Wesleyan Methodists]

Baptisms, 1872-1925; circuit schedule book, 1866-93.   **MIC.1E/9, 15**

DERRYGONNELLY METHODIST CHURCH,
CO. FERMANAGH
[*see under* INISHMACSAINT]

DERRYGORTREAVY CHURCH OF IRELAND PARISH,
CO. TYRONE
[*see under* CLONFEACLE]

DERRYHEEN CHURCH OF IRELAND PARISH,
CO. CAVAN
[*see under* ANNAGELLIFF]

DERRYKEIGHAN, CO. ANTRIM

C.I. Derrykeighan (Connor diocese)
[Earliest registers destroyed in Dublin]

Vestry minutes, 1802-26, including list of the poor,
1817.   **T.1182**

Baptisms, 1878-; marriages, 1845-; burials, 1882-; vestry
minutes, 1827-; registers of vestrymen, 1875-; preachers'
books, 1835-.   **In local custody**

P. Benvarden
Baptisms, 1864-1913; marriages, 1864-1912; session and
communicants' rolls, 1864-1912; session minutes,
1894-1912; session and committee minutes, 1889-93.   **MIC.1P/19**

P. Dervock
    Baptisms, 1827-38 and 1850-1970; marriages, 1828-41
    and 1845-1903.   **MIC.1P/30**

R.C. [*see under* **BALLYMONEY**]

**DERRYLANE CHURCH OF IRELAND PARISH,
CO. CAVAN**
    [*see under* **KILLASHANDRA**]

DERRYLEE METHODIST CHURCH, CO. ARMAGH
    [*see under* **TARTARAGHAN**]

DERRYLORAN, COS TYRONE and LONDONDERRY

B. Cookstown and Lisnagleer
    Marriages, 1873-; burials, 1866-.   **In local custody**

C.I. Derryloran (Armagh diocese)
    Baptisms, 1795-1875; marriages, 1797-1845; burials,
    1797-1879; vestry minutes, 1816-95; confirmation lists,
    1828, 1833, 1837, 1840, 1843, 1846, 1849, 1852 and 1856.   **MIC.1/15/1**

    List of incumbents, 1367-c.1866; extracts from preachers'
    book, 1830-1910; census of rural deanery of
    Derryloran, 1832; extracts from vestry minutes, 1816-38,
    and from births, marriages and deaths, 1795-1825.   **T.2574**

    Baptisms, 1876-; marriages, 1852-.   **In local custody**

M. Cookstown
    Baptisms, 1873-; marriages, 1864.   **In local custody**

P. 1st Cookstown
    Baptisms, 1836-1950; marriages, 1845-88.   **MIC.1P/43, 139**

P. 2nd Cookstown
    Baptisms, 1852-; marriages, 1845-; session minutes, 1853-. **In local custody**

P. 3rd Cookstown (now Molesworth Street)
    Session minutes, 1834-1966.   **T.2750/1**

    Baptisms, 1835-; marriages, 1845-; session minutes, 1834-. **In local custody**

R.C. Desertcreight and Derryloran (Cookstown)
    (Armagh diocese)

    [This parish forms part of the Roman Catholic parish of
    Desertcreight and Derryloran - *see under*
    DESERTCREAT]

DERRYNEIL BAPTIST CHURCH, CO. DOWN
[*see under* **DRUMGOOLAND**]

DERRYNOOSE, CO. ARMAGH

C.I. Derrynoose (Armagh diocese)
Baptisms, 1710-46, with gaps, and 1822-70; marriages,
1712-43, 1825-9 and 1835-45; burials, 1835-1939; vestry
minutes, 1709-12, 1720-50, 1756 and 1811-1958;
confirmations, 1833-79, with gaps; list of emigrants to
America and Scotland, 1840-c.1855.   **MIC.1/14; T.679/10**

Baptisms, 1870-; marriages, 1845-; registers of
vestrymen, 1870-.   **In local custody**

C.I. Killylea
[*see under* **TYNAN**]

P. 1st Keady (or The Temple)
Baptisms, 1838-1938; marriages, 1845-1920.   **MIC.1P/296**

R.C. Derrynoose (Keady) (Armagh diocese)
[Derrynoose Roman Catholic parish consists of
Derrynoose and Keady parishes]

Baptisms, 1835-7 and 1846-81; marriages, 1846-81;
deaths, 1846-51.   **MIC.1D/40**

**DERRYVALLEY PRESBYTERIAN CHURCH,
CO. MONAGHAN**
[*see under* **BALLYBAY**]

DERRYVULLAN, CO. FERMANAGH

C.I. Castle Archdale (Clogher diocese)
Baptisms and burials, 1842-; marriages, 1892-; vestry
minutes, 1887-.   **In local custody**

C.I. Derryvullen or Derryvullan (or Derryvullen South)
[Sometimes spelt Derryvollan] (Clogher diocese)

[Earliest registers destroyed in Dublin]

Baptisms, 1877-1916; marriages, 1845-1903; register of
vestrymen, 1870-1974; preachers' book, 1894-1910;
vestry minutes, 1864-1920.   **MIC.1/308**

Burials, 1902-.   **In local custody**

C.I. Derryvullen [or Derryvullan] North (Clogher diocese)
[Originally a chapel of ease]

Baptisms, 1803-1909; marriages, 1803-1934; burials,
1804-1902; vestry minutes, 1804-73; poor list, 1823-40.   **MIC.1/34; T.679/15;
C.R.1/37**

Register of vestrymen, 1870-; preachers' books, 1873-.   **In local custody**

C.I. Garvary (Clogher diocese)
[Partly in Derryvullan parish - *see under*
ENNISKILLEN]

M. Irvinestown [Wesleyan Methodists]
Baptisms, 1829-1913 (circuit); marriages, 1863-1918.   **MIC.1E/37**

Baptisms, 1829-44.   **MIC.429/1/217**

M. Yellow Church [Wesleyan Methodists]
[Formed part of Irvinestown Circuit - *see under*
Irvinestown above]

P. Irvinestown
Baptisms, 1842-1918; marriages, 1846-1934; list of
members and of communicants, 1913.   **MIC.1P/66**

R.C. Enniskillen [Derryvullan is partly in the Roman Catholic
parish of Enniskillen - *see under* **ENNISKILLEN**]

R.C. Derryvullen (Irvinestown) or Whitehill/Whitehall
(Clogher diocese)

Baptisms, 1846-81; marriages, 1851-82.   **MIC.1D/14**

DERVER CHURCH OF IRELAND PARISH, CO. LOUTH
[*see under* **DARVER**]

DERVOCK PRESBYTERIAN CHURCH, CO. ANTRIM
[*see under* **DERRYKEIGHAN**]

DESERTCREAT, CO. TYRONE

C.I. Altedesert
[Partly in Desertcreat parish - *see under* **POMEROY**].

C.I. Desertcreat (Armagh diocese)
Baptisms, 1812-73; marriages, 1812-45; burials,
1812-1960; vestry minutes, 1740-1901; confirmation
lists, 1828 and 1840.   **MIC.1/9; T.679/5**

Notes on attendances, baptisms and marriages and a list
of clergy, 1829-46.   **C.R.1/10**

Confirmation list, 1870.   **DIO.4/32/D/5/7/1**

P. Sandholes
Baptisms, 1863-70; marriages, 1845-70.   **MIC.1P/42**

R.C. Desertcreight and Derryloran (Cookstown)
(Armagh diocese)

Baptisms and marriages, 1827-81.   **MIC.1D/36**

R.P. Grange
Baptisms, 1844-93; session minutes, 1812-83; committee
minutes, 1804-25.   **D.392/1-3**

DESERTEGNY, CO. DONEGAL

C.I. Desertegny (St Ignatius) (Formerly Derry diocese but
now Raphoe diocese)

Baptisms, 1878-1966; marriages, 1848-1929; burials,
1879-1981; vestry minutes, 1869-1947.   **MIC.1/184**

R.C. Desertegny and Lower Fahan (Buncrana)
(Derry diocese)

[Desertegny forms part of the Roman Catholic parish of
Desertegny and Lower Fahan]

Baptisms, 1864-81; marriages, 1871-82.   **MIC.1D/54**

DESERTLYN, CO. LONDONDERRY

C.I. Desertlyn (Armagh diocese)
Baptisms, 1797-1871; marriages, 1797-1845; burials,
1798-1891; confirmations, 1824-59; vestry minutes,
1837-77.   **MIC.1/10A**

Baptisms, 1871-; marriages, 1845-; burials, 1891-;
accounts, 1837-58 and 1877-; registers of vestrymen,
1870-.   **In local custody**

R.C. Ardtrea and Desertlin (Moneymore)
[Part of Desertlyn parish is in the Roman Catholic parish
of Ardtrea and also in the Roman Catholic parishes of
Lissan and Magherafelt - *see under* **ARTREA, LISSAN**
and **MAGHERAFELT**]

DESERTMARTIN, CO. LONDONDERRY

C.I. Desertmartin (Derry diocese)
Baptisms, 1785-1880; marriages, 1784-1869; burials,
1783, 1788, 1829 and 1842-1936; vestry minutes, 1751-
1870, with some baptism entries for 1752.   **MIC.1/16; T.679/6**

Baptisms, 1881-; marriages, 1870-; register of vestrymen,
1870-; list of tithes, 1794.   **In local custody**

P. Lecumpher
    Baptisms and marriages, 1825-.   **In local custody**

R.C. Desertmartin and Kilcronaghan (Derry diocese)
    Baptisms, 1848-81; marriages, 1848-80; deaths,
    1848-82.   **MIC.1D/60**

DESERTOGHILL, CO. LONDONDERRY

C.I. Desertoghill (Derry diocese)
    [Earliest registers destroyed in Dublin)

    Baptisms, 1873-; marriages, 1845-; burials, 1879-; vestry
    minutes, 1870-.   **In local custody**

P. Moneydig
    Baptisms, 1857-1923; marriages, 1852-1928.   **MIC.1P/93; T.2421**

R.C. Kilrea
    [Part of Desertoghill parish is in the Roman Catholic
    parish of Kilrea, along with Kilrea and
    Tamlaght O'Crilly - *see under* **KILREA** and
    TAMLAGHT O'CRILLY and is also partly in the
    Roman Catholic parish of Errigal - *see under*
    ERRIGAL]

DEVENISH, CO. FERMANAGH

C.I. Devenish (Clogher diocese)
    Baptisms, 1800-73; marriages, 1800-24 and 1829-61;
    burials, 1801-22 and 1828-74; vestry minutes,
    1739-1829.   **MIC.1/31**

    Vestry minutes, 1830-; register of vestrymen, 1870-;
    preachers' books, 1869-; census, 1874.   **In local custody**

C.I. Garrison (Chapel of Ease) (Clogher diocese)
    Baptisms, 1879-1924; marriages, 1849-1935; burials,
    1877-1924.   **MIC.1/266**

C.I. Kiltyclogher
    [Partly in Devenish parish - *see under* **CLOONCLARE**]

M. Kilcoo
    Baptisms, 1877-1986; marriages, 1902-28.   **MIC.1E/17-18**

M. Springfield (Originally Primitive Wesleyan Methodists)
    Baptisms, 1871-1985; marriages, 1879-1936.   **MIC.1E/16**

R.C. Garrison (Devenish) (Clogher diocese)
[Devenish parish is the head of the Roman Catholic
parish of Devenish or Derrygonnelly comprising also
parts of Inishmacsaint and Boho parishes, with
chapels at Garrison, Monea and Derrygonnelly]

Baptisms, 1860-81; marriages, 1860-80.   **MIC.1D/12**

R.C. Devenish (Botha, Derrygonnelly) (Clogher diocese)
Baptisms, 1853-79.   **MIC.1D/10**

**DIAMOND, THE, CHURCH OF IRELAND PARISH,
CO. ARMAGH**
[*see under* **KILMORE**]

DOAGH, GRANGE OF, CO. ANTRIM

C.I [*see under* **DONEGORE** and *under* **KILBRIDE**]

M. Ballyclare
Baptisms, 1834-46.   **MIC.429/1/341, 436**

Baptisms, 1843-; marriages, 1868-.   **In local custody**

M. Ballyclare (New Connexion)
Baptisms, 1843-; marriages, 1875-.   **In local custody**

M. Doagh
Baptisms, 1843-. [At Ballyclare]   **In local custody**

N.S.P. Ballyclare
Baptisms, 1839-1920; marriages, 1839-1933; legal
papers relating to a dispute over church property, 1862. **MIC.1B/7; C.R.4/1E;
C.R.4/19**

P. Ballyclare
Baptisms, 1857-1906; marriages, 1857-1909; burials,
1817-1928; communicants' roll, 1862-1909.   **MIC.1P/324; T.1602**

R.C. Ballyclare (Down and Connor diocese)
[Originally part of the Roman Catholic parish of Larne
and Carrickfergus - *see under* **LARNE** and then became
part of the Roman Catholic parish of Ballyclare -
see under **RALOO**]

R.P. Ballyclare
Marriages, 1864-1925; printed financial report, 1867. **MIC.1C/9B; C.R.5/1**

DONACAVEY, CO. TYRONE

C.I. Barr (Clogher diocese)
[Formed out of the parishes of Kilskeery, Donacavey and Dromore - *see under* **KILSKEERY**]

C.I. Clanabogan (Derry diocese)
[Formed out of the parishes of Drumragh (Derry diocese) and Donacavey (Clogher diocese) - *see under* **DRUMRAGH**]

C.I. Donacavey or Fintona (Clogher diocese)
Baptisms, 1800-61 and 1864-1936; marriages, 1800-1902; burials, 1800-1903; vestry minutes, 1779-1930, with lists of the poor, 1783-1841.   **MIC.1/45; D.1048/4, 14**

Names of incumbents, 1615-1707.   **DIO.2/9/465**

M. Cavan
Circuit schedule book, 1879-94.   **MIC.1E/25**

M. Fintona
Circuit schedule books, 1866-1908; membership register and quarterly class roll, 1863-1939; minutes of quarterly meetings of stewards and leaders, 1859-1953; membership register of Fintona Band of Hope and Temperance Society, 1894-1965, with gaps.   **MIC.1E/24-25**

Baptisms, 1878-; marriages, 1882-.   **In local custody**

P. Fintona
Baptisms, 1836-75; marriages, 1836-1929.   **MIC.1P/283**

R.C. Donacavey (Fintona) (Clogher diocese)
Baptisms, 1857-81; marriages, 1857-80.   **MIC.1D/14**

DONACLONEY PRESBYTERIAN CHURCH, CO. DOWN
[*see under* **DONAGHCLONEY**]

DONAGH, CO. DONEGAL

C.I. Donagh (Derry diocese)
[Earliest registers destroyed in Dublin]

Baptisms, 1874-; marriages, 1846-; burials, 1878-; vestry minutes, 1782-; churchwardens' accounts, 1871-; registers of vestrymen, 1873-; preachers' books, 1889-.   **In local custody**

P. Carndonagh
Baptisms, 1830-1928; marriages, 1830-1950; marriage notices, 1845-1984.   **MIC.1P/237; MIC.1P/ 230/2B**

R.C. Carndonagh (Donagh) (Derry diocese)
Baptisms, 1847-81; marriages, 1849-81.   **MIC.1D/54**

DONAGH, CO. MONAGHAN

C.I. Donagh (Clogher diocese)
Baptisms, 1736 and 1796-1880; marriages, 1736 and
1797-1923; banns, 1807-37; burials, 1736 and 1797-1901;
vestry minutes, 1731-1912; confirmation list, 1846; census
1832; poor list, 1775; tithe applotment book, 1833.   **MIC.1/127**

List of incumbents, 1721-1816.   **DIO.2/9/477**

P. Glennan
Baptisms, 1805-1981; marriages, 1805-20 and 1845-1905.   **MIC.1P/155**

R.C. Donagh (Glaslough) (Clogher diocese)
Baptisms, 1836-81; marriages, 1836-82.   **MIC.1D/17; C.R.2/11**

DONAGHADEE, CO. DOWN

C.I. Donaghadee (Down diocese)
Baptisms, 1771-1893; marriages, 1772-1844; burials,
1771-86 and 1817-41; vestry minutes, 1779-1870; list of
parishioners, 1797.   **MIC.1/17; T.679/44;**
                                                 C.R.1/54

Indexes to baptisms, 1771-1845, marriages, 1772-1844,
and burials, 1771-1841.   **In Public Search Room**

Vestry minutes, 1871-; cess applotment, 1779-1870;
preachers' books, 1825-1934; Sustentation Fund book,
1870-79.   **In local custody**

C.I. Carrowdore (Down diocese)
[Earliest registers destroyed in Dublin]

Baptisms, 1873-; marriages, 1846-; burials, 1875-; vestry
minutes, 1841-; registers of vestrymen, 1870-.   **In local custody**

Correspondence relating to the building of the church,
tithes, the parish school etc., 1837-74.   **C.R.1/50**

M. Donaghadee
Baptisms, 1815-45, and marriages, 1834-45, kept by
Matthew Lanktree, an itinerant preacher attached to the
circuit, 1815-45.   **C.R.6/6**

Baptisms, 1845-6 (circuit).   **MIC.429/1/140**

Baptisms, 1827-.   **In local custody**

P. Ballycopeland
Baptisms, 1906-41; marriages, 1903-06.   MIC.1P/382

Baptisms, 1773-1818.   **In Presbyterian
                                                      Historical Society**

P. Ballyfrenis
Baptisms, 1862-1917; marriages, 1864-1901; communion
lists recording emigrations, deaths and marriages,
1862-1901.   MIC.1P/315

P. Carrowdore
Baptisms, 1843-1940; marriages, 1843-4 and 1864-1907;
session minutes with lists of new communicants, 1843-67;
marriage notices, 1879-1906.   MIC.1P/316;
                                                      MIC.1P/230/6

P. 1st Donaghadee
Baptisms, 1793-1950; marriages, 1805-06 and 1813-1936;
session and committee minutes, 1783-1826.   MIC.1P/167

P. Donaghadee, Shore Street
Baptisms, 1849-1966; marriages, 1850-1936.   MIC.1P/341

P. Millisle
Baptisms, 1773-1941; marriages, 1845-1936; marriage
notice books, 1845-1941; list of elders and members of the
congregation, 1777; call to the Rev. Hanna signed by 82
members of the congregation, 1815.   MIC.1P/230/7;
                                                      MIC.1P/382;
                                                      D.1759/1C/1

R.C. Newtownards (Down diocese)
[Donaghadee parish is in the Roman Catholic parish of
Newtownards - *see under* **NEWTOWNARDS**]

DONAGHCLONEY, CO. DOWN

C.I. Donaghcloney (Dromore diocese)
Baptisms, 1697-1878; marriages, 1697-1848; burials,
1697-1890; vestry minutes, 1772-1833; parish accounts,
1745-8; parochial school account book, 1868-76; minutes
of Young Men's Society, 1863-6; Donaghcloney Infant
School register, 1869-70.   MIC.1/92-93

Births, marriages and burials, 1697-1772; vestry minutes,
1883-; cess applotment books, 1834-; vestrymen's lists,
1871-; Sustentation Fund book, 1870-72.   **In local custody**

P. Donacloney
Baptisms, 1798-1950; marriages, 1826-1909; burials,
1920-87; accounts, 1831-78; list of new communicants,

1830-79; session minutes, 1830-51; discipline cases,
1826-53 and 1862-7; poor accounts, 1831-51 and 1877-8;
lists of new elders, 1826-37.   **MIC.1P/342**

P. Waringstown
Baptisms, 1862-1985; marriages, 1854-1926.   **MIC.1P/270**

R.C. Tullylish
[Donaghcloney parish forms part of the Roman Catholic
parish of Tullyish - *see under* **TULLYLISH**]

DONAGHEDY, CO. TYRONE

C.I. Donagheady (Derry diocese)
Baptisms, 1697-1723, 1753-65, 1818-19 and 1826-74;
marriages, 1697-1726, 1754-64 and 1826-44; marriage
licences, 1817 and 1829-53; burials, 1698-1726, 1754-7
and 1826-89; vestry minutes, 1697-1723 and 1754-1919;
accounts, 1829-1922; confirmation lists, 1872, 1875,
1877, 1880, 1883 and 1886.   **MIC.1/35-36; C.R.1/26**

Baptisms, 1874-; marriages, 1845-; burials, 1889-;
churchwardens' account books, 1793 and 1871-;
preachers' books, 1855-.   **In local custody**

C.I. Dunnalong (Derry diocese)
Baptisms, 1877-; marriages, 1868-; burials, 1902-;
registers of vestrymen, 1870-.   **In local custody**

P. 1st Donagheady
Baptisms, 1875-; marriages, 1860-; stipend books,
1804-60, 1867-96 and 1898-1914.   **In local custody**

P. 2nd Donagheady
Baptisms and marriages, 1838-.   **In local custody**

P. Donemana
Baptisms, 1856-1943; marriages, 1845-1926.   **MIC.1P/425**

P. Magheramason
Baptisms, 1878-1939; marriages, 1881-1927.   **MIC.1P/369**

R.P. Bready
Baptisms, 1866-1984; marriages, 1864-1936; session
minutes, 1872-1932.   **MIC.1C/11**

R.C. Donagheady (Donemana, Donamanagh)
(Derry diocese)

[Donagheady parish is part of the Roman Catholic parish
of Donagheady, including also Leckpatrick]

Baptisms, 1854-80; marriages, 1857/8-1859, 1862-3;
deaths, 1857-9.   **MIC.1D/55-56**

DONAGHENRY, CO. TYRONE

C. Donaghy
Baptisms, 1861-; marriages, 1863-.   **In local custody**

C.I. Brackaville (Armagh diocese)
[Formed out of Killyman, Tullyniskan and Clonoe
parishes]

Baptisms, 1836-71; marriages, 1840-45; burials,
1862-1930; vestry minutes, 1844 and 1848-70;
confirmation lists, 1837, 1840, 1843, 1846, 1849, 1852
and 1863; banns, 1897-1955.   **T.697/267-268**

Baptisms, 1872-; marriages, 1845-; burials, 1930.   **In local custody**

C.I. Donaghenry or Donaghendry (Armagh diocese)
Baptisms, 1733-4, 1754-68, 1802-04 and 1810-71;
marriages, 1733-5, 1754-68, 1763-1804 and 1811-45;
burials, 1735, 1754-68 and 1811-71; vestry minutes,
1738-1895; confirmation lists, 1816-59.   **T.679/40, 318-322,
331, 336**

Confirmation register, 1843-91; census of the parish,
c.1830; plan of graveyard, c.1830.   **C.R.1/38**

Baptisms, 1872-; marriages, 1845-; burials, 1872-.   **In local custody**

M. Newtownkelly (Coalisland)
Baptisms, 1830-; marriages, 1944-.   **In local custody**

M. Stewartstown
Baptisms, 1868-; marriages, 1869-.   **In local custody**

P. 1st Stewartstown
Baptisms, 1814-71.   **MIC.1P/48**

P. 2nd Stewartstown
Baptisms, 1827-; marriages, 1845-.   **In local custody**

R.C. Coalisland and Stewartstown (Armagh diocese)
Baptisms, 1861-80; marriages, 1862-79; deaths, 1861-8.   **MIC.1D/34**

R.C. Donaghenry and Ballyclog (Coalisland)
(Armagh diocese)

[Donaghenry parish is united to that of Ballyclog and part
of Clonoe to form the Roman Catholic parish of
Stewartstown with chapels at Stewartstown and
Coalisland]

Baptisms, 1822-40 and 1849-81; marriages, 1822-41 and
1853-80; deaths, 1822-39 and 1854-69.   **MIC.1D/8, 34**

DONAGHMORE, CO. DONEGAL

C.I. Donaghmore (formerly in Derry diocese now in Raphoe
diocese)

[Earliest registers destoyed in Dublin]

Baptisms, 1818-19, 1824-9, 1884, 1886 and 1896-1902;
marriages, 1817, 1825-8 and 1845-1917; burials, 1825-8
and 1898-1984; vestry minutes, 1815-70; register of
members, 1907-10; registers of vestrymen, 1870-1948.   **MIC.1/209**

Cess applotment book, 1807-73.   **In local custody**

C.I. Meenglass (St Anne's) (formerly in Derry diocese but
now in Raphoe diocese)

Marriages, 1864-1953.   **MIC.1/169B**

Baptisms, 1877-; burials, 1877-; vestry minutes, 1870-;
register of vestrymen, 1870-; preachers' books, 1868-. **In local custody**

C.I. Monellan (Chapel of Ease)
(formerly in Derry diocese but now in Raphoe diocese)

Baptisms, 1833-87 and 1906; marriages, 1836-45 and
1874-1955; burials, 1849-81; register of vestrymen,
1870-1948; register of members, 1907-10.   **MIC.1/209**

Burials, 1889-; vestry minutes, 1870-.   **In local custody**

M. Castlefin
Baptisms, c.1829-1867; marriages may be in with Strabane
marriages, 1865-1935; circuit schedule books, 1865-1909;
membership register, 1897-1947; minutes of quarterly
leaders' meetings, 1880-1910; circuit stewards' books,
1872-86.   **MIC.1E/46**

P. Carnone
Baptisms, 1834-1984; marriages, 1846-1916.   **MIC.1P/221**

P. Donaghmore
Baptisms, 1835-1961; marriages, 1819-42 and 1845-1905. **MIC.1P/217**

R.C. Donaghmore (Derry diocese)
Baptisms, 1840-80; marriages, 1846-83.   **MIC.1D/62**

DONAGHMORE, CO. DOWN

C.I. Donaghmore (Dromore diocese)
Baptisms, 1783-1958, with an index for 1783-1851;
marriages, 1795-1845, with an index for 1795-1844;
burials, 1784-1858, 1861-1932 and 1950-58, with an
index for 1784-1858; confirmation list, 1835; preachers'
book, 1920-38.

**MIC.1/54/2; C.R.1/48;
D.2034/3/4; D.2034/5/8**

Marriages, 1845-.

In local custody

P. Donaghmore
Baptisms, 1804-37 and 1845-1968; marriages, 1845-1936.

MIC.1P/129

Burials of Presbyterian ministers, 1765, 1771, 1803, 1854
and 1927.

MIC.1/54/2

P. Fourtowns
Baptisms, 1820-97; marriages, 1845-1936.

MIC.1P/437

R.C. Donoughmore (Dromore diocese)
Baptisms, 1835-80; marriages, 1825-82; funerals,
1840-71.

MIC.1D/22

DONAGHMORE, CO. TYRONE

C.I. Donaghmore (Armagh diocese)
Baptisms, 1748-1937; marriages, 1741-1883; burials,
1741-1901; index of baptisms, 1748-1883; index of
marriages, 1741-1883; index of burials, 1741-1883;
vestry minutes, 1781-2; confirmations, 1823-75.

**T.679/19; MIC.1/106/
1-2; T.786; D.750**

Marriages, 1871-; vestry minutes, 1783-; registers of
vestrymen, 1873-.

In local custody

C.I. Donaghmore Upper (Armagh diocese)
[Earliest registers destroyed in Dublin]

Baptisms, 1877; marriages, 1846-; burials, 1878-; vestry
minutes, 1852-.

In local custody

M. Castlecaufield
Baptisms, 1830-.

In local custody

P. Carland
Baptisms, 1759-99 and 1847-1986; marriages, 1770-1802
and 1845-1914.

MIC.1P/28

P. Castlecaulfield
Baptisms, 1855-1947; marriages, 1834-1919; session
minutes, 1855-65 and 1885-1963; committee minutes,
1898-1934.

MIC.1P/121

R.C. Donaghmore (Armagh diocese)
[Other entries may be found in the Roman Catholic parish
of Pomeroy - *see under* **POMEROY**, and there may be
earlier entries in Killeeshil registers - *see under*
KILLEESHIL]

Baptisms, 1837-80; marriages, 1837-68.   **MIC.1D/33-34**

DONAGHMOYNE, CO. MONAGHAN

C.I. Broomfield
[Partly in Donaghmoyne parish - *see under*
CLONTIBRET]

C.I. Donaghmoine (Clogher diocese)
[After 1921 included also Inniskeen]

Baptisms, 1877-1955; marriages, 1845-1949; burials,
1878-1969; confirmation lists, 1860-66, 1900, 1903,
1906, 1932 and 1950; vestry minutes, 1876-1948;
preachers' books, 1872-1969.   **MIC.1/140**

P. Broomfield
Baptisms, 1841-1973; marriages, 1842-1956; list of
ministers, 1841-1955; Sabbath attendance register, 1847.   **MIC.1P/192**

R.C. Donaghmoyne (Clogher diocese)
Baptisms, 1863-80; marriages, 1872-80.   **MIC.1D/15**

R.C. Inniskeen
[Donaghmoyne parish is partly in the Roman Catholic
parish of Inniskeen - *see under* **INISHKEEN**]

DONAGHY CONGREGATIONAL CHURCH, CO. TYRONE
[*see under* **DONAGHENRY**]

DONEGAL, CO. DONEGAL

C.I. Donegal (Raphoe diocese)
Baptisms, 1808-72; marriages, 1812-1944; burials,
1812-24 and 1838-75.   **MIC.1/146**

Notes of baptism and marriage entries, 1826-49.   **D.2535/1**

Vestry minutes, 1870-; registers of vestrymen, 1870-;
preachers' books, 1839-.   **In local custody**

M. Donegal Mission [Included chapels at St John's Point,
Ardara, Dunkineely and Ballyederland]

Baptisms, 1833-1982; marriages, 1855-6 and 1864-1902;
membership register, 1833-73.   **MIC.1E/34**

Baptisms, 1833-42.   **MIC.429/1/547**

M. North Donegal Mission Stations
Baptisms, 1865-82.   **C.R.3/12**

R.C. Tawnawilly (Raphoe diocese)
Baptisms, 1872-81; marriages, 1873-82.   **MIC.1D/86**

**DONEGAL (1ST) PRESBYTERIAN CHURCH,
CO. DONEGAL**
[*see under* **DRUMHOME**]

**DONEGAL (2ND) PRESBYTERIAN CHURCH,
CO. DONEGAL**
[*see under* **KILLYMARD**]

DONEGORE, CO. ANTRIM

C.I. Donegore (Connor diocese)
[Formerly united with Kilbride]

[Earliest registers destroyed in Dublin]

Vestry minutes, 1818-71.   **MIC.1/82**

Baptisms and burials, 1878-.   **In local custody**

P. 1st Donegore
Baptisms, 1806-96; marriages, 1806-1916; committee
minutes, 1896-1951; communicants' roll, 1871-91.   **MIC.1P/79; D.1759/1A**

P. 2nd Donegore
Baptisms, 1848-1957; marriages, 1845-1936; session
minutes, 1847-73 and 1933-72; committee minutes,
1891-1976; communicants' roll, 1892-1933.   **MIC.1P/153; C.R.3/23**

DONEMANA PRESBYTERIAN CHURCH, CO. TYRONE
[*see under* **DONAGHEDY**]

**DONOUGHMORE ROMAN CATHOLIC PARISH,
CO. DOWN**
[*see under* **DONAGHMORE**]

DOUGLAS PRESBYTERIAN CHURCH, CO. TYRONE
[*see under* **ARDSTRAW**]

DOWN, CO. DOWN

C.I. Down or Downpatrick (Down diocese)
Baptisms, 1733-4, 1750-1815 and 1818-99;
marriages, 1701-1969; burials, 1718-36 and 1752-1876;
vestry minutes, 1704-1951; preachers' books, 1898-1925
and 1942-69; briefs read out in church after which money
was collected, 1716-35; list of poor widows and others
exempted from hearth money tax, 1733; vestry accounts,
1753-69; register of vestrymen, 1871-1970; minutes of
the select vestry, 1873-1975.   **MIC.1/38-40; T.679/41; C.R.1/33**

Copy of baptisms, 1750-1813 and 1817-29, marriages,
1752-1829, and burials, 1752-1829.   **T.684**

Marriage notice books, 1845-55 and 1873-1957.   **D.1563**

Applotment for Down parish, 1794.   **T.553/4**

Copy of baptisms, 1733-1856, marriages, 1701-1875,
and burials, 1719-1876.   **D.1759/1D/3**

C.I. Down Cathedral
Baptisms, 1867-; marriage licences, 1856-69; burials,
1864-.   **In local custody**

C.I. Hollymount (Down diocese)
[Earliest registers destroyed in Dublin]

Marriages, 1851-1935; preachers' book, 1936-85.   **C.R.1/33**

Baptisms, 1883-; burials, 1899-; vestry minutes, 1868-;
registers of vestrymen, 1870-; preachers' books, 1876-.   **In local custody**

M. Downpatrick [Wesleyan Methodists]
Baptisms, 1829-42.   **MIC.429/1/407**

Baptisms, 1829-; marriages, 1863-.   **In local custody**

N.S.P. Downpatrick
Memoranda and account books, c.1740-c.1850.   **T.1268**

Baptisms, 1834-7 and 1870-1978; marriages, 1834-43
and 1845-1936; burials, 1834-7; marriage notice books,
1845-92, 1918-30 and 1938; ministers' certificate
books, 1846-59 and 1918-38.   **C.R.4/8**

P. Downpatrick
Baptisms, 1827-1977; marriages, 1827-1913; session
minutes, 1836-1955; committee minutes, 1888-1963;
marriage notices, 1845-1906 (for Down Presbytery which
includes details for Downpatrick).   **MIC.1P/156**

R.C. Downpatrick (Down and Connor diocese)
   Baptisms, 1851-82; marriages, 1853-82, (one entry
   possibly for 1852); deaths, 1851-82.   MIC.1D/74

**DOWNSHIRE ROAD, NEWRY, PRESBYTERIAN CHURCH,
CO. DOWN**
   [*see under* **NEWRY**]

DOWRA CHURCH OF IRELAND PARISH, CO. CAVAN
   [*see under* **KILLINAGH**]

**DRAPERSTOWN PRESBYTERIAN CHURCH,
CO. LONDONDERRY**
   [*see under* **BALLYNASCREEN**]

**DRIMBOLG REFORMED PRESBYTERIAN CHURCH,
CO. LONDONDERRY**
   [*see under* **TAMLAGHT O'CRILLY**]

**DROGHEDA (ST PETER'S) CHURCH OF IRELAND
PARISH, CO. LOUTH**
   [*see under* **ST PETER'S**]

DROGHEDA METHODIST CHURCH, CO. LOUTH
   [*see under* **ST PETER'S**]

**DROGHEDA (ST PETER'S) ROMAN CATHOLIC
PARISH, CO. LOUTH**
   [*see under* **ST PETER's**]

**DROMAHAIRE ROMAN CATHOLIC CHURCH,
CO. LEITRIM**
   [*see under* **DRUMLEASE**]

DROMARA, CO. DOWN

   C.I. Dromara (Dromore diocese)
      [Earliest registers destroyed in Dublin]

      Baptisms, 1844-75; vestry minutes, 1804-1900.   MIC.1/117

      Baptisms, 1881-; marriages, 1845-; burials, 1889-.   **In local custody**

C.I. Magherahamlet (Dromore diocese)
[Earliest registers destroyed in Dublin]

Returns from parish registers, 1823-63.   **DIO.1/14/5**

Baptisms, 1881-; marriages, 1845-; burials, 1883-; vestry
minutes, 1819-; preachers' book, 1884-; confirmation
lists, 1892-; registers of vestrymen, 1925-.   **In local custody**

P. 1st Dromara
Baptisms, 1762-1959; marriages, 1799-1802, 1810-13 and
1817-1922; session minutes, 1763-1871; accounts,
1762-99.   **MIC.1P/89; T.1447**

History of the church, 1713-1913.   **D.2453/85**

P. 2nd Dromara
Baptisms, 1853-1952; marriages, 1847-1936; lists of
communicants, 1853-79.   **MIC.1P/393**

P. Magherahamlet
[Previously in Dromara parish, but now in Magherahamlet -
see under **MAGHERAHAMLET**]

R.C. Dromara (Dromore diocese)
Baptisms, marriages and funerals, 1844-80.   **MIC.1D/24; C.R.2/3**

R.P. Dromara
Baptisms, 1874-1933; marriages, 1876-1922; session
minutes and lists of communicants, 1874-1909; list of
stipend payers, c.1874-1937; stipend accounts,
1875-1937.   **MIC.1C/17**

DROMIN CHURCH OF IRELAND PARISH, CO. LOUTH
[*see under* **COLLON**]

**DROMINTEE ROMAN CATHOLIC CHURCH,
CO. ARMAGH**
[*see under* **KILLEVY**]

DROMORE, CO. DOWN

B. Ballykeel
Marriages, 1893-.   **In local custody**

C.I. Dromore (Dromore diocese)
Baptisms, 1784-1871; marriages, 1784-1845; burials,
1784-1812 and 1816-73; confirmation lists, 1823-46
(with gaps).   **T.679/395, 398-406,
410**

Marriages, 1845-; churchwardens' accounts, 1801-36; preachers' books, 1847-; vestry minutes, 1870-; registers of vestrymen, 1891-.	**In local custody**

C.I. Kilwarlin [partly in Dromore parish]
[*see under* **HILLSBOROUGH**]

M. Dromore [Wesleyan Methodists]

Baptisms, 1832-1952; marriages, 1864-1908.	**MIC.1E/43**
Baptisms, 1827-44 (Moira and Dromore Circuit).	**MIC.429/1/496**

N.S.P. Dromore

Marriages, 1845-95; marriage notice books, 1845-61; stipend books, 1852-1921; session and committee minutes, 1860-1911.	**C.R.4/14; T.2705**

P. 1st Dromore

Baptisms, 1832-54 and 1857-1913; marriages, 1845-1910; committee minutes, 1871-94; membership list, 1835; lists of new communicants, 1836-55.	**MIC.1P/140**

P. Dromore, Banbridge Road

Baptisms, 1851-72; marriages, 1870.	**MIC.1P/62**

P. Drumlough

Baptisms, 1827-1943; marriages, 1871-1936.	**MIC.1P/359**
Marriage notices, 1853-1953.	**C.R.3/9**

R.C. Dromore and Garvaghy (Dromore diocese)
(The Roman Catholic parish of Dromore consists of the parishes of Dromore and Garvaghy)

Baptisms, 1823-81; marriages and deaths, 1821-82.	**MIC.1D/29**

DROMORE, CO. TYRONE

C.I. Barr
[Partly in Dromore Parish - *see under* **KILSKEERY**]

C.I. Clanabogan (Derry diocese)
[Clanabogan Church of Ireland parish was formed out of part of Dromore parish - *see under* **DRUMRAGH**]

C.I. Dromore (Clogher diocese)
[Earliest registers destroyed in Dublin]

Baptisms, 1874-; marriages, 1845-; burials, 1880-; vestry minutes, 1762-.	**In local custody**

P. Dromore
  Baptisms, 1835-1925; marriages, 1835-1914; session
  minutes, 1836-48 and 1851-69; committee minutes
  1865-1908; lists of families, c.1830 and c.1860; list of
  communicants, 1836-40.   **MIC.1P/247**

R.C. Dromore (Clogher diocese)
  Baptisms, 1835-81; marriages, 1833-81.   **MIC.1D/11**

DROMORE PRESBYTERIAN CHURCH, CO. LONDONDERRY
  [*see under* **MACOSQUIN**]

DRUM METHODIST CHURCH, CO. MONAGHAN
  [*see under* **CURRIN**]

DRUM (1ST AND 2ND) PRESBYTERIAN CHURCHES, CO. MONAGHAN
  [*see under* **CURRIN**]

DRUMACHOSE, CO. LONDONDERRY

C.I. Drumachose (Derry diocese)
  Baptisms, 1730-52 and 1804-98; marriages, 1728-53 and
  1805-45; burials, 1730-36 and 1804-81; vestry minutes,
  1729-77, 1787 and 1794-1881, which include a list of
  those who attended church on Easter Day, 1754;
  confirmation lists, 1833-77; census, 1830.   **T.679/3, 394, 396-397, 416-417**

M. Limavady
  Baptisms, 1841-2 (circuit).   **MIC.429/1/534**

  Baptisms, 1841-; marriages, 1878-.   **In local custody**

P. Derramore
  Baptisms, 1825-1935; communicants, 1870-1925.   **MIC.1P/423**

P. Drumachose
  Baptisms, 1837-1913; committee minutes, 1833-1903;
  account book, 1834-83; communicants' roll, c.1880-1902.   **MIC.1P/422**

P. 1st Limavady
  Baptisms, 1832-9 and 1861-1905; marriages, 1832-41
  and 1845-1905; notices of marriages, 1845-53, 1854-69,
  1879 and 1907-09; minutes of session and committee,
  1861-1906; stipend book, 1837-1906; accounts, 1857-1908. **MIC.1P/34**

P. 2nd Limavady
  Marriages, 1845-1904.   **MIC.1P/410**

**R.C. Drumachose, Tamlaght Finlagan and part of Aghanloo
(Limavady)** (Derry diocese)
   Baptisms, 1855-80; marriages, 1856-81; burials, 1859-69.   **MIC.1D/56**

R.P. Broadlane (later Limavady)
   Baptisms, 1843-1982; marriages, 1865-1931; deaths,
   1887-1982; admissions, 1896-1982; removals from
   membership, 1896-1933; communicants' rolls and lists
   of members, 1862-1922; emigrations, 1887-93; list of
   members of Total Abstinence Association, 1870-1946.   **MIC.1C/21**

DRUMALOOR CHURCH OF IRELAND PARISH, CO. CAVAN
   [*see under* **ANNAGH**]

DRUMAROAD ROMAN CATHOLIC PARISH, CO. DOWN
   [*see under* **KILMEGAN**]

DRUMBALLYRONEY, CO. DOWN

C.I. Drumballyroney (Dromore diocese)
   Baptisms, 1838-71; marriages, 1838-46; burials, 1839-73;
   vestry minutes, 1870-1902; registration book, 1870.   **T.679/335, 350, 352**

   Preachers' books, 1869-.   **In local custody**

P. Ballyroney
   Baptisms, 1819-63; marriages, 1818-29 and
   1833-1906; stipend accounts, c.1830-1848.   **MIC.1P/168; C.R.3/30**

P. Brookvale
   Baptisms, 1891-1968; marriages, 1867-1936.   **MIC.1P/132**

R.C. Annaghlone
   [Drumballyroney parish forms part of the Roman
   Catholic parish of Annaghlone - *see under*
   ANNACLONE]

DRUMBANAGHER CHURCH OF IRELAND PARISH, CO. ARMAGH
   [*see under* **KILLEVY**]

DRUMBEG, COS ANTRIM AND DOWN

C.I. Drumbeg (Down diocese)
   Baptisms, 1807-76; marriages, 1823-45; burials,
   1818-1909; confirmation lists, 1865 and 1868.   **MIC.1/41**

   Vestry minutes, 1823-1919.   **In local custody**

N.S.P. Dunmurry
  Baptisms, 1807-12 and 1815-17; notes about the history
  of the church, c.1686-1820; lists of collectors of stipend,
  1807-10.   **CR.4/1**

  Burials in churchyard, 1781-1954.   **T.1602**

P. Dunmurry
  Marriage notices, 1871-1901.   **MIC.1P/230/5**

  Baptisms, 1860-.   **In local custody**

P. Legacurry
  Baptisms, 1866-1950; (no pre-1900 marriages held). **MIC.1P/345**

R.C. [Part of Drumbeg is in the Roman Catholic parish of
    Blaris - *see under* **BLARIS**]

DRUMBO, CO. DOWN

C.I. Drumbo (Down diocese)
  Baptisms, 1791-1931; marriages, 1791-1845; burials,
  1792-1877.   **MIC.1/41**

  Vestry minutes, 1788-; preachers' books, 1824-;
  churchwardens' accounts, 1873-; registers of vestrymen,
  1870-.   **In local custody**

P. Ballycairn
  Baptisms, 1860-; marriages, 1845-.   **In local custody**

P. Carryduff
  Baptisms, 1854-1914; marriages, 1846-1970.   **MIC.1P/154**

  Marriage notices, 1871-89.   **MIC.1P/230/5**

P. Drumbo
  Baptisms, 1699-1723, 1764-73, 1781-92, 1802 and
  1827-1980; marriages, 1706-21, 1772, 1782-3, 1786-91
  and 1845-1921.   **MIC.1P/291;
                                                      D.1759/1D/1**

  Printed history of the congregation from the early 17th
  century-1991.   **C.R.3/54**

**DRUMBOLG (or DRIMBOLG) REFORMED
PRESBYTERIAN CHURCH, CO. LONDONDERRY**
    [*see under* **TAMLAGHT O'CRILLY**]

**DRUMCLAMPH CHURCH OF IRELAND PARISH,
CO. TYRONE**
    [*see under* **ARDSTRAW**]

DRUMCLIFF, CO. CLARE

M. Ennis
Baptisms, 1844-58.   **MIC.429/1/540**

DRUMCREE, CO. ARMAGH

C.I. Drumcree (Armagh diocese)
Baptisms, 1788-1881; marriages, 1802-45; burials,
1804-84.   **MIC.1/21, 42-43**

Vestry minutes, 1767-1935; cess applotment book, 1767.   **In local custody**

C.I. The Diamond
[Partly in Drumcree and partly in Kilmore parishes -
see under **KILMORE**]

C.I. Portadown (St Mark's) (Armagh diocese)
Baptisms, 1826-77; marriages, 1827-45.   **MIC.1/66**

Baptisms, 1878-; marriages, 1845-; burials, 1856-; vestry
minutes, 1826-; preachers' books, 1827-; register of
vestrymen, 1870-.   **In local custody**

M. Derryall
Baptisms, 1830-.   **In local custody**
[At Thomas Street Church, Portadown]

M. Derryanvil
Baptisms, 1830-; marriages 1952.   **In local custody**
[At Thomas Street Church, Portadown]

M. Edenderry
Baptisms, 1830-.   **In local custody**
[At Thomas Street Church, Portadown]

M. Mahon
Baptisms, 1830-; marriages 1938-.   **In local custody**
[At Thomas Street Church, Portadown]

M. Portadown (Thomas Street) [Wesleyan Methodists]
Baptisms, 1830-1904; marriages, 1863-1903.   **MIC.1E/8**

M. Portadown (Scotch Street)
Baptisms, 1830-; marriages, 1863-.   **In local custody**

M. Portadown [Primitive Methodists]
Baptisms, 1847-1901.   **MIC.1E/8**

M. Portadown [Primitive Wesleyan Methodists]
Baptisms, 1871-9. [Includes baptisms in the parishes of
Drumcree, Seagoe, Kilmore and Shankill and in Tandragee
and Mullavilly]   **MIC.1E/8**

P. Portadown (Armagh Road or 2nd)
Baptisms, 1868-1985; marriages, 1869-1930.   **MIC.1P/269**

R.C. Drumcree (Portadown) (Armagh diocese)
Baptisms, 1844-81 (incomplete in 1845 and last quarter
of 1871); marriages, 1844-81 (incomplete in 1844 and
1845 and August 1871-July 1872); burials, 1863-80;
souvenir booklet and photograph, 1977.   **MIC.1D/37; C.R.2/8**

DRUMGATH, CO. DOWN

C.I. Drumgath (Dromore diocese)
[Earliest registers destroyed in Dublin]

Vestry minutes and churchwardens' account book,
1822-91.   **T.679/353**

Preachers' book, 1818-60.   **T.1453**

Baptisms, 1881-; marriages, 1846-; preachers' books,
1893-.   **In local custody**

P. 1st Rathfriland
Baptisms, 1827-1970; marriages, 1782-1811 and
1845-1936.   **MIC.1P/131; T.1037;
                                                             D.1759/1D/14**

P. 2nd Rathfriland
Baptisms, 1804-1934; marriages, 1805-43 and 1845-1935;
deaths, 1849-58; session minutes, 1805-49; lists of new
communicants, 1849-60; committee minutes, 1866-c.1900;
communion roll, 1865-79.   **MIC.1P/387; T.1539**

P. 3rd Rathfriland
Baptisms, 1834-1934; marriages, 1834-1935; communion
roll, 1865-79.   **MIC.1P/388; T.1539/3**

Minute book of Sunday School, 1833-82, and roll book,
1853-80, with gaps.   **T.1537**

R.C. Drumgath (Dromore diocese)
Baptisms, 1829-81; marriages and burials, 1837-80.   **MIC.1D/24**

R.P. Rathfriland
Baptisms, 1857-1916; marriages, 1864-1943; deaths,
1857-68 and 1925-84; admissions, 1857-1972; lists of
members with details of emigrations, deaths and
marriages, 1884-1944; lists of members removed,
1924-45; session minutes, 1857-1908; history of the
church, published in 1977.   **MIC.1C/20**

DRUMGLASS, CO. TYRONE

    C.I. Drumglass (Armagh diocese)
    [Also includes Tullyniskan up to 1793]

       Baptisms, 1665-1767, 1774-1802 and 1814-76; marriages,
       1677-1766, 1791-2, 1799-1804 and 1809-45; burials,
       1672-1767 and 1814-1948; vestry minutes, 1693-1866;
       confirmations, 1824, 1828, 1841, 1843, 1849, 1852,
       1856, 1859, 1863 and 1866.　　　　　　　　**MIC.1/18, 36-37**

       Baptisms, 1876-; marriages, 1855-; vestry minutes,
       1870-.　　　　　　　　　　　　　　**In local custody**

       Printed history of the parish of Drumglass, 1967.　　**DIO.4/32/D/18/10/1**

    M. Dungannon
       Baptisms, 1819-46.　　　　　　　　　　**MIC.429/1/416**

       Baptisms, 1830-; marriages, 1865-.　　　　**In local custody**

    P. 1st Dungannon
       Baptisms, 1790-1886; marriages and notices of marriages,
       with rebukes for irregular marriages, 1789-1845.　　**MIC.1P/3A**

    P. 2nd Dungannon
       Baptisms, 1830-; marriages, 1825-.　　　　**In local custody**

    R.C. Dungannon (Armagh diocese)
    [The Roman Catholic parish of Dungannon consists of
    the parishes of Drumglass, Killyman and Tullyniskin]

       Baptisms, marriages and burials, 1821-81.　　**MIC.1D/31-32**

DRUMGOOLAND, CO. DOWN

    B. Derryneil
       Marriages, 1869-1906.　　　　　　　　**In local custody**

    C.I. Drumgooland (Dromore diocese)
       Baptisms, 1779-92 and 1833-72; marriages, 1779-91 and
       1834-45; burials, 1839-41 and 1860-1959.　　**MIC.1/40**

       Parochial account book, 1872-1925; Sustentation Fund
       book, 1880-81; registers of vestrymen, 1870-.　　**In local custody**

    P. Drumgooland
       Baptisms, 1836-1912; marriages, 1836-44 and 1856-1935;
       communion roll, 1867-90.　　　　　　**MIC.1P/304**

    P. Drumlee
       Baptisms, 1826-1980; marriages, 1845-1920; session
       minutes, 1826-54.　　　　　　　　　**MIC.1P/133**

P. Leitrim
  Baptisms, 1839-1901; marriages, 1836-1936; deaths,
  1837-43 and 1888-92; communicants' roll, 1837-1936;
  session minutes, 1838-64.   **MIC.1P/264**

R.C. Drumgooland Lower (Dromore diocese)
  Baptisms, marriages and deaths, 1832-81.   **MIC.1D/22**

R.C. Drumgooland Upper (Dromore diocese)
  Baptisms and marriages, 1827-80; deaths, 1828-81.   **MIC.1D/22; T.2637/1**

DRUMGOON, CO. CAVAN

C.I. Dernakesh (Kilmore diocese)
  Baptisms, 1837-1985; marriages, 1838-73 and
  1875-1942; burials, 1837-1985.   **MIC.1/279**

C.I. Drumgoon (Kilmore diocese)
  Baptisms, 1802-14 and 1825-1909; marriages, 1813 and
  1825-1957; burials, 1825-47 and 1850-1915;
  confirmation lists, 1827, 1852, 1855, 1857, 1864, 1871,
  1875 and 1878.   **MIC.1/280**

M. Cootehill [Primitive Wesleyan Methodists]
  Marriages, 1877-8.   **MIC.1E/54**

M. Cootehill [Wesleyan Methodists]
  Baptisms, 1835-6 and 1843-1910; marriages, 1871-1955;
  register of members, 1847-78.   **MIC.1E/54**

P. 1st Cootehill
  Baptisms, 1870-1982.   **MIC.1P/178**

P. 2nd Cootehill
  Baptisms, 1822-1921; marriages, 1845-63 and 1879.   **MIC.1P/177**

R.C. Drumgoon (Cootehill) (Kilmore diocese)
  Baptisms, 1829-79; marriages, 1829-72.   **MIC.1D/81**

DRUMHILLERY, CO. ARMAGH
  [*see under* **TYNAN**]

DRUMHOME, CO. DONEGAL

C.I. Drumholm (Raphoe diocese)
  Baptisms, 1719-20, 1739-48, 1764, 1783-1873;
  marriages, 1691-1718, 1764 and 1783-1869; burials,
  1696-1715, 1764 and 1783-1873; confirmation list, 1853.   **MIC.1/148; T.607/2**

  Vestry minutes, 1783-; census, 1831.   **In local custody**

C.I. Laghey (Raphoe diocese)
Baptisms, 1877-1903; marriages, 1847-71; burials,
1877-1909.   **MIC.1/155**

C.I. Rossnowlagh (Raphoe diocese)
Baptisms, 1879-1972; marriages, 1845-1953.   **MIC.1/144**

Burials 1902-; vestry minutes, 1879-; register of
vestrymen, 1870-.   **In local custody**

M. Ballintra
Baptisms, 1835-1984; marriages, 1875-1954.   **MIC.1E/35-36**

M. Ballyshannon Circuit
[Part of Drumhome parish is in Ballyshannon Circuit -
see under **KILBARRON**]

P. 1st Donegal
[After 1885 1st and 2nd Donegal united - *see also under*
KILLYMARD]

Baptisms, 1824-85; marriages, 1824-43 and 1845-1947;
deaths, 1860-83; census, 1861-2.   **MIC.1P/6; D.2535/1**

R.C. Drumholm (Ballintra) (Raphoe diocese)
Baptisms and marriages, 1866-81.   **MIC.1D/86**

DRUMINISKILL CHAPEL OF EASE (CHURCH OF IRELAND), CO. FERMANAGH
[*see under* **KILLESHER**]

DRUMKEEN PRESBYTERIAN CHURCH, CO. MONAGHAN
[*see under* **AGHABOG**]

DRUMKEERAN PRESBYTERIAN CHURCH, CO. CAVAN
[*see under* **KILLASHANDRA**]

DRUMKEERAN, CO. FERMANAGH

C.I. Drumkeeran (Clogher diocese)
Baptisms, 1801-1944; marriages, 1801-1904; burials,
1836-1943.   **MIC.1/37; T.679/7A-D**

Vestry minutes, 1794-; register of vestrymen, 1871-;
preachers' books, 1863-.   **In local custody**

C.I. Lack (or Colaghty)
[Partly in Drumkeeran parish - *see under*
MAGHERACULMONEY]

M. Pettigo [Wesleyan Methodists]
    Baptisms, 1835-1910; marriages, 1872-1937.   **MIC.1E/35, 38**

    Baptisms, 1835-46.   **MIC.429/1/473**

M. Terwinney
    Baptisms, 1829-1913; marriages, 1878-1927.   **MIC.1E/37**

P. Pettigo
    Baptisms, 1844-1917; marriages, 1846-1926.   **MIC.1P/66**

R.C. Drumkeeran (Blackbog) (Clogher diocese)
    [United with the parishes of Templecarne
    Magheraculmoney and Belleek - *see under*
    TEMPLECARN]

DRUMKEERAN CHURCH OF IRELAND PARISH, CO. LEITRIM
    [*see under* **INISHMAGRATH**]

DRUMLANE, CO. CAVAN

C.I. Drumlane (Kilmore diocese)
    [Earliest registers destroyed in Dublin]

    Baptisms, 1874-1985; marriages, 1845-1932; burials,
    1877-1982; vestry minutes, 1796-1888.   **MIC.1/219**

C.I. Quivvy (Kilmore diocese)
    Baptisms, 1854-1938; marriages, 1857-1940.   **MIC.1/242**

R.C. Drumlane (Staghall) (Kilmore diocese)
    Baptisms, 1836-81; marriages, 1870-80.   **MIC.1D/75**

DRUMLEASE, CO. LEITRIM

C.I. Drumlease (Kilmore diocese)
    Baptisms, 1827-1984; marriages, 1828-1951; burials,
    1827-48.   **MIC.1/265**

R.C. Drumlease (Dromahaire) (Kilmore diocese)
    Baptisms, 1859-79; marriages, 1859-81.   **MIC.1D/77**

DRUMLEE PRESBYTERIAN CHURCH, CO. DOWN
    [*see under* **DRUMGOOLAND**]

DRUMLEGAGH (or 2ND ARDSTRAW) PRESBYTERIAN CHURCH, CO. TYRONE
    [*see under* **ARDSTRAW**]

DRUMLOUGH PRESBYTERIAN CHURCH, CO. DOWN
   [*see under* **DROMORE, CO. DOWN**]

DRUMMAUL, CO. ANTRIM

C.I. Drummaul (Connor diocese)
   Baptisms, 1823-75; marriages, 1823-46; burials, 1823-77.   **MIC.1/104**

   Marriages, 1845-; vestry minutes, 1851-; preachers'
   books, 1891-.   **In local custody**

M. Randalstown
   Baptisms, 1829-1987; circuit schedule books, 1860-94;
   membership register, 1826-91.   **MIC.1E/58**

P. Old Randalstown
   Baptisms, 1853-1944; marriages, 1845-1922.   **MIC.1P/364**

P. 1st Randalstown
   Marriages, 1845-1934.   **MIC.1P/99**

P. 2nd Randalstown
   Baptisms, 1850-1986; marriages, 1845-1936; session
   minutes, 1850-95.   **MIC.1P/86**

R.C. Drummaul (Randalstown) (Down and Connor diocese)
   [Includes the civil parishes of Drummaul and Cranfield
   and up to 1873 the parish of Antrim]

   Baptisms, 1825-81; marriages, 1825-84; deaths, 1837-48.   **MIC.1D/70-71**

DRUMMINIS PRESBYTERIAN CHURCH, CO. ARMAGH
   [*see under* **KILDARTON**]

DRUMMULLY, COS FERMANAGH AND MONAGHAN

C.I. Drummully (Clogher diocese)
   Baptisms, 1830-73; marriages, 1829-1956; burials,
   1836-1970; vestry minutes, 1808-70.   **MIC.1/134**

   Vestry minutes, 1808-70 (with baptism and marriage
   entries for St Mary's Parish, Drumcrin, 1801-13).   **C.R.1/30/D/1**

   Baptisms, 1873-; vestry minutes, 1871-.   **In local custody**

P. Ballyhobridge
   Baptisms, 1846-1985; marriages, 1854-1936; accounts,
   1846-51.   **MIC.1P/274**

R.C. Drummully (Currin, Scotshouse) (Clogher diocese)
[Drummully Roman Catholic parish consists of the
parishes of Drummully, Currin and Galloon - *see also
under* **GALLOON**]

Baptisms, 1845-81; marriages, 1864-81. **MIC.1D/15**

**DRUMNAKILLY CHURCH OF IRELAND PARISH,
CO. TYRONE**
[*see under* **TERMONMAGUIRK**]

**DRUMOGHILL ROMAN CATHOLIC CHURCH,
CO. DONEGAL**
[*see under* **ALL SAINTS**]

DRUMQUIN METHODIST CHURCH, CO. TYRONE
[*see under* **LONGFIELD EAST**]

DRUMQUIN PRESBYTERIAN CHURCH, CO. TYRONE
[*see under* **LONGFIELD EAST**]

DRUMQUIN ROMAN CATHOLIC CHURCH, CO. TYRONE
[*see under* **LONGFIELD EAST AND WEST**]

DRUMRAGH, CO. TYRONE

C.I. Drumragh (Derry diocese)
Baptisms, 1801-95; marriages, 1804-45; burials, 1830-95. **T.679/13-14;
MIC.1/40-41**

Marriages, 1845-; vestry minutes, 1792-; churchwardens'
accounts, 1874-80 and 1931-; registers of vestrymen,
1870-; grave register, 1874-; preachers' books, 1871-. **In local custody**

C.I. Clanabogan (Derry diocese)
[In Drumragh, Donacavey and Dromore parishes]

Baptisms, 1863-1960; burials, 1864-1934. **MIC.1/5**

Marriages, 1865-; vestry minutes, 1864-; register of
vestrymen, 1870-; preachers' books, 1863-. **In local custody**

M. Omagh [Wesleyan Methodists]
Baptisms, 1832-1953; circuit schedule books, 1866-1909;
membership registers, 1863-1907; minutes about rebuilding
Omagh chapel, 1855-7; quarterly meeting minute book,
1859-1902; circuit stewards' book, 1829-85. **MIC.1E/24**

Baptisms, 1831-46.   **MIC.429/1/253**

P. 1st Ballynahatty
Baptisms, 1843-1968; marriages, 1845-1936.   **MIC.1P/97**

P. 2nd Ballynahatty (or Creevan)
Baptisms, 1867-1984; marriages, 1846-1934.   **MIC.1P/97**

P. Gillygooley
Baptisms, 1848-66 and 1869-1984; marriages, 1845-1934;
communcants' roll, 1892-1918.   **MIC.1P/234**

P. 1st Omagh
Baptisms, 1856-1968; marriages, 1845-1927; committee
minutes, 1861-5; session minutes, 1874-1913.   **MIC.1P/128**

P. 2nd Omagh or Omagh Trinity
Baptisms, 1821-41 and 1849-1942; marriages, 1846-1900;
building committee minutes and accounts, 1855-64 and
1866-70; communicants' roll, 1896-1910.   **MIC.1P/235**

R.C. Drumragh (Omagh) (Derry diocese)
Baptisms, marriages and deaths, 1846 and 1853-81;
index to baptisms, 1846-79; printed history of the parish,
mainly from the 17th century to c.1900.   **MIC.1D/60; C.R.2/9**

DRUMREAGH PRESBYTERIAN CHURCH, CO. ANTRIM
    [*see under* **BALLYMONEY**]

DRUMREILLY, CO. LEITRIM

C.I. Corrawallen (Kilmore diocese)
Baptisms, 1877-1921; marriages, 1859-1950; burials,
1877-1981.   **MIC.1/258**

C.I. Dowra (Kilmore diocese)
[Formed out of part of Drumreilly parish - *see under*
KILLINAGH]

R.C. Drumreilly Lower (Kilmore diocese)
Baptisms, 1867-80.   **MIC.1D/78**

DRUMSNAT, CO. MONAGHAN

R.C. Drumsnat and Kilmore (Clogher diocese)
[Kilmore parish is united to Drumsnat]

Baptisms, 1875-81; marriages, 1836-72 and 1875-83;
deaths, 1862-80.   **MIC.1D/18; C.R.2/13**

DRUMTULLAGH, GRANGE OF, CO. ANTRIM

C.I. Drumtullagh (Connor diocese)
[Earliest registers destroyed in Dublin]

Baptisms, 1895-; marriages, 1876-; burials, 1916-; vestry
minutes, 1875-; preachers' books, 1875-; registers of
vestrymen, 1875-.   **In local custody**

DRUNG, CO. CAVAN

C.I. Drung (Kilmore diocese)
Baptisms, 1759-1936; marriages, 1785-1957; burials,
1774-1925, together with details of the total number of
families in each parish in 1810 and a list of children and
their parents, 1814.   **MIC.1/300**

R.C. Drung (Kilmore diocese)
Baptisms, 1847-83.   **C.R.2/10**

DUBLIN

C. York Street, Dublin
Marriages, 1827-45 and 1937-42; minutes of church
meetings, 1858-1949; minutes of deacons' meetings,
1883-8, 1901-37 and 1945-8; committee minutes, with
subscription lists, 1830-60; Mutual Improvement Society
minutes, 1900-14; minutes relating to church building
improvements, 1857-60; accounts, 1909-39; reports and
statements of accounts, 1867-1937, with gaps; printed
rules, 1803.   **C.R.7/3**

C. Zion Chapel, Dublin
Baptisms, 1820-84, with an index, and marriages, 1820-57;
minutes and lists of church members, 1819-40; minutes of
deacons' meetings, 1871-7; accounts, 1842-90.   **C.R.7/4**

C. Kingstown
Baptisms, 1881-1935; minutes of meetings of church
members, 1869-1923 and 1936-8; committee minutes,
1887-1900; minutes of deacons' meetings, 1937-8; lists of
members, 1849-61 and 1881-1925; communicants' roll,
1890-91.   **C.R.7/5**

C. Oriel Street, Dublin
Account book, 1902-09.   **C.R.7/6**

M. Dublin [Wesleyan Methodists]
Leaders' meetings minutes, 1822-39.   **C.R.6/7**

M. Dublin [Primitive Wesleyan Methodists]
Society minutes, 1817-54.   **C.R.6/6**

M. Dublin [Primitive Methodists]
   [In the parishes of St Thomas', St Mary's, St Mark's,
   St George's, St Peter's and St Andrew's, Dublin]

   Baptisms, 1870-81; marriages, 1878-81.   **MIC.1E/20**

MOR. Dublin
   Baptisms, 1748-1977; marriages, 1799-1854 and
   1866-1980; burials, 1765-1979; registers of members,
   1750-1837 and 1861-85; diaries, 1749-1917; elders'
   conference minutes, 1748-1829; committee minutes,
   1773-1940; poor account books, 1771-1907; cash books,
   1750-1829; ledgers, 1806-30.   **MIC.1F/4**

P. Clontarf (Lower Gloucester Street)
   Baptisms, 1836-1992; marriages, 1836-41 and 1847-1932;
   session minutes, 1843-55 and 1862-90; committee minutes,
   1845-1910; stipend book, 1877-86.   **MIC.1P/430**

DUNAGHY, CO. ANTRIM

C.I. Dunaghy (Connor diocese)
   Baptisms, 1877-1958; burials, 1894-1934; register of
   vestrymen, 1870-1937.   **MIC.1/298-299**

   Notebook of the Rev. Andrew Rowan, 1672-80.   **T.796/1**

P. Clough
   Baptisms, 1865-1987; transcripts of marriages, 1855-76;
   marriages, 1873-1907; communicants' roll, 1866-92;
   committee and session minutes, 1839-1903.   **MIC.1P/312;**
                                                                   T.3054/B/2

R.C. Glenravel and Braid (Down and Connor diocese)
   [Glenravel and Braid Roman Catholic parish consists of
   part of the parishes of Dunaghy, Racavan and Skerry and
   all of Newtowncrommelin - *see under* **RACAVAN**;
   the other part of Dunaghy is in the Roman Catholic
   parish of Dunloy and Cloughmills - *see under* **FINVOY**]

DUNBIN, CO. LOUTH

R.C. Dunbin, Haggardstown (Kilkerley) (Armagh diocese)
   [Dunbin, Haggardstown, part of Baronstown, Heynstown,
   Ballybarrack and Philipstown]

   Baptisms and marriages, 1752-1880; deaths, 1752-1806
   and 1831-8.   **MIC.1D/45**

DUNBOE, CO. LONDONDERRY

C.I. Castlerock (Derry diocese)
Baptisms, 1870-1982; marriages, 1871-1971; burials, 1874-1982; vestry minutes, 1920-32; general vestry register, 1920-82; account book, 1869-83; registers of vestrymen, c.1870 and 1903; select vestry minutes, 1871-86; confirmation lists, 1889-1953.   **MIC.1/137**

C.I. Dunboe, St Paul's (Derry diocese)
[Earliest registers destroyed in Dublin]

Baptisms, 1839-1982; marriages, 1845-1974; burials, 1845-1982; vestry minutes, 1783-1864 and 1920-32; general vestry register, 1920-82.   **MIC.1/135, 137**

Preachers' books, 1875-.   **In local custody**

C.I. Fermoyle (Derry diocese)
Baptisms, 1860-1975; marriages, 1844-1935 and 1965; burials, 1864-1972; vestry minutes, 1920-32; general vestry register, 1920-82.   **MIC.1/136-137**

P. 1st Dunboe
Baptisms, 1805-12, 1825-6 and 1843-1949; marriages, 1845-1934; session and committee minutes, 1828, 1841-54 and 1859; male communicants, 1826-66; list of the poor, 1830; seatholders' account book, 1853-65; receipt and expenditure book, 1847-72.   **MIC.1P/412**

P. 2nd Dunboe
Baptisms, 1864-1983; marriages, 1845-1913; session minutes, including entries for baptisms, marriages and communicants, 1835-68; stipend book, 1894-1951; details about persons emigrating, 1841-7 and 1866.   **MIC.1P/149**

R.C. [*see under* **COLERAINE**]

DUNDALK, CO. LOUTH

C.I. Dundalk, St Nicholas' (Armagh diocese)
Baptisms, 1729-1924; marriages, 1750-1929; burials, 1727-1985.   **MIC.1/204**

Plans and elevations for alterations and extensions to the church, c.1935-1939.   **C.R.1/57**

Vestry minutes, 1807-.   **In local custody**

M. Dundalk
Baptisms, 1837-50.   **MIC.429/1/11**

R.C. Dundalk (Armagh diocese)
   [Also includes Castletown and Kane parishes]

   Baptisms, 1790-1802 and 1814-81; marriages, 1790-1802
   and 1817-31; deaths, 1790-1802.   MIC.1D/46

DUNDELA CHURCH OF IRELAND PARISH, HOLYWOOD, CO. DOWN
   [*see under* HOLYWOOD]

DUNDERMOT, GRANGE OF, CO. ANTRIM

   C.I. [Attached to Dunaghy - *see under* DUNAGHY]

DUNDONALD, CO. DOWN

   C.I. Dundonald (Down diocese)
      Baptisms and marriages, 1811-45; burials, 1823-42;
      vestry minutes, 1811-98.   MIC.1/46

      Vestry minutes, 1810-; baptisms, 1845-; marriages,
      1845-; registers of vestrymen, 1891-; preachers' books,
      1871-.   In local custody

   P. Dundonald
      Baptisms, 1678-; marriages, 1678-.   In local custody

      Marriage notices, 1892-1924.   D.2643

   R.C. Newtownards
      [Part of Newtownards Roman Catholic parish - *see under*
      NEWTOWNARDS]

DUNDROD PRESBYTERIAN CHURCH, CO. ANTRIM
   [*see under* GLENAVY]

DUNDRUM METHODIST CHURCH, CO. DOWN
   [*see under* KILMEGAN]

DUNDRUM ROMAN CATHOLIC CHURCH, CO. DOWN
   [*see under* KILMEGAN]

DUNEANE, CO. ANTRIM

   C.I. Duneane (Connor diocese)
      [Earliest registers destroyed in Dublin]

Baptisms, 1879-; marriages, 1846-; burials, 1878-; vestry
minutes, 1896-; churchwardens' accounts, 1894-;
registers of vestrymen, 1895-; preachers' books, 1893-.   **In local custody**

P. Duneane
Baptisms, 1864-; marriages, 1845-.   **In local custody**

R.C. Duneane (Down and Connor diocese)
Baptisms, 1834-61; marriages, 1835-61.   **MIC.1D/70**

**DUNFANAGHY CHURCH OF IRELAND PARISH,
CO. DONEGAL**
[*see under* **CLONDAHORKY**]

DUNFANAGHY PRESBYTERIAN CHURCH, CO. DONEGAL
[*see under* **CLONDAHORKY**]

DUNGANNON METHODIST CHURCH, CO. TYRONE
[*see under* **DRUMGLASS**]

**DUNGANNON (1ST AND 2ND) PRESBYTERIAN
CHURCHES, CO. TYRONE**
[*see under* **DRUMGLASS**]

DUNGANNON ROMAN CATHOLIC PARISH, CO. TYRONE
[*see under* **DRUMGLASS**]

DUNGIVEN, CO. LONDONDERRY

C.I. Dungiven (Derry diocese)
Baptisms, 1795-1886; marriages, 1795-1844; burials,
1824-90; vestry minutes, 1778-1896, with baptisms and
marriages; preachers' book, 1850-62.   **T.679/70; MIC.1/88-89**

Baptisms, 1778-94; marriages, 1778-94 and 1845-;
registers of vestrymen, 1870-; preachers' books, 1862-.   **In local custody**

P. Dungiven
Baptisms, 1835-; marriages, 1834-.   **In local custody**

R.C. Dungiven (Derry diocese)
Baptisms, 1825-34 and 1847-81; marriages, 1825-34
and 1864-82; deaths, 1825-32 and 1870-71.   **MIC.1D/59**

P. Scriggan
Baptisms, 1864-84; marriages, 1876-1905.   **In local custody**

DUNGLOE ROMAN CATHOLIC CHURCH, CO. DONEGAL
    [*see under* **LETTERMACAWARD**]

DUNKINEELY METHODIST CIRCUIT AND CHURCH,
CO. DONEGAL
    [*see under* **KILLAGHTEE**]

DUNLEER, CO. LOUTH

    R.C. Dunleer (Armagh diocese)
        [United to parishes of Dromin, Cappoge, Mosstown and
        Richardson]

        Baptisms, 1847-81; marriages, 1772-98 and 1848-82;
        deaths, 1847-58 and 1877-82.   **MIC.1D/50**

DUNLEWEY CHURCH OF IRELAND PARISH,
CO. DONEGAL
    [*see under* **TULLAGHOBEGLEY**]

DUNLOY PRESBYTERIAN CHURCH, CO. ANTRIM
    [*see under* **FINVOY**]

DUNLOY ROMAN CATHOLIC PARISH, CO. ANTRIM
    [*see under* **FINVOY**]

DUNLUCE, CO. ANTRIM

    C.I. Dunluce (Connor diocese)
        Baptisms, 1809-98; marriages, 1826-45; burials,
        1826-97; vestry minutes, 1778-1931; preachers' books,
        1847-1902.   **MIC.1/90-91**

        Churchwardens' account book, 1888-; confirmation lists,
        1880-; registers of vestrymen, 1870-.   **In local custody**

    P. Dunluce
        Baptisms, 1865-1953; marriages, 1845-1912.   **MIC.1P/367**

    R.C. Portrush and Bushmills (Down and Connor diocese)
        [Dunluce parish is partly in the Roman Catholic parish
        of Ballymoney - *see under* **BALLYMONEY** and partly
        in the Roman Catholic parish of Portrush - *see under*
        BALLYWILLIN]

DUNMORE ROMAN CATHOLIC PARISH, CO. DOWN
    [*see under* **MAGHERADROOL**]

**DUNMOYLE CHURCH OF IRELAND PARISH,
CO. TYRONE**
   [*see under* **TERMONMAGUIRK**]

**DUNMURRY NON-SUBSCRIBING PRESBYTERIAN
CHURCH, CO. ANTRIM**
   [*see under* **DRUMBEG**]

DUNMURRY PRESBYTERIAN CHURCH, CO. ANTRIM
   [*see under* **DRUMBEG**]

**DUNNALONG CHURCH OF IRELAND PARISH,
CO. TYRONE**
   [*see under* **DONAGHEADY**]

**DUNSEVERICK CHURCH OF IRELAND PARISH,
CO. ANTRIM**
   [*see under* **BALLINTOY**]

DUNSFORT, CO. DOWN

   C.I. Dunsford (Down diocese)
      [Earliest registers destroyed in Dublin]

      Vestry minutes, 1814-1926; preachers' books, 1887-1944.   **MIC.1/118; T.2841**

      Baptisms, 1895-; marriages, 1846-; burials, 1884-;
      registers of vestrymen, 1870-.   **In local custody**

   R.C. Dunsford and Ardglass (Down and Connor diocese)
      Baptisms, 1845-81; marriages, 1845-80; deaths, 1848-68.   **MIC.1D/72**

**EDENDERRY CHURCH OF IRELAND PARISH,
CO. TYRONE**
   [*see under* **CAPPAGH**]

EDENDERRY METHODIST CHURCH, CO. ARMAGH
   [*see under* **DRUMCREE**]

EDENDERRY PRESBYTERIAN CHURCH, CO. TYRONE
   [*see under* **CAPPAGH**]

**EDENGROVE PRESBYTERIAN CHURCH,
BALLYNAHINCH, CO. DOWN**
   [*see under* **MAGHERADROOL**]

**EDERNEY ROMAN CATHOLIC CHURCH,
CO. FERMANAGH**
[*see under* **MAGHERACULMONEY**]

**EGLANTINE (ALL SAINTS) CHURCH OF IRELAND
PARISH, CO. ANTRIM**
[*see under* **BLARIS**]

EGLISH, CO. ARMAGH

C.I. Eglish (Armagh diocese)
Baptisms, 1803-1935, with index; marriages, 1804-1936,
with index; burials, 1803-1935, with index;
confirmations, 1824-8, 1833-52 and 1894-1933, with
index; preachers' book, 1836-1925; notes from vestry
minutes about erection of new church, 1820-30.   **MIC.1/1A-B; T.679/20**

Vestry minutes, 1803-.   **In local custody**

M. Killymaddy
Baptisms, 1815-.   **In local custody**

P. Knappagh
[No pre-1900 baptism registers]

Marriages, 1846-1923; printed history, 1839-1989, which
includes a congregational list, 1884.   **MIC.1P/402**

R.C. Eglish (Armagh diocese)
Baptisms, 1862-81; marriages, 1862-82.   **MIC.1D/36**

EGLISH PRESBYTERIAN CHURCH, CO. TYRONE
[*see under* **CLONFEACLE**]

EMATRIS, CO. MONAGHAN

C.I. Ematris (Clogher diocese)
Baptisms, 1811-1980; marriages, 1811-1952; burials,
1811-83; vestry minutes, 1767-1869 with baptisms,
1753-91, and marriages, 1753-75; preachers' book,
1823-52; collections for, and distribution to, the poor
of the parish, 1830-51.   **MIC.1/132**

Burials, 1884-.   **In local custody**

C.I. Rockcorry (Clogher diocese)
Baptisms, 1880-1978; marriages, 1857-1948; plans of
church, 1854.   **C.R.1/28**

Burials, 1880-; vestry minutes, 1870-; register of
vestrymen, 1870-; preachers' books, 1855-.   **In local custody**

M. Rockcorry
Baptisms, 1835-6 and 1843-1910; marriages may be in
with Cootehill marriages, 1871-1955; register of members,
1842-72.   **MIC.1E/54**

P. Rockcorry
Baptisms, 1860-1982; marriages, 1861-1955.   **MIC.1P/195**

R.C. Ematris (Rockcorry) (Clogher diocese)
Baptisms, 1848-76; marriages, 1850-61.   **MIC.1D/21**

ENNIS METHODIST CHURCH, CO. CLARE
[*see under* **DRUMCLIFF**]

ENNISKEEN, CO. CAVAN

M. Kingscourt [Wesleyan Methodists]
Baptisms, 1838-6 and 1843-1970; marriages, 1871-1952;
lists of members, 1847-78.   **MIC.1E/49, 54**

ENNISKILLEN, CO. FERMANAGH

C.I. Enniskillen (Clogher diocese)
[Formerly known as Enniskeen or Inniskeen]

[Earliest registers destroyed in Dublin]

Extracts of baptisms, 1667-1789, marriages, 1668-1794,
and burials, 1667-1781; baptisms, 1861-1922; burials,
1879-1907 and 1941-50; vestry minutes, 1731-1920;
copy deeds, 1796-9; select vestry minutes, 1871-80;
register of church members, 1871 and 1946-50.   **MIC.1/94, 110;**
                                                             C.R.1/21; D.2296

Extracts from baptism, marriage and burial registers,
1666-1826.   **T.3548/1**

Preachers' book, 1895-1928.   **D.1358**

Printed copy of *Old Enniskillen Vestry Book*, with
extracts of births, marriages and deaths, 1666-c.1797.   **D.3007/T/578**

Extracts from vestry minutes, 1666-1912, which include
some baptisms, marriage and burial entries.   **D.1588/6**

Marriages, 1845-.   **In local custody**

C.I. Clabby (Clogher diocese)
Baptisms, 1862-77; marriages, 1867-1901.   **T.679/354; C.R.1/31**

Burials, 1870-.   **In local custody**

C.I. Garvary (Clogher diocese)
[Partly in Enniskillen parish]

[Earliest baptism register destroyed in Dublin]

Baptisms, 1877-1991; marriages, 1869-1930; burials,
1870-1942; accounts and vestry minutes, 1872-1942.   **MIC.1/309**

Registers of vestrymen, 1872-.   **In local custody**

C.I. Tempo (Clogher diocese)
Baptisms, 1836-1954; marriages, 1837-45; burials,
1837-1944.   **MIC.1/85-86; C.R.1/32**

Marriages, 1845-; vestry minutes, 1902-; register of
vestrymen, 1870-.   **In local custody**

M. Clabby
Baptisms, 1879-1933; marriages, 1891-1936; circuit
schedule books, 1881-1910; quarterly meeting minutes,
1900-37; membership lists, 1884, 1887, 1889 and c.1890.   **MIC.1E/47**

M. Enniskillen [Wesleyan Methodists]
Baptisms, 1823-1953; marriages, 1864-1906; circuit
schedule book, 1866-80; quarterly meeting minutes,
1877-93.   **MIC.1E/15**

Baptisms, 1823-43.   **MIC.429/1/198**

M. Enniskillen [Primitive Wesleyan Methodists]
Baptisms, 1871-9; marriages, 1873-9.   **MIC.1E/13**

M. Pubble [Primitive Wesleyan Methodists]
Baptisms, 1872-1925; quarterly schedule book, 1880-93.   **MIC.1E/9**

M. Tempo
Baptisms, 1841-1954; circuit schedule books, 1865-1909.   **MIC.1E/28**

P. Enniskillen
Baptisms, 1819-35 and 1837-1986; marriages, 1819-34 and
1838-45; lists of ministers, 1688-1947; accounts, 1859-74. **MIC.1P/282**

P. Tempo
Baptisms, 1874-1951; marriages, 1845-1934; committee
minutes, 1849-1951.   **MIC.1P/96**

R.C. Enniskillen (Clogher diocese)
Baptisms, 1838-81; marriages, 1817-80.   **MIC.1D/10-11**

R.C. Tempo (Pubble) (Clogher diocese)
Baptisms, 1845-81; marriages, 1845-82.   **MIC.1D/13**

ERRIGAL, CO. LONDONDERRY

C.I. Errigal (Derry diocese)
[Earliest registers destroyed in Dublin]

Baptisms, 1873-; marriages, 1845-; burials, 1879-; vestry
minutes, 1911-.   **In local custody**

P. 1st Garvagh
Baptisms, 1795-1816, 1822-49 and 1859-1945; marriages,
1795-1802, 1807-14 and 1822-89; census of congregation,
1796 and 1840.   **MIC.1P/257**

P. 2nd or Main Street Garvagh
Baptisms, 1830-1921; marriages, 1830-1934; burials,
1853-96; session and committee minutes, 1827-76;
communicants' roll, 1832-6, 1854-5 and 1887-1918.   **MIC.1P/17**

P. 3rd Garvagh
Baptisms, 1872-1907; marriages, 1864-96.   **MIC.1P/403**

R.C. Errigal (Garvagh) (Derry diocese)
Baptisms, 1846-81; marriages, 1873-84.   **MIC.1D/59**

ERRIGAL KEEROGUE, CO. TYRONE

C.I. Errigal Keerogue (Armagh diocese)
Baptisms, 1812-75; marriages, 1825-45; burials, 1817-75;
confirmations, 1843-9 and 1851-63; vestry minutes,
1757 and 1829-1941; banns, 1819-21.   **MIC.1/2**

Baptisms, 1875-; marriages, 1845-; burials, 1876-; vestry
minutes, 1941-; preachers' books, 1845-; confirmation
register, 1870-.   **In local custody**

C.I. Ballygawley
[In Errigal Keerogue and Carnteel - *see under*
CARNTEEL]

R.C. Errigal Kieran (Ballygawley) (Armagh diocese)
Baptisms, 1847-81.   **MIC.1D/35**

R.C. Errigal Kieran (Ballymacelroy) (Armagh diocese)
Marriages, 1864-81.   **MIC.1D/35**

P. Ballygawley
Baptisms, 1842-1984; marriages, 1842-1927.   **MIC.1P/61**

Marriage notices, 1860-1906.   **MIC.1P/230/4B**

**ERRIGAL PORTCLARE CHURCH OF IRELAND PARISH,
CO. LONDONDERRY**
  [*see under* **ERRIGAL TROUGH**]

**ERRIGAL SHANCO CHURCH OF IRELAND PARISH,
CO. MONAGHAN**
  [*see under* **ERRIGAL TROUGH**]

ERRIGAL TROUGH, COS MONAGHAN AND TYRONE

  C.I. Errigal Shanco (Clogher diocese)
      [Earliest registers destroyed in Dublin]

      Baptisms, 1877-1961; marriages, 1845-1949; burials,
      1877-1974.   **MIC.1/128**

      Vestry minutes, 1913-.   **In local custody**

  C.I. Errigal Trough (Clogher diocese)
      Baptisms, marriages and burials, 1671-2, 1719-20,
      1722-3 and 1728-9; baptisms, 1801-1980; marriages,
      1803-1927; burials, 1802-1980; Trough Relief Fund
      registers, c.1845 and c.1847.   **MIC.1/125**

      Vestry minutes, 1852-.   **In local custody**

  C.I. St Mary's, Portclare (Clogher diocese)
      [Earliest registers destroyed in Dublin]

      Marriages, 1845 (one entry).   **MIC.1/125**

      Baptisms, 1835-; vestry minutes, 1882-.   **In local custody**

  R.C. Errigal Trough (Clogher diocese)
      Baptisms, 1835-52 and 1861-81; marriages, 1837-49 and
      1862-81.   **MIC.1D/19**

      Births, marriages, deaths and parish accounts, 1837-79. **DIO(RC).1/9**

**ESKYLANE REFORMED PRESBYTERIAN (LATER
PRESBYTERIAN) CHURCH, CO. ANTRIM**
  [*see under* **SHILVODAN, GRANGE OF**]

FAHAN LOWER, CO. DONEGAL

  C.I. Fahan Lower (Raphoe diocese, previously in Derry
          diocese)

      Baptisms, 1817-1980; marriages, 1817-1939; marriage
      banns, 1817-1942; burials, 1822-1983.   **MIC.1/181**

Vestry minutes, 1857-; churchwardens' accounts book, 1890-; register of vestrymen, 1870-; preachers' books, 1890-.   **In local custody**

P. Buncrana
Baptisms, 1836-1966; marriages, 1845-1937.   **MIC.1P/32**

R.C. Desertegney and Lower Fahan
[*see under* **DESERTEGNEY**]

FAHAN UPPER, CO. DONEGAL

C.I. Fahan Upper (Raphoe diocese, previously in Derry diocese)

Baptisms, 1762-1824, 1827 and 1835-1921; marriages, 1814 and 1817-1909; burials, 1832, 1843 and 1849-1934; vestry minutes, 1792-1908; accounts, 1870-95; cess applotment, 1793-1813 and 1830-91.   **MIC.1/180**

Register of vestrymen, 1870-; preachers' books, 1866-.   **In local custody**

P. Fahan
Baptisms, 1899-1986; marriages, 1845-1955.   **MIC.1P/306**

R.C. [Upper Fahan forms part of the Roman Catholic parish of Desertegney and Lower Fahan - *see under* **DESERTEGNY**]

FANNET PRESBYTERIAN CHURCH, CO. DONEGAL
[*see under* **TULLYFERN**]

FAUGHAN REFORMED PRESBYTERIAN CHURCH, CO. LONDONDERRY
[*see under* **CLONDERMOT**]

FAUGHANVALE, CO. LONDONDERRY

C.I. Faughanvale (Derry diocese)
Baptisms, 1802-85; marriages, 1802-45; burials, 1802-1906; vestry minutes, 1847-72; census, 1803.   **MIC.1/7B**

Baptisms, 1886-; marriages, 1846-; burials, 1906-; vestry minutes, 1872-; preachers' books, 1875-.   **In local custody**

P. Faughanvale
Baptisms, 1819-1983; marriages, 1845-1968; lists of contributors to Sustentation Fund, 1890, 1891 and 1893.   **MIC.1P/190; C.R.3/19**

R.C. **Faughanvale and Cumber Lower (Creggan)**
(Derry diocese)

Baptisms, 1863-81; marriages, 1860-80.   **MIC.1D/57**

FAUGHART, CO. LOUTH

C.I. **Faughart** (Armagh diocese)
[Earliest registers destroyed in Dublin]

Marriages, 1848-64.   **MIC.1/205**

R.C. **Faughart** (Armagh diocese)
[Also includes part of Ballymascanlon parish and
Jonesborough parish]

Baptisms, 1851-81, with an index, 1851-96; marriages,
1851-82, with an index, 1851-1900.   **MIC.1D/47**

**FEENY CHURCH OF IRELAND CHURCH,
CO. LONDONDERRY**
[*see under* **BANAGHER**]

FERMOY, CO. CORK

M. **Fermoy and Mallow**
Baptisms, 1839-41.   **MIC.429/1/545**

**FERMOYLE CHURCH OF IRELAND PARISH,
CO. LONDONDERRY**
[*see under* **DUNBOE**]

FINNER CHURCH OF IRELAND PARISH, CO. DONEGAL
[*see under* **INISHMACSAINT**]

**FINTONA (OR DONACAVEY) CHURCH OF IRELAND
PARISH, CO. TYRONE**
[*see under* **DONACAVEY**]

**FINTONA METHODIST CIRCUIT AND CHURCH,
CO. TYRONE**
[*see under* **DONACAVEY**]

FINTONA PRESBYTERIAN CHURCH, CO. TYRONE
[*see under* **DONACAVEY**]

FINTOWN ROMAN CATHOLIC CHURCH, CO. DONEGAL
[*see under* INISHKEEL]

FINVOY, CO. ANTRIM

C.I. Finvoy (Connor diocese)
Baptisms, 1811-80; marriages, 1812-45; burials, 1811-85;
vestry minutes, 1791-1901.   **MIC.1/48;**
                                                                    T.679/21A-B

Notes on history of Finvoy parish, compiled c.1950.   **T.1397**

Baptisms, 1881-; marriages, 1845-; burials, 1886-;
registers of vestrymen, 1870-; preachers' books, 1862-;
churchwardens' account book, 1870-.   **In local custody**

P. Dunloy
Baptisms, 1841-1925; marriages, 1842-1936; notices of
marriage, 1862-1911.   **MIC.1P/117**

P. Finvoy
Baptisms, 1843-1933; marriages, 1843-1907;
communicants' lists, 1843-92; session minutes, 1844-89.   **MIC.1P/321**

List of ministers, c.1690-1734.   **T.985/1**

R.C. Dunloy and Cloughmills (Down and Connor diocese)
[Contains part of Dunaghy parish also]

Baptisms, 1840-81; marriages and burials, 1877-81.   **MIC.1D/71**

[Part of Finvoy parish is in the Roman Catholic parish of
Rasharkin - *see under* RASHARKIN]

FIVEMILEHILL BAPTIST CHURCH, CO. ARMAGH
[*see under* BALLYMORE]

FIVEMILEHILL METHODIST CHURCH, CO. ARMAGH
[*see under* BALLYMORE]

FIVEMILETOWN CHURCH OF IRELAND PARISH,
CO. TYRONE
[*see under* CLOGHER]

FIVEMILETOWN WESLEYAN METHODIST AND
PRIMITIVE WESLEYAN METHODIST CHURCHES,
CO. TYRONE
[*see under* CLOGHER]

FLORENCECOURT METHODIST CHURCH,
CO. FERMANAGH
    [*see under* **KILLESHER**]

FORKHILL, CO. ARMAGH

    C.I. Forkhill (Armagh diocese)
        [Earliest registers destroyed in Dublin]

        Baptisms and burials, 1887-; marriages, 1845-.   **In local custody**

    R.C. Dromintee
        [This Roman Catholic parish may be partly in Forkhill
        parish - *see under* **KILLEVY**]

    R.C. Forkhill (Mullaghbawn) (Armagh diocese)
        Baptisms, 1845-79; marriages, 1844-78.   **MIC.1D/38**

        Notice books recording announcements made each
        Sunday and lists of the sick and dead and of masses,
        1924-45; account books, 1910-41; correspondence,
        1914-24.   **C.R.2/15**

FOURTOWNS PRESBYTERIAN CHURCH, CO. DOWN
    [*see under* **DONAGHMORE, CO. DOWN**]

FRANKFORD OR 2ND CASTLEBLANEY PRESBYTERIAN
CHURCH, CO. MONAGHAN
    [*see under* **MUCKNO**]

FREEDUFF PRESBYTERIAN CHURCH, CO. ARMAGH
    [*see under* **CREGGAN**]

GALLOON, CO. FERMANAGH

    C.I. Galloon (Clogher diocese)
        Baptisms, 1798-1863; marriages, 1798-1844; burials,
        1798-1881; vestry minutes, 1799-1914.   **MIC.1/51**

        Baptisms, 1864-; marriages, 1845-; burials, 1882-;
        register of vestrymen, 1870-; preachers' books, 1883-.   **In local custody**

    C.I. Sallaghy (Clogher diocese)
        Baptisms, 1857-; marriages, 1847-; burials, 1884-; vestry
        minutes, 1885-; register of vestrymen, 1874-82 and 1931;
        graveyard register, 1906-.   **In local custody**

    M. Newtownbutler
        Baptisms, 1873-1942; marriages, 1869-1935.   **MIC.1E/29**

R.C. Galloon (Drummully and Newtownbutler)
(Clogher diocese)

Baptisms, 1853-9 and 1863-81; marriages, 1847-79.　　　　**MIC.1D/15**

GALWAY, CO. GALWAY

M. Galway
Baptisms, 1836-42.　　　　**MIC.429/1/539**

GARDENMORE PRESBYTERIAN CHURCH, LARNE, CO. ANTRIM
[*see under* **LARNE**]

GARRISON CHURCH OF IRELAND PARISH, CO. FERMANAGH
[*see under* **DEVENISH**]

GARRISON ROMAN CATHOLIC PARISH, CO. FERMANAGH
[*see under* **DEVENISH**]

GARRYDUFF PRESBYTERIAN CHURCH, CO. ANTRIM
[*see under* **BALLYMONEY**]

GARTAN, CO. DONEGAL

C.I. Gartan (Raphoe diocese)
[Earliest registers destroyed in Dublin]

Baptisms, 1881-1959; marriages, 1845-1946.　　　　**MIC.1/210**

Burials, 1889-; vestry minutes, 1841-; vestrymen's lists, 1870-.　　　　**In local custody**

GARTREE CHURCH OF IRELAND CHURCH, CO. ANTRIM
[*see under* **KILLEAD**]

GARVAGH (1ST, 2ND AND 3RD) PRESBYTERIAN CHURCHES, CO. LONDONDERRY
[*see under* **ERRIGAL**]

GARVAGHY, CO. DOWN

C.I. Garvaghy (Dromore diocese)
[Earliest registers destroyed in Dublin]

Baptisms, 1877-; marriages, 1845-; burials, 1885-; vestry
minutes, 1872-; registers of vestrymen, 1872-.   **In local custody**

P. Garvaghy
Baptisms, 1809-1969; marriages, 1845-1926; list of new
communicants, 1837.   **MIC.1P/135**

P. Kilkinamurry
[Pre-1900 baptisms destroyed]

Marriages, 1845-1926; communion roll giving details
of emigration to America, 1873-1930.   **MIC.1P/305**

R.C. Dromore and Garvaghy
[*see under* **DROMORE**]

**GARVARY CHURCH OF IRELAND PARISH,
CO. FERMANAGH**
[*see under* **ENNISKILLEN**]

GILFORD CHURCH OF IRELAND PARISH, CO. DOWN
[*see under* **TULLYLISH**]

GILFORD METHODIST CHURCH, CO. DOWN
[*see under* **TULLYLISH**]

GILFORD PRESBYTERIAN CHURCH, CO. DOWN
[*see under* **TULLYLISH**]

GILLYGOOLEY PRESBYTERIAN CHURCH, CO. TYRONE
[*see under* **DRUMRAGH**]

GILNAHIRK PRESBYTERIAN CHURCH, CO. DOWN
[*see under* **KNOCKBREDA**]

GLANGEVLIN ROMAN CATHOLIC PARISH, CO. CAVAN
[*see under* **TEMPLEPORT**]

GLASCAR PRESBYTERIAN CHURCH, CO. DOWN
[*see under* **AGHADERG**]

**GLASDRUMMOND ROMAN CATHOLIC CHURCH,
CO. DOWN**
[*see under* **KILKEEL**]

GLASLECK PRESBYTERIAN CHURCH, CO. CAVAN
[*see under* **SHERCOCK**]

GLASTRY METHODIST CHURCH, CO. DOWN
[*see under* **ST ANDREW'S**]

GLASTRY PRESBYTERIAN CHURCH, CO. DOWN
[*see under* **ST ANDREW'S**]

GLENADE ROMAN CATHOLIC PARISH, CO. LEITRIM
[*see under* **ROSSINVER**]

GLENALLA CHURCH OF IRELAND PARISH, CO. DONEGAL
[*see under* **AUGHNISH**]

GLENARM OR TICKMACREVAN CHURCH OF IRELAND PARISH, CO. ANTRIM
[*see under* **TICKMACREVAN**]

GLENARM METHODIST CHURCH, CO. ANTRIM
[*see under* **TICKMACREVAN**]

GLENARM NON-SUBSCRIBING PRESBYTERIAN CHURCH, CO. ANTRIM
[*see under* **TICKMACREVAN**]

GLENARM PRESBYTERIAN CHURCH, CO. ANTRIM
[*see under* **TICKMACREVAN**]

GLENARM ROMAN CATHOLIC PARISH, CO. ANTRIM
[*see under* **TICKMACREVAN**]

GLENAVY, CO. ANTRIM

    C.I. Glenavy (Connor diocese)
      [Includes also Camlin and Tullyrusk]

        Baptisms, 1707-1908; marriages, 1707-1845, 1857-64
        and 1874-1915; burials, 1707-1918; vestry minutes,
        1707-1884; tithe applotments, 1826-7; census of united
        parishes of Glenavy, Camlin and Tullyrusk, taken in
        1856-7 but revised in 1858-9 and 1873; communicants
        and confirmations, 1814-24 and 1886-97.

        MIC.1/43-44, 44A, 74;
        C.R.1/53; T.679/1, 74

Registers of vestrymen, 1870-.   **In local custody**

M. Glenavy (Antrim and Glenavy Circuit)
Baptisms, 1879-c.1900; annual report, 1899; register of
members, 1879-91; minute book of leaders and stewards,
1879-87; circuit schedule book, 1880-94.   **MIC.1E/58**

Marriages, 1881-.   **In local custody**

R.C. Glenavy and Killead (Down and Connor diocese)
[Includes the parishes of Glenavy, Killead, Camlin and
part of Ballinderry]

Baptisms, 1849-81; marriages, 1848-83.   **MIC.1D/63**

GLENCAR CHURCH OF IRELAND PARISH, CO. LEITRIM
[*see under* **KILLASNET**]

GLENCOLUMBKILLE, CO. DONEGAL

C.I. Glencolumbkille (Raphoe diocese)
Baptisms, 1827-1984; marriages, 1845-1954; burials,
1827-1975.   **MIC.1/187**

Vestry minute book, 1870-.   **In local custody**

GLENCRAIG CHURCH OF IRELAND PARISH, CO. DOWN
[*see under* **HOLYWOOD**]

**GLENDERMOTT CHURCH OF IRELAND PARISH,
CO. LONDONDERRY**
[*see under* **CLONDERMOT**]

**GLENDERMOTT PRESBYTERIAN CHURCH,
CO. LONDONDERRY**
[*see under* **CLONDERMOT**]

**GLENDERMOTT ROMAN CATHOLIC PARISH,
WATERSIDE, LONDONDERRY**
[*see under* **CLONDERMOT**]

**GLENEELY CHURCH OF IRELAND PARISH,
CO. DONEGAL**
[*see under* **CULDAFF**]

GLENELLY PRESBYTERIAN CHURCH, CO. TYRONE
[*see under* **BODONEY UPPER**]

GLENFIN ROMAN CATHOLIC PARISH, CO. DONEGAL
[*see under* KILTEEVOGUE]

GLENHOY PRESBYTERIAN CHURCH, CO. TYRONE
[*see under* CLOGHER, CO. TYRONE]

GLENLOUGH CHURCH OF IRELAND PARISH, CO. LEITRIM
[*see under* KILLASNET]

GLENMANUS REFORMED PRESBYTERIAN CHURCH, PORTRUSH, CO. ANTRIM
[*see under* BALLYWILLIN]

GLENNAN PRESBYTERIAN CHURCH, CO. MONAGHAN
[*see under* DONAGH)

GLENRAVEL ROMAN CATHOLIC PARISH, CO. ANTRIM
[*see under* RACAVAN]

GLENSWILLY ROMAN CATHOLIC CHURCH, CO. DONEGAL
[*see under* CONWALL]

GLENTIES CHURCH OF IRELAND PARISH, CO. DONEGAL
[*see under* INISHKEEL]

GLENTIES ROMAN CATHOLIC CHURCH, CO. DONEGAL
[*see under* INISHKEEL]

GLENWHIRRY, CO. ANTRIM

P. Glenwhirry
Baptisms, 1845-1978; marriages, 1845-1927.　　　　MIC.1P/151

R.C. [Part of Glenwhirry parish is in the Roman Catholic parish of Kirkinnola - *see under* KIRKINRIOLA and part is in the Roman Catholic parish of Ballyclare - *see under* RALOO]

GLYNN, CO. ANTRIM

    C.I. Glynn (Connor diocese)
        Baptisms, 1838-1969; marriages, 1842-5; burials,
        1838-1991; account book, 1877-1900; preachers' book,
        1935-60.   **MIC.1/105: C.R.1/61**

        Marriages, 1845-; vestry minutes, 1867-; vestrymen's
        lists, 1870-.   **In local custody**

    P. Magheramorne
        Baptisms, 1880-1930; marriages, 1881-1919.   **MIC.1P/349**

    R.C. [*see under* **LARNE**]

GORTAHORK ROMAN CATHOLIC CHURCH,
CO. DONEGAL
    [*see under* **TULLAGHOBEGLY**]

GORTIN PRESBYTERIAN CHURCH, CO. TYRONE
    [*see under* **BODONY LOWER**]

GORTLEE REFORMED PRESBYTERIAN CHURCH,
CO. DONEGAL
    [*see under* **CONWALL**]

GORTNESSY PRESBYTERIAN CHURCH,
CO. LONDONDERRY
    [*see under* **CLONDERMOT**]

GOWNA CHURCH OF IRELAND PARISH, CO. CAVAN
    [*see under* **SCRABBY**]

GRACEFIELD MORAVIAN CHURCH,
CO. LONDONDERRY
    [*see under* **ARTREA**]

GRACEHILL MORAVIAN CHURCH, CO. ANTRIM
    [*see under* **AHOGHILL**]

GRANGE, CO. ARMAGH

    C.I. Grange (Armagh diocese)
        Baptisms, 1780-1892; marriages, 1780-1845; burials,
        1783-1805, 1807, 1816-52 and 1880-92;

confirmations, 1837, 1840, 1843, 1846, 1859, 1863 and
1866.

MIC.1/65; T.2540;
T.2706/122-149

Vestry minutes, 1854-; preachers' books, 1828-.

In local custody

R.C. [Grange parish forms part of the district of Armagh -
see under **ARMAGH**]

**GRANGE COOLEY ROMAN CATHOLIC CHURCH,
CO. LOUTH**
[*see under* **CARLINGFORD**]

GRANGE OF BALLYSCULLION PARISH, CO. ANTRIM
[*see under* **BALLYSCULLION, GRANGE OF**]

GRANGE OF DOAGH PARISH, CO. ANTRIM
[*see under* **DOAGH, GRANGE OF**]

GRANGE PRESBYTERIAN CHURCH, CO. ANTRIM
[*see under* **BALLYSCULLION, GRANGE OF**]

**GRANGE REFORMED PRESBYTERIAN CHURCH,
CO. TYRONE**
[*see under* **DESERTCREAT**]

**GRANGE RELIGIOUS SOCIETY OF FRIENDS,
CO. ARMAGH**
[*see under* **KILMORE, CO. ARMAGH**]

**GREAT JAMES' STREET PRESBYTERIAN CHURCH,
LONDONDERRY**
[*see under* **TEMPLEMORE**]

GREENAN CHURCH OF IRELAND PARISH, CO. TYRONE
[*see under* **BODONY LOWER**]

GREENBANK PRESBYTERIAN CHURCH, CO. DONEGAL
[*see under* **MUFF**]

**GREENCASTLE (ST FINIAN'S) CHURCH OF IRELAND
PARISH, CO. DONEGAL**
[*see under* **MOVILLE LOWER**]

**GREENCASTLE ROMAN CATHOLIC CHURCH,
CO. ANTRIM**
[*see under* **CARNMONEY**]

**GREENCASTLE ROMAN CATHOLIC CHURCH,
CO. TYRONE**
[*see under* **BODONEY LOWER**]

**GREENLOUGH ROMAN CATHOLIC CHURCH,
CO. LONDONDERRY**
[*see under* **TAMLAGHT O'CRILLY**]

**GREENWELL STREET, NEWTOWNARDS,
PRESBYTERIAN CHURCH, CO. DOWN**
[*see under* **NEWTOWNARDS**]

GREYABBEY, CO. DOWN

    C.I. Greyabbey (Down diocese)

Baptisms, 1807-93; marriages, 1807-73; burials,
1807-73; vestry minutes, 1789-1823; preachers' book,
1849-70 and 1874-7; list of abbots, rectors and curates,
1222-37, 1557 and 1633-1928.   **MIC.1/48-49**
                                                            T.2688/1

Map of graveyard with key to burials, 1857.   **T.1619**

Registers of vestrymen, 1870-.   **In local custody**

    N.S.P. Greyabbey

Baptisms, 1835-40 and 1848-1988; marriages, 1835-43
and 1845-1935; burials, 1914-88; list of families, 1835-6
and 1839.   **MIC.1B/9**

    P. Greyabbey

Baptisms, 1873-1932; marriages, 1845-1936;
communicants' roll, 1873-87; register of pews, c.1850;
pew rent book, 1863-78; subscription list for the church
building fund, 1902-04.   **MIC.1P/323**

Marriage notice books, 1879-1906.   **MIC.1P/230/6/1-2**

Baptisms, 1835-40; marriages, 1835-42; lists of families,   **In Presbyterian**
1835-54.   **Historical Society**

    R.C. [*see under* **ARDKEEN**]

GROGEY METHODIST CHURCH, CO. FERMANAGH
[*see under* **AGHALURCHER**]

**GROOMSPORT CHURCH OF IRELAND PARISH,
CO. DOWN**
   [*see under* **BANGOR**]

GROOMSPORT PRESBYTERIAN CHURCH, CO. DOWN
   [*see under* **BANGOR**]

**GWEEDORE CHURCH OF IRELAND PARISH,
CO. DONEGAL**
   [*see under* **TEMPLECRONE**]

GWEEDORE ROMAN CATHOLIC PARISH, CO. DONEGAL
   [*see under* **TULLAGHOBEGLY**]

HAGGARDSTOWN, CO. LOUTH

   R.C. Dunbin, Haggardstown (Kilcurley or Kilkerley
      [*sic* Kilcurly]) (Armagh diocese)

      [Haggardstown is part of the Roman Catholic parish of
      Kilcurley or Kilkerley which also includes the parishes
      of Dunbin, Heynestown, Ballybarrack, Philipstown
      and part of Baronstown - *see under* **DUNBIN**]

**HANNAHSTOWN ROMAN CATHOLIC CHURCH,
CO. ANTRIM**
   [*see under* **DERRYAGHY**]

HEYNESTOWN, CO. LOUTH

   C.I. Heynestown (Armagh diocese)
      Baptisms, 1869-1984; marriages, 1855-1951; burials,
      1871-1983; confirmations, 1888-1964.   **MIC.1/274**

      Vestry minutes, 1827-; preachers' books, 1845-; registers
      of vestrymen, 1870-.   **In local custody**

   R.C. Heynestown (Armagh diocese)
      [Part of Kilcurley or Kilkerley Roman Catholic parish -
      see under **HAGGARDSTOWN**]

**HIGH KIRK PRESBYTERIAN CHURCH, BALLYMENA,
CO. ANTRIM**
   [*see under* **KIRKINRIOLA**]

HILLHALL PRESBYTERIAN CHURCH, CO. DOWN
[*see under* **LAMBEG**]

HILLSBOROUGH, CO. DOWN

C.I. Hillsborough (Down diocese)
Baptisms, 1686-95, 1763-9 and 1772-1928; marriages,
1688-95, 1772-4 and 1782-1845; burials, 1688-1735,
1772-3, 1784 and 1823-1953; vestry minutes, 1709-1870;
confirmations, 1823, 1886, 1895, 1898, 1901, 1904, 1907
and 1913.   **MIC.1/62-64**

Vestry minutes, 1871-.   **In local custody**

C.I. Kilwarlin (St John's) (Down Diocese)
[Partly in Hillsborough parish and partly in Dromore and
Moira parishes]

[Earliest registers destroyed in Dublin]

Baptisms, 1877-; marriages, 1846-; burials, 1877-; vestry
minutes, 1870-; registers of vestrymen, 1870-.   **In local custody**

MOR. Kilwarlin
Baptisms, 1845-1902; marriages, 1845-53 and 1867-90;
burials, 1846-1903; confirmations, 1845-1901; diaries,
1834-5 and 1845-98; register of members, c.1830-1844;
committee minutes, 1844-66 and 1875-1900.   **MIC.1F/2**

P. Annahilt
Baptisms, 1780-1801 and 1803-1939; marriages,
1838-1931; marriage notices, 1889-1901.   **MIC.1P/360;**
                                                             MIC.1P/230/5/2

P. Hillsborough
Baptisms, 1833-90; marriages, 1845-83 and 1893-1915;
session minutes, 1832-76; lists of communicants, 1841-3
and 1877.   **MIC.1P/46**

R.C. [Hillsborough parish is part of the Roman Catholic parish
of Blaris - *see under* **BLARIS**]

HILLTOWN PRESBYTERIAN CHURCH, CO. DOWN
[*see under* **CLONDUFF**]

HOLLYMOUNT CHURCH OF IRELAND PARISH, CO. DOWN
[*see under* **DOWN**]

HOLY TRINITY, CROM, CHURCH OF IRELAND PARISH, CO. FERMANAGH
[*see under* **KINAWLEY**]

HOLYWOOD, CO. DOWN

C.I. Dundela (Down diocese)
Baptisms, 1869-89.   **MIC.1/53**

C.I. Glencraig
Baptisms, 1878-; marriages, 1871-; vestry minutes,
1873-; registers of vestrymen, 1870-; preachers' books,
1861-.   **In local custody**

C.I. Holywood (Down diocese)
Baptisms, 1806-73; marriages, 1823-44; burials, 1823-93;
banns, 1822-70; vestry minutes, 1826-70.   **MIC.1/43**

Notes relating to the parish of Holywood, c.1600-c.1850.   **T.1308**

Baptisms, 1874-; marriages, 1845-; vestry minutes, 1871-;
registers of vestrymen, 1870-; preachers' books, 1844-.   **In local custody**

M. Holywood
Baptisms, 1867-1981; marriages, 1873-1972; circuit
schedule book, 1968-80.   **MIC.1E/60**

P. 1st Holywood
Baptisms, 1840-1916; marriages, 1845-1903; marriage
notices, 1871-7; session minutes, 1838-64.   **MIC.1P/68;
                                                           MIC.1P/230/5/1**

P. 2nd Holywood (High Street)
Baptisms, 1857-1984; marriages, 1858-1934.   **MIC.1P/243**

R.C. Holywood (Down and Connor diocese)
Baptisms, 1866-80; marriages, 1867-83.   **MIC.1D/67**

HYDEPARK METHODIST CHURCH, CO. ANTRIM
[*see under* **TEMPLEPATRICK**]

HYDEPARK PRESBYTERIAN CHURCH, CO. ANTRIM
[*see under* **TEMPLEPATRICK**]

INCH, CO. DONEGAL

C.I. Inch (Derry diocese)
Baptisms, 1868-1951; marriages, 1846-1946; burials,
1868-1965.   **MIC.1/182**

Baptisms, 1815-28; marriages, 1816-57; vestry minutes,
1818-57 and 1868-.   **In local custody**

P. Inch
Marriages, 1845-1947.   **MIC.1P/313**

R.C. Inch
[Forms part of the Roman Catholic parish of Iskahan,
Burt and Inch - *see under* **BURT**]

INCH, CO. DOWN

C.I. Inch (Down diocese)
Baptisms, 1767-1878; marriages, 1764 and 1791-1846;
burials, 1788-1876.   **MIC.1/49**

Manuscript copy of baptisms and marriages, 1796-1933.   **D.1759/1D/4**

Baptisms, 1879-; marriages, 1847-; burials, 1877-; vestry
minutes, 1757-; churchwardens' accounts, 1871-;
registers of vestrymen, 1871-.   **In local custody**

R.C. [Inch parish forms part of the Roman Catholic parish of
Kilmore - *see under* **KILMORE, CO. DOWN**]

INISHARGY, CO. DOWN

C.I. Inishargy (St Andrew's) (Down diocese)
Baptisms, 1783-1800 and 1805-80 [includes Kircubbin];
marriages, 1783-1850; burials, 1783-1850; vestry minutes,
1706-84, which include baptisms, 1728-69, marriages,
1728-69 and burials, 1769-71; vestry minutes, 1783-1850.   **T.679/278; MIC.1/96**

Baptisms, 1881-; marriages, 1851-; burials, 1851-;
churchwardens' accounts, 1706-70; cess applotment,
1875; preachers' book, 1894-.   **In local custody**

C.I. Kircubbin (Down diocese)
[For baptisms, c.1847-1880 *see under* **Inishargy** above]

Baptisms, 1880-; marriages, 1867-1932 and 1938-;
burials, 1896-; vestry minutes, 1894-; churchwardens'
accounts, 1862-; register of vestrymen, 1870-1932;
preachers' book, 1872-; confirmation register, 1919-37.   **In local custody**

P. Kircubbin
Baptisms, 1778-1949; marriages, 1781-1935;
collections and accounts, 1777-87.   **MIC.1P/396;
                                                                        D.1759/1D/12**

R.C. [*see under* **ARDKEEN**]

INISHKEEL, CO. DONEGAL

C.I. Ardara (Raphoe diocese)
[Partly in Inishkeel parish and partly in Killybegs parish]

Baptisms, 1829-1954; marriages, 1845-1956; burials, 1876-1984.   **MIC.1/192**

Vestry minutes, 1872-; register of vestrymen, 1870-.   **In local custody**

C.I. Inishkeel (Raphoe diocese)
Baptisms, 1699-1700 and 1818-1948; marriages, 1699, 1818-48 and 1851; burials, 1699-1700 and 1819-1983; vestry minutes, 1828-97.   **MIC.1/189; C.R.1/51**

Marriages, 1845-.   **In local custody**

C.I. Glenties (Raphoe diocese)
Baptisms, 1898-1977; burials, 1898-1982.   **MIC.1/190**

Marriages, 1856-; register of vestrymen, 1870-.   **In local custody**

M. Ardara [Wesleyan Methodists]
Baptisms, 1833-97; marriages, 1863-1920; register of members, 1833-73; minutes and accounts of quarterly leaders' meetings, 1869-1904.   **MIC.1E/31-32, 34**

R.C. Ardara(Raphoe diocese)
[Part of Innishkeel and Killybegs Lower]

Baptisms, 1869-80; marriages, 1867-75.   **MIC.1D/86**

R.C. Inniskeel (Glenties and Fintown) (Raphoe diocese)
Baptisms and marriages, 1866-81.   **MIC.1D/86**

INISHKEEN, COS LOUTH AND MONAGHAN

C.I. Inniskeen (Clogher diocese)
[United to Killany in 1903 and then with Donaghmoine after 1921 - *see also under* **KILLANNY** and **DONAGHMOYNE**]

[Earliest registers destroyed in Dublin]

Preachers' books, 1905-45; vestry minutes, 1870-98; register of vestrymen, 1870-91; tithe applotment, 1823.   **MIC.1/141**

Baptisms, 1878-; marriages, 1846-; burials, 1877-.   **In local custody**

R.C. Iniskeen (Clogher diocese)
[The Roman Catholic parish of Inishkeen includes Inishkeen parish and part of Donaghmoyne parish]

Baptisms, 1837-81; marriages, 1839-50.   **MIC.1D/5, 18; C.R.2/2**

INISHMACSAINT, COS FERMANAGH AND DONEGAL

C.I. Finner (Clogher diocese)
Baptisms, 1815-1950; marriages, 1817-1925; burials,
1815-1980; vestry minutes, 1847-1926.   **MIC.1/295**

C.I. Inishmacsaint (Clogher diocese)
Baptisms, 1813-85; marriages, 1813-1934; burials,
1813-87; vestry minutes, 1765-1818 and 1837-70;
confirmations, 1866, 1870, 1873, 1876, 1879 and 1882.   **MIC.1/50; C.R.1/56;**
                                                          T.679/64, 66-67

Extracts from baptisms, 1660-72 and 1800-15, marriages,
1663-72 and 1801-15, and burials, 1662-72 and 1802-15.   **T.808/15274-15276**

Extracts from baptisms, marriages and burials,
1660-1814.   **T.3548**

Extracts from baptisms, marriages and burials,
1660-1866, with gaps.   **C.R.1/7**

Typescript history of the parish giving the succession of
rectors, curates and churchwardens and a list of the
townlands in the parish, compiled c.1920.   **T.2849/1**

Baptisms, 1886-; burials, 1887-; vestry minutes, 1871-;
register of vestrymen, 1870-; preachers' books, 1859-66
and 1916-.   **In local custody**

C.I. Slavin (Clogher diocese)
Marriages, 1847-1935.   **MIC.1/272**

Baptisms, 1836-; burials, 1883-.   **In local custody**

M. Bundoran
Baptisms, 1835-1932; marriages may be in with
Ballyshannon Church, 1890-1956.   **MIC.1E/35**

M. Churchill [Wesleyan Methodists]
Baptisms, 1877-1986; marriages, 1879-1934; circuit
schedule book, 1866-80.   **MIC.1E/15, 17**

M. Derrygonnelly
Baptisms, 1871-1985; marriages, 1879-1936
(Springfield Circuit).   **MIC.1E/16**

R.C. Innismacsaint (Maghene, Bundoran)
(Clogher diocese)

[Parts of Inishmacsaint are united to Boho, Devenish and
Bundoran Roman Catholic districts - *see also under*
DEVENISH]

Baptisms and marriages, 1847-80.   **MIC.1D/12**

INISHMAGRATH, CO. LEITRIM

C.I. Innishmagrath or Drumkeeran (Kilmore diocese)
Baptisms, 1877-1985; burials, 1877-1983.   **MIC.1/234**

C.I. Dowra
[Formed out of part of Inishmagrath - *see under*
KILLINAGH]

INISKEEN ROMAN CATHOLIC PARISH, CO. LOUTH
[*see under* **INISHKEEN**]

INISHMORE METHODIST CHURCH, CO. FERMANAGH
[*see under* **DERRYBRUSK**]

INISPOLLAN, GRANGE OF, CO. ANTRIM

C.I. [*see under* **LAYD**]

R.C. [*see under* **CULFEIGHTRIN**]

INVER, CO. ANTRIM

C.I. Inver and Larne (Connor diocese)
Baptisms, 1806-71; marriages, 1817-20 and 1826-45;
burials, 1826-1905; vestry minutes, 1763-1870; cess
applotment book, 1833.   **MIC.1/49; T.679/38,
58-59, 78, 80**

Marriages, 1845-; burials, 1906-.   **In local custody**

P. 1st Larne
Baptisms, 1813 and 1824-1902; marriages, 1846-1902.   **MIC.1P/335**

Stipend and other account books, 1828-89.   **D.2009/1**

R.C. [Inver parish forms part of the Roman Catholic parish of
Larne and Carrickfergus - *see under* **LARNE** and *under*
CARRICKFERGUS]

INVER, CO. DONEGAL

C.I. Inver (Raphoe diocese)
Baptisms, 1805-1920; marriages, 1805-1949; burials,
1818-1984; vestry minutes, 1782-1924; parochial account
book, 1878-1921.   **MIC.1/159**

Baptisms, 1920-; register of vestrymen, 1870-.   **In local custody**

C.I. Mountcharles (Raphoe diocese)
Baptisms, 1877-1920; marriages, 1861-1913; deaths,
1860-67; vestry minutes, 1860-1924; register of
vestrymen, 1897-1924; list of persons who emigrated,
1860-67.   **MIC.1/158**

Baptisms, 1920-; marriages, 1913-.   **In local custody**

M. Inver
Baptisms, 1860-1982; marriages, 1889-1955.   **MIC.1E/34**

R.C. Inver (Raphoe diocese)
Baptisms, 1861-81; marriages, 1861-7 and 1875-81.   **MIC.1D/86**

**IRVINESTOWN METHODIST CHURCH,
CO. FERMANAGH**
[*see under* **DERRYVULLAN**]

**IRVINESTOWN PRESBYTERIAN CHURCH,
CO. FERMANAGH**
[*see under* **DERRYVULLAN**]

ISKAHEEN ROMAN CATHOLIC PARISH, CO. DONEGAL
[*see under* **MUFF**]

ISLANDMAGEE, CO. ANTRIM

C.I. Islandmagee (Connor diocese)
[Earliest registers destroyed in Dublin]

Baptisms, 1879-1917; burials, 1878-1915; vestry
minutes, 1879-99.   **MIC.1/87**

P. 1st Islandmagee
Baptisms, 1829-1935; marriages, 1829-1905;
communicants' roll, 1874-1903; committee minutes with
printed stipend lists, 1859-75.   **MIC.1P/326**

P. 2nd Islandmagee
Baptisms, 1854-1937; marriages, 1848-1933.   **MIC.1P/337**

R.C. [*see under* **LARNE**]

JONESBOROUGH, CO. ARMAGH

C.I. Jonesborough (Armagh diocese)
Baptisms, and burials, 1833-; marriages, 1834-44 and
1940-; vestry minutes, 1799-; preachers' books, 1845-.   **In local custody**

R.C. Faughart
[Jonesborough parish forms part of the Roman Catholic parish of Faughart - *see under* **FAUGHART**]

JORDANSTOWN CHURCH OF IRELAND PARISH, CO. ANTRIM
[*see under* **CARNMONEY**]

KATESBRIDGE PRESBYTERIAN CHURCH, CO. DOWN
[*see under* **NEWRY**]

KEADY, CO. ARMAGH

C.I. Keady (Armagh diocese)
Baptisms, 1780-1818 and 1825-71; marriages, 1780-1845; burials, 1815-18 and 1826-80; confirmations, 1828 and 1833.   **MIC.1/51-52; T.679/8, 8A-B**

Baptisms, 1872-; marriages, 1845-; burials, 1871-; vestry minutes, 1814-.   **In local custody**

C.I. Armaghbreague (Armagh diocese)
[Partly in Keady parish and partly in Lisnadill parish]

[Earliest registers destroyed in Dublin]

Baptisms, 1877-; marriages, 1845-; burials, 1877-; vestry minutes, 1832.   **In local custody**

M. Keady
Baptisms, 1815-. (At Armagh)   **In local custody**

P. Armaghbreague
Baptisms, 1908-84; marriages, 1848-1936.   **MIC.1P/297**

P. 2nd Keady
Baptisms, 1826- (a few entries 1819); marriages, 1819-.   **In local custody**

P. Tassagh
Baptisms and marriages, 1843-.   **In local custody**

R.C. [Keady parish forms part of the Roman Catholic parish of Derrynoose - *see under* **DERRYNOOSE**]

1ST KEADY PRESBYTERIAN CHURCH, CO. ARMAGH
[*see under* **DERRYNOOSE**]

KELLS PRESBYTERIAN CHURCH, CO. ANTRIM
[*see under* **CONNOR**]

KELLSWATER REFORMED PRESBYTERIAN CHURCH, CO. ANTRIM
[*see under* CONNOR]

KENAGH METHODIST CHURCH, CO. LONGFORD
[*see under* KILCOMMOCK]

KERRY AND THE MINES METHODIST MISSION, CO. KERRY

M. Baptisms, 1838-45.   **MIC.429/1/541**

KILBARRON, CO. DONEGAL

C.I. Kilbarron (Raphoe diocese)
Baptisms, 1785-93 and 1812-1960; marriages,
1785-1801, 1815-48 and 1865-1926; burials, 1785-1801,
1813-28 and 1830-1948.   **MIC.1/156**

Marriages, 1845-65; vestry minutes, 1691-1781 and
1809-; registers of vestrymen, 1871-; preachers' books,
1854-.   **In local custody**

M. Ballyshannon [Wesleyan Methodists]
Baptisms, 1835-1932, with an index for 1874-1908 entries;
marriages, 1890-1956.   **MIC.1E/35**

Baptisms, 1835-46.   **MIC.429/1/473**

P. Ballyshannon
Baptisms, 1836-1962; marriages, 1837-1952; committee
minutes, 1857-1946; session minutes, 1836-1928.   **MIC.1P/5**

R.C. Kilbarron (Ballyshannon) (Raphoe diocese)
Baptisms, 1854-81; marriages, 1858-81.   **MIC.1D/88**

KILBRIDE, CO. ANTRIM

C.I. Kilbride (Connor diocese)
[Formerly united with Donegore]

[Earliest registers destroyed in Dublin]

Vestry minutes, 1818-71.   **MIC.1/82**

Baptisms and burials, 1878-.   **In local custody**

P. Kilbride
Baptisms, 1848-1923; marriages, 1849-1934.   **MIC.1P/331**

R.C. [*see under* **RALOO**]

KILBRIDE, CO. OFFALY (KING'S COUNTY)

M. Tullamore
    Baptisms, 1830-46.   **MIC.429/1/97**

KILBRONEY, CO. DOWN

C.I. Kilbroney (Dromore diocese)
    Baptisms, 1814-71; marriages, 1818-45; burials,
    1814-94; vestry minutes, 1798-1860 and 1870-1937.   **MIC.1/87-88**

    Parish registers, 1784-1867.   **DIO.1/14/1**

    Churchwardens' accounts, 1849-84 and 1904-22;
    preachers' books, 1813-85, 1890-94 and 1901-35;
    Sustentation Fund accounts, 1871-9; annual statements,
    1873-1930.   **In local custody**

P. Rostrevor
    Baptisms, 1851-1986; marriages, 1852-1910; committee
    minutes, 1848-56; session minutes, 1901-23; accounts,
    1847-82, with baptisms, 1847-9; list of communicants,
    1848; papers relating to property, 1816-35, 1847 and
    1850-53.   **MIC.1P/260**

R.C. Kilbroney (Dromore diocese)
    Baptisms, marriages and burials, 1808-81.   **MIC.1D/24-25**

KILCAR, CO. DONEGAL

C.I. Kilcar (Raphoe diocese)
    Baptisms, 1819-1957; marriages, 1819-1938; burials,
    1818-1930; vestry minutes, 1869-1916.   **MIC.1/191**

    Marriage notice book, 1872-81.   **In local custody**

R.C. Kilcar (Raphoe diocese)
    Baptisms, 1848-81.   **MIC.1D/86**

KILCLIEF, CO. DOWN

C.I. Kilclief (Down diocese)
    [Earliest registers destroyed in Dublin]

    Baptisms, 1860-70 and 1877-; marriages, 1845-; burials,
    1871-; vestry minutes, 1819-60 and 1870-1911;
    preachers' books, 1871-2 and 1881; registers of
    vestrymen, 1870-.   **In local custody**

R.C. Kilclief and Strangford (Down and Connor diocese)
[Part of Kilclief parish is in the Roman Catholic parish
of Bright - *see under* **BRIGHT**]

Baptisms, 1866-81; marriages, 1865-81.   MIC.1D/72

KILCLOONEY, CO. ARMAGH

C.I. Kilcluney (Armagh diocese)
[Part of Mullaghbrack parish before 1794 - *see also
under* **MULLAGHBRACK**]

Baptisms, 1832-; marriages, 1835-; burials, 1837-.   **In local custody**

P. Cladymore
Baptisms, 1848-; marriages, 1845-.   **In local custody**

P. Redrock
Baptisms, 1808-1986; marriages, 1812-1936; stipend and
other accounts, 1807-58; lists of new communicants,
1808-97; transfer certificates, 1808-47.   **MIC.1P/285**

R.C. Ballymacnabb (Kilcluney) (Armagh diocese)
[Includes the parishes of Kilclooney, part of
Mullaghbrack, and Lisnadill]

Baptisms, 1844-81; marriages, 1844-80.   **MIC.1D/37-38**

KILCLUNEY CHURCH OF IRELAND PARISH, CO. ARMAGH
[*see under* **KILCLOONEY**]

KILCOMMOCK, CO. LONGFORD

M. Kenagh [Wesleyan Methodists]
Baptisms, 1840-1987; marriages, 1868-1955.   **MIC.1E/48**

KILCOO, CO. DOWN

C.I. Kilcoo or Bryansford (Dromore diocese)
Baptisms, 1786-1883; marriages, 1828-45; burials, 1829,
1836-7, 1839-40 and 1854-1932; publication of banns,
1838 and 1841.   **MIC.1/55; DIO.1/14/
10; T.679/57**

Baptisms, 1884-; marriages, 1845-; vestry minutes,
1828-1935; preachers' books, 1828-53 and 1903-;
register of vestrymen, 1870-1937.   **In local custody**

C.I. Newcastle (Dromore diocese)
    Baptisms, 1843-1957.   **MIC.1/70**

    Marriages, 1864-; burials, 1899-; register of vestrymen,
    1870-; preachers' books, 1855-.   **In local custody**

M. Newcastle
    Baptisms, 1881-; marriages, 1892-.   **In local custody**

P. Newcastle
    Baptisms, 1881-1921; marriages, 1846-1912.   **MIC.1P/383**

R.C. Bryansford and Newcastle (Down and Connor diocese)
    [Part of Kilcoo parish is in the Roman Catholic parish
    of Bryansford or Maghera - *see under* **MAGHERA**]

R.C. Kilcoo (Down and Connor diocese)
    Baptisms, 1832-80.   **MIC.1D/72**

KILCOO METHODIST CHURCH, CO. FERMANAGH
    [*see under* **DEVENISH**]

KILCRONAGHAN, CO. LONDONDERRY

B. Carndaisy and Tobermore
    Marriages, 1863-; roll of church members, 1848-94 and
    1896-; correspondence and business records, 1848-94.   **In local custody**

C.I. Kilcronaghan (Derry diocese)
    Baptisms, 1790-1936; marriages, 1748-1845; burials,
    1828-9 and 1831-92.   **MIC.1/52**

    Marriages, 1845-; vestry minutes, 1749-; parish church
    arrears fund, 1898-1941; registers of vestrymen, 1870-.   **In local custody**

P. Tobermore
    Baptisms, 1860-1905; marriages, 1845-1918; committee
    minutes, 1860-1912; session minutes, 1867-1904;
    communion rolls, 1882-1904.   **MIC.1P/344; C.R.3/48**

R.C. [Kilcronaghan parish forms part of the
    Roman Catholic parish of Desertmartin and
    Kilcronaghan - *see under* **DESERTMARTIN**]

KILCURLEY ROMAN CATHOLIC PARISH, CO. LOUTH
    [*see under* **HAGGARDSTOWN**]

KILDALLON, CO. CAVAN

C.I. Kildallon (Kilmore diocese)
Baptisms, 1856-1986; marriages, 1845-1923; burials,
1877-1985.   **MIC.1/257**

P. Killeshandra (formerly known as Croghan)
Baptisms, 1743-81, 1799, 1800-34 and 1841-96;
marriages, 1741-76; register of members, c.1835, with
dates of birth of children in each family, the earliest being
in 1790; session minutes, 1842-65; accounts, 1743-80.   **MIC.1P/164**

R.C. Kildallon and Tomregan (Ballyconnell)
(Kilmore diocese)

Baptisms and marriages, 1867-81.   **MIC.1D/78**

KILDARTON, CO. ARMAGH

C.I. Kildarton (Armagh diocese)
[Originally a perpetual curacy formed out of Armagh,
Lisnadill, Loughgall and Mullabrack parishes.]

[Earliest registers destroyed in Dublin]

Baptisms, 1877-; marriages, 1845-; burials, 1877-;
vestry minutes, 1841-84 and 1886-.   **In local custody**

P. Drumminis
[Originally in Mullaghbrack parish]

Marriages, 1846-1936.   **MIC.1P/286**

KILDOLLAGH, COS ANTRIM AND LONDONDERRY

C.I. Kildollagh (Connor diocese)
[Earliest registers destroyed in Dublin]

Baptisms, 1879-; marriages, 1856-; burials, 1890-; vestry
minutes, 1870-; preachers' books, 1857-.   **In local custody**

KILDRESS, CO. TYRONE

C.I. Kildress (Armagh diocese)
Baptisms, 1794-1920; marriages, 1794-1923; burials,
1828-94; vestry minutes, 1709-1876.   **MIC.1/107**

Tithes due, 1737.   **D.2395/9**

Register of vestrymen, 1870-; preachers' books, 1845-.   **In local custody**

M. Tullyroan
Baptisms, 1874-; marriages, 1899- (at Moy Church : earlier records at Armagh). **In local custody**

P. Orritor
Baptisms, 1831-; marriages, 1827-. **In local custody**

R.C. Kildress (Armagh diocese)
Baptisms and marriages, 1835-81, with gaps; deaths, 1835-42. **MIC.1D/37**

KILDRUMFERTON CHURCH OF IRELAND PARISH, CO. CAVAN
[*see under* CROSSERLOUGH]

KILDRUMSHERDAN OR KILLERSHERDONY, CO. CAVAN

C.I. Ashfield (Kilmore diocese)
Baptisms, 1821-7 and 1839-1907; marriages, 1845-1956; burials, 1818-27 and 1856-1935. **MIC.1/282**

C.I. Killesherdoney (Kilmore diocese)
Baptisms, 1796-1805 and 1810-1982; marriages, 1796-1803 and 1812-45; burials, 1797-1802, 1811-24 and 1827-1929. **MIC.1/281**

M. Cortubber [*sic* Cortober]
Baptisms, 1877-1910; marriages, 1882-1950. **MIC.1E/54**

R.C. Kilsherdany (Kilmore diocese)
Baptisms, 1803-14, 1826-49 and 1855-60; marriages, 1803-14,1835, 1843-9 and 1855-7. **MIC.1D/75**

KILFENNAN PRESBYTERIAN CHURCH, LONDONDERRY
[*see under* TEMPLEMORE]

KILGLASS, CO. LONGFORD

M. Deer Park [Wesleyan Methodists]
Baptisms, 1840-1987; marriages, 1868-1955. **MIC.1E/48**

KILKEEL, CO. DOWN

C.I. Kilkeel (Dromore diocese)
Baptisms, 1816-1937, with indexes, 1816-42; marriages, 1816-1972, with indexes, 1816-26; burials, 1816-1937; vestry minutes, 1811-1956; preachers' book, 1887-1960; account book, 1826-38. **MIC.1/53-54; C.R.1/15**

C.I. Annalong (Kilhorne) (Dromore diocese)
Baptisms, 1842-1913; marriages, 1873-1960; burials,
1845-1959; preachers' books, 1842-1967; minutes of
general vestry, 1926-1963; minutes of select vestry,
1884-1967; accounts, 1866-1957.   **T.679/63, 108;**
                                                          C.R.1/12

C.I. Carginagh (Pratt Memorial Church) (Dromore diocese)
Minute books, 1926-30; preachers' books, 1906-66.   **C.R.1/15**

C.I. Mullartown Church Hall (Dromore diocese)
Preachers' book, 1946-56; details of services and
collections, 1950-54.   **C.R.1/12**

MOR. Kilkeel
Diaries recording births, marriages and burials,
1844-1915.   **D.1052**

P. Kilkeel
Baptisms, 1842-71 and 1875-1964; marriages, 1842-1957;
session minutes, 1843-54; accounts, 1842-50; list of
seatholders, c.1850; account book, 1842-71.   **MIC.1P/205; T.1604**

P. Mourne
Baptisms, 1839-1946; marriages, 1845-1903; communion
roll, 1882-1929; stipend books, 1838-57; committee
minutes, 1882-1929; session minutes, 1888-1944.   **MIC.1P/365**

P. Annalong
Baptisms, 1840-1951; marriages, 1840-1918; marriage
notices, 1857-63.   **MIC.1P/421**

R.C. Kilkeel (Down and Connor diocese)
Baptisms, 1839-81; marriages, 1839-76.   **MIC.1D/73**

Baptisms and marriages, 1839-76.   **T.1529**

R.C. Lower Mourne (Glasdrummond)
(Down and Connor diocese)

Baptisms, 1842-81; marriages, 1839-80.   **MIC.1D/74**

KILKENNY, CO. KILKENNY

M. Kilkenny
Baptisms, 1837-45.   **MIC.429/1/542**

KILKINAMURRY PRESBYTERIAN CHURCH, CO. DOWN
[*see under* **GARVAGHY**]

**KILLADEAS CHURCH OF IRELAND PARISH,
CO. FERMANAGH**
   [*see under* **TRORY**]

KILLAGAN, CO. ANTRIM

   C.I. Killagan (Connor diocese)
   [Earliest registers destroyed in Dublin]

   Baptisms, 1880-1937; marriages, 1845-1935; burials
   (Killagan and Dunaghy), 1894-1939; register of
   vestrymen, 1896-1937.   **MIC.1/298-299**

   R.C. Dunloy and Cloughmills
   [*see under* **FINVOY**]

KILLAGHTEE, CO. DONEGAL

   C.I. Killaghtee (Raphoe diocese)
      Baptisms, 1873-1983; marriages, 1857-1947; burials,
      1874-1983; vestry minutes, 1875-1904; confirmation
      roll, 1890-1949; account book, 1888-1909.   **MIC.1/157**

      Baptisms, 1810-31; marriages, 1814-31; burials, 1819-22;
      marriage banns, 1809-14.   **DIO.3/Box 27**

      Vestry minutes, 1748-1874.   **DIO.3/Box 40**

   M. Ballyederland (*sic* Ballyederlan)
      Baptisms, 1833-1951; circuit schedule book, 1894-1909;
      register of members, 1833-73.   **MIC.1E/31, 34**

   M. Dunkineely
      Baptisms, 1833-1951; marriages, 1863-1904; circuit
      schedule book, 1894-1909; register of members, 1833-63. **MIC.1E/31, 34**

   M. St John's Point
      Baptisms, 1833-c.1860; marriages, 1855-6; register of
      members, 1833-73.   **MIC.1E/34**

   R.C. Killaghtee (Raphoe diocese)
      Baptisms, 1845-7, 1850-53 and 1857-81; marriages,
      1857-81.   **MIC.1D/88**

**KILLAIG PRESBYTERIAN CHURCH,
CO. LONDONDERRY**
   [*see under* **AGHADOWEY**]

KILLALOE, CO. CLARE

M. Killaloe
Baptisms, 1844-58.   **MIC.429/1/540**

KILLANEY, CO. DOWN

C.I. Killaney (Down diocese)
Baptisms, 1857-1961; burials, 1865-1961.   **MIC.1/62**

Baptisms, 1836-57; marriages, 1860-; vestry minutes,
1870-; preachers' books, 1836-56 and 1936-.   **In local custody**

P. 1st Boardmills
Baptisms, 1782-1933; marriages, 1782-1814 and
1823-1929; session minutes, 1784-1816 and 1849-89;
accounts, 1785-93; private censures, 1784-1816 and
1824-42; transfer certificates, 1824-42.   **MIC.1P/72;**
                                                              D.1759/1D/2

P. Killaney
Baptisms, 1846-1925; marriages, 1865-1923; list of
families, 1846; lists of new communicants, 1846-1930; list
of communicants, 1886; session minutes, 1931-66.   **MIC.1P/102;**
                                                              D.1759/1D/2

KILLANN ROMAN CATHOLIC PARISH, CO. CAVAN
[*see under* BAILIEBOROUGH]

KILLANNY, COS LOUTH AND MONAGHAN

C.I Killany (Clogher diocese)
Baptisms, 1825-1954; marriages, 1830-33 and
1853-1955; burials, 1825-1974; vestry minutes,
1860-1932 (Killany and Inniskeen); preachers' books,
1852-71 and 1891-1964.   **MIC.1/142**

R.C. Killanny (Clogher diocese)
Baptisms, 1857-81; marriages, 1862-82.   **MIC.1D/17**

KILLANUMMERY, CO. LEITRIM

C.I. Killenumery (Kilmore diocese)
Baptisms, 1884-1961; marriages, 1845-1905; burials,
1856-1943.   **MIC.1/264**

KILLARGA, CO. LEITRIM

C.I. Killargue (Kilmore diocese)
Baptisms, 1879-1957; marriages, 1894-1953; burials,
1879-1981.   **MIC.1/233**

C.I. Dowra
　　[Formed out of part of Killarga - *see under*
　　KILLINAGH]

R.C. Killargue (Kilmore diocese)
　　Baptisms and marriages, 1852-81.　　　　　　　　　　　　　　**MIC.1D/77**

KILLASHANDRA, CO. CAVAN

C.I. Arvagh (Kilmore diocese)
　　Baptisms, 1877-1905; marriages, 1845-1956; burials,
　　1877-1921.　　　　　　　　　　　　　　　　　　　　　　　**MIC.1/291**

C.I. Derrylane (Kilmore diocese)
　　Baptisms, 1845-1917; marriages, 1846-1925; burials,
　　1875-1958.　　　　　　　　　　　　　　　　　　　　　　　**MIC.1/221**

C.I. Killeshandra (Kilmore diocese)
　　Baptisms, 1735-1982; marriages, 1735-1955; burials,
　　1735-1985.　　　　　　　　　　　　　　　　　　　　　　　**MIC.1/220**

M. Corlespratten [*sic* Corlisbrattan]
　　Baptisms, c.1853-1986; marriages, 1864-1950; circuit
　　schedule book, 1894-1910; quarterly meeting minute
　　book, 1894-1910.　　　　　　　　　　　　　　　　　　　**MIC.1E/51-52**

M. Killeshandra
　　Baptisms, 1840-1986; quarterly meeting minute book,
　　1910-27; circuit schedule book, 1894-1910.　　　　　　　**MIC.1E/51-52**

　　Baptisms, 1840-44.　　　　　　　　　　　　　　　　　　**MIC.429/1/175**

P. Drumkeeran
　　Baptisms, 1835-99; marriages, 1835-7 and 1845-1947;
　　session minutes, 1848 and 1855-6; history of the
　　congregation, 1834-55.　　　　　　　　　　　　　　　　　**MIC.1P/166**

P. Kilmount
　　Baptisms, 1862-4 and 1866-1972; marriages, 1862-1907;
　　communicants' roll, 1866-79 (giving some details of
　　marriages, deaths and emigration etc.,); session minutes,
　　1867; list of ministers, 1862-1954.　　　　　　　　　　　**MIC.1P/213**

R.C. Killeshandra (Kilmore diocese)
　　Baptisms, 1835-80; marriages, 1835-40 and 1849-81.　　**MIC.1D/78-79**

KILLASHEE, CO. LONGFORD

C.I. Killashee (Ardagh diocese)
　　Speculum Gregis, 1846-48, a survey of families in the
　　parish with details of births from c.1780.　　　　**MIC.1/122; C.R.1/14**

KILLASNET, CO. LEITRIM

C.I. Glenlough or Glencar (Kilmore diocese)
Marriages, 1846-1950; burials, 1878-1982.   MIC.1/269

C.I. Killasnett (Kilmore diocese)
Baptisms, 1877-1984; marriages, 1846-1950; burials,
1862-1986.   MIC.1/269

C.I. Lurganboy Chapel of Ease (Kilmore diocese)
Marriages, 1863-1956; burials, 1862-1986.   MIC.1/269

R.C. Killasnet (Kilmore diocese)
Baptisms, 1852-69 and 1878-81; marriages, 1852-71 and
1878-81.   MIC.1D/83

KILLEA, CO. DONEGAL

C.I. Killea (Raphoe diocese)
Baptisms, 1877-1922; marriages, 1845-1931.   MIC.1/175

Burials, 1880-; vestry minutes, 1788-; registers of
vestrymen, 1895; preachers' books, 1894-.   In local custody

R.C. [Killea parish forms part of the Roman Catholic parish
of All Saints, Raymochy and Taughboyne - *see under*
ALL SAINTS]

KILLEAD, CO. ANTRIM

C.I. Gartree (Connor diocese)
[Earliest registers destroyed in Dublin]

Baptisms, 1901-; marriages, 1935-; burials, 1899-.   In local custody

C.I. Killead (Connor diocese)
[Earliest registers destroyed in Dublin]

Baptisms, 1838-1966; burials, 1873-1942; vestry
minutes, 1829-1900; cash book, 1874-1925.   MIC.1/293

Marriages, 1845-.   In local custody

P. Killead
Baptisms, 1826-49; marriages, 1826-1901; session
minutes, 1891-1951; communicants' lists, 1826-49.   MIC.1P/419; C.R.3/3

P. Loanends
Baptisms, 1834-43 and 1874-1922; marriages, 1845-1902;
deaths, 1845-7; communicants' roll, 1864; session
minutes, 1832-1921; list of subscribers, 1862-4.   MIC.1P/418; C.R.3/6

R.C. [Killead parish forms part of the Roman Catholic parish of Glenavy - *see under* **GLENAVY**]

KILLEAVEY CHURCH OF IRELAND PARISH, CO. ARMAGH
   [*see under* **KILLEVY**]

KILLEAVEY ROMAN CATHOLIC PARISH, CO. ARMAGH
   [*see under* **KILLEVY**]

KILLEESHIL, CO. TYRONE

C.I. **Killeshill** (Armagh diocese)
[Earliest registers destroyed in Dublin]

Vestry minutes, 1913-58; plans of alterations to church, c.1860-1861.   **C.R.1/60**

Baptisms, 1881-9 and 1923-; marriages, 1845-; burials, 1881-; vestry minutes, 1819-.   **In local custody**

P. Clonaneese Lower
Baptisms, 1811-1963; marriages, 1845-71; deaths, 1865-75; session minutes, 1865-1963; communion roll, 1865-1942.   **MIC.1P/45; C.R.3/38**

P. Clonaneese Upper
Baptisms, 1868-1902; marriages, 1860-69.   **MIC.1P/44; C.R.3/37**

R.C. Killeeshil
Baptisms, 1816-80; marriages, 1816-83; deaths, 1816-75 and 1880-81.   **MIC.1D/33**

KILLEEVAN, CO. MONAGHAN

C.I. Killeevan (Clogher diocese)
Baptisms, 1811-1982; marriages, 1811-1930; burials, 1812-1983; vestry minutes, 1888-1920; district register, 1876-80; general register, 1880-1904; register of vestrymen, 1890-1904.   **MIC.1/154**

C.I. Newbliss (Clogher diocese)
Baptisms, 1841-; marriages, 1880-; burials, 1837-; preachers' books, 1852-.   **In local custody**

P. Newbliss
Baptisms, 1856-1984; marriages, 1845-1923.   **MIC.1P/275**

R.C. Killeevan (Newbliss) (Clogher diocese)
[Includes also Aghabog parish]

Baptisms, 1871-81; marriages, 1871-81.   **MIC.1D/20**

**KILLEGAR CHURCH OF IRELAND PARISH,
CO. LEITRIM**
[*see under* **CARRIGALLEN**]

KILLELAGH, CO. LONDONDERRY

C.I. Killelagh (Derry diocese)
[Earliest registers destroyed in Dublin]

Baptisms, 1892-; marriages, 1845-; burials, 1894-;
register of vestrymen, 1870-; preachers' books, 1908-.   **In local custody**

[Some entries, 1785-1860, in registers for Maghera
parish - *see under* **MAGHERA**]

R.C. [Killelagh parish forms part of the Roman Catholic parish
of Maghera - *see under* **MAGHERA**]

**KILLENKERE, CHURCH OF IRELAND PARISH,
CO. CAVAN**
[*see under* **KILLINKERE**]

**KILLENUMERY CHURCH OF IRELAND PARISH,
CO. LEITRIM**
[*see under* **KILLANUMMERY**]

**KILLESHANDRA CHURCH OF IRELAND PARISH,
CO. CAVAN**
[*see under* **KILLASHANDRA**]

KILLESHANDRA METHODIST CHURCH, CO. CAVAN
[*see under* **KILLASHANDRA**]

KILLESHANDRA PRESBYTERIAN CHURCH, CO. CAVAN
[*see under* **KILDALLON**]

**KILLESHANDRA ROMAN CATHOLIC PARISH,
CO. CAVAN**
[*see under* **KILLASHANDRA**]

KILLESHER, CO. FERMANAGH

C.I. Druminiskill Chapel of Ease (Kilmore diocese)
Baptisms, 1862-1910.   **C.R.1/27**

C.I. Killesher (Kilmore diocese)
Baptisms, 1798-1910; marriages, 1798-1909; burials,
1800-23 and 1827-95; vestry minutes, 1832-1920.   **MIC.1/56, 122;**
                                                                         T.679/48; C.R.1/27

M. Florencecourt [Wesleyan Methodists]
Baptisms, 1877-1966; marriages, 1868-1937.   **MIC.1E/12, 14**

R.C. Killesher (Kilmore diocese)
Baptisms, marriages and burials, 1855-81.   **MIC.1D/78**

KILLERSHERDONEY CHURCH OF IRELAND PARISH, CO. CAVAN
[*see under* **KILDRUMSHERDAN**]

KILLESHILL CHURCH OF IRELAND PARISH, CO. TYRONE
[*see under* **KILLEESHIL**]

KILLETER PRESBYTERIAN CHURCH, CO. TYRONE
[*see under* **TERMONAMONGAN**]

KILLEVY, CO. ARMAGH

C.I. Camlough (Armagh diocese)
Baptisms, 1832-72; marriages, 1835-45; burials, 1833-71;
vestry minutes, 1819-82; confirmation lists, 1840-1945,
with gaps.   **T.679/311-314**

Baptisms, 1873-; marriages, 1874-; burials, 1872-.   **In local custody**

C.I. Drumbanagher (Armagh diocese)
Baptisms, 1838-85; marriages, 1839-44; burials,
1841-1910; vestry minutes, 1858-9; confirmations,
1849 and 1866.   **MIC.1/11; T.679/11**

Baptisms, 1885-; marriages, 1845-; burials, 1910-; vestry
minutes, 1861-; confirmations, 1912-.   **In local custody**

C.I. Killeavey (formerly Meigh) (Armagh diocese)
[Earliest registers destroyed in Dublin]

Incomplete burial register, 1879-1962.   **T.2432**

Baptisms, 1878-; marriages, 1845-; burials, 1879-; vestry
minutes, 1879-; preachers' books, 1883-.   **In local custody**

C.I. Mullaglass [was a district curacy of Killeavy up to 1870]
Baptisms and burials, 1877-; marriages, 1845-.   **In local custody**

M. Bessbrook
Baptisms, 1830-; marriages, 1904-.   **In local custody**

P. Bessbrook
Baptisms, 1854-; marriages, 1857-.   **In local custody**

R.C. Dromintee
Baptisms, 1853-79; marriages, 1853-77.   **MIC.1D/41**

R.C. Lower Killeavy (Bessbrook)
Baptisms, 1835-81; marriages, 1835-62, 1868-9 and
1874-8; deaths, 1858-62.   **MIC.1D/39**

R.C. Upper Killeavey (Cloghogue)
Baptisms, 1832-80; marriages, 1832-82.   **MIC.1D/39**

KILLINAGH, CO. CAVAN

C.I. Dowra (Kilmore diocese)
Baptisms, 1877-1985; burials, 1877 and 1901-83.   **MIC.1/234-235**

C.I Killinagh (Kilmore diocese)
Baptisms, 1877-1941; burials, 1877-1986.   **MIC.1/231**

M. Blacklion
Baptisms, 1877-1966; marriages, 1868-1954.   **MIC.1E/12**

R.C. Killinagh (Kilmore diocese)
Baptisms, 1869-81; marriages, 1869-81 (there are some
marriages amongst the baptisms); burials, 1875-81.   **MIC.1D/83**

KILLINCHY, CO. DOWN

C.I. Killinchy (Down diocese)
Baptisms, 1819-77; marriages, 1825-45; burials,
1824-76; vestry minutes, 1716-57, 1779 and 1800-1944;
accounts, 1778-90, 1794 and 1809-33; preachers' books,
1824-73 and 1878-1947; printed list of rectors,
1637-1885.   **T.679/61-62, 109,**
                                                                            109A; C.R.1/16

Baptisms, 1878-; marriages, 1845-; burials, 1877-; vestry
minutes, 1801-77; preachers' books, 1824-44 and
1878-1928; churchwardens' accounts, 1872-88; register
of vestrymen, 1870-.   **In local custody**

N.S.P. Killinchy
>[Includes records relating to Killinchy Presbyterian Church prior to the setting up of the Non-Subscribing Presbyterian Church in 1835]
>
>Baptisms, 1812-54; marriages, 1813-45 (with gaps); indexes to baptisms and marriages, 1812-54; marriage notice book, 1845-54; pew rent book, c.1785; accounts, 1781-1835 ; lists of names of heads of families and their children, 1841; printed list of stipend payers, 1881-2; typescript history of the church, 1835-1935; stipend and other accounts, 1875-6.　　　**C.R.4/17; D.1759/1D**

P. Ballygowan
>Baptisms, 1870-97; marriages, 1845-1900.　　　**MIC.1P/406**

P. Killinchy
>[*see also under* **N.S.P. Killinchy**]
>
>Baptisms, 1835-1974; marriages, 1835-1907.　　　**MIC.1P/404; D.1759/1D**
>
>Manuscript history of the church, mainly from the 17th century to 1874.　　　**C.R.3/5**

P. Raffrey
>Baptisms, 1843-1968; marriages, 1845-1915; committee minutes, 1892-1919; session minutes, 1919-42.　　　**MIC.1P/130; D.1759/1D/7**

R.C. Carrickmannon and Saintfield (Down and Connor diocese)
>[Killinchy parish forms part of the Roman Catholic parish of Carrickmannon and Saintfield - *see under* **SAINTFIELD**]

KILLINCOOLE, CO. LOUTH

C.I. Killincoole (Armagh diocese)
>Baptisms, 1877-1954; marriages, 1849-1944; burials, 1886-1965.　　　**MIC.1/276**
>
>Vestry minutes, 1803-.　　　**In local custody**

R.C. [Killincoole parish forms part of the Roman Catholic parish of Darver - *see under* **DARVER**]

KILLINKERE, CO. CAVAN

C.I. Billis (Kilmore diocese)
>Baptisms, 1844-96; marriages, 1851-1900; burials, 1851-1987.　　　**MIC.1/262**

C.I. Killenkere (Kilmore diocese)
Baptisms, 1840-44 and 1878-99; marriages, 1840-42,
1845-74 and 1877-98; burials, 1877-1900; Sustentation
Fund account books, 1883-1900; parochial accounts,
1872-1901; vestry minutes, 1826-70.   **MIC.1/254, 261-262**

P. Seafin
Marriages, 1846-1956.   **MIC.1P/144**

R.C. Killinkere (Kilmore diocese)
Baptisms, 1766-90, 1842-62 and 1864-80; marriages,
1766-89, 1842-61 and 1864-80.   **MIC.1D/82**

KILLOGHTER CHURCH OF IRELAND PARISH, CO. CAVAN
[*see under* **ANNAGH**]

KILLOUGH CHURCH OF IRELAND PARISH, CO. DOWN
[*see under* **RATHMULLAN**]

KILLOUGH ROMAN CATHOLIC CHURCH, CO. DOWN
[*see under* **BRIGHT**]

KILLOWEN, CO. LONDONDERRY

C.I. Killowen (Derry diocese)
Baptisms, 1824-69; marriages, 1824-45; burials,
1825-30, 1843-81 and 1893-1901; confirmations, 1844,
1849 and 1855.   **MIC.1/61**

Baptisms, 1870-; marriages, 1845-; vestry minutes,
1747-; churchwardens' accounts, 1869-; register of
vestrymen, 1870-; preachers' book, 1873-.   **In local custody**

R.C. [Killowen parish forms part of the Roman Catholic parish
of Coleraine - *see under* **COLERAINE**]

KILLYBEGS LOWER, CO. DONEGAL

C.I. Ardara
[Partly in Lower Killybegs parish and partly in Inishkeel
parish - *see under* **INISHKEEL**]

M. Ardara
Baptisms, 1833-97; marriages, 1863-1920; minutes and
accounts of quarterly leaders' meetings, 1869-1904;
register of members, 1833-73.   **MIC.1/31-32, 34**

R.C. Ardara (Raphoe diocese)
Baptisms, 1869-80; marriages, 1878-80.   **MIC.1D/86**

KILLYBEGS UPPER, CO. DONEGAL

C.I. Killybegs (Raphoe diocese)
Baptisms, 1809-1983; marriages, 1810-40 and
1863-1944; burials, 1820-1983; preachers' book, 1844-55,
which also contains poor accounts, 1848, 1853-5 and
1867-70.   **MIC.1/186**

Baptisms, 1787-96; marriages, 1841-62; vestry minutes,
1788-; registers of vestrymen, 1870-; preachers' books,
1844-.   **In local custody**

R.C. Killybegs (Raphoe diocese)
Baptisms, 1850-81.   **MIC.1D/88**

KILTYCLOGHER CHURCH OF IRELAND PARISH, CO. FERMANAGH
[*see under* **CLOONCLARE**]

KILLYGARVAN, CO. DONEGAL

C.I. Killygarvan (Raphoe diocese)
Baptisms, 1706-99 and 1881-1982; marriages, 1706-37
and 1845-1902; burials, 1706-99 and 1881-1969; vestry
minutes, 1706-1911; register of vestrymen, 1870-1923.   **MIC.1/166**

M. Rathmullen
Baptisms, 1829-67; circuit schedule book, 1865-79; circuit
stewards' book, 1872-81.   **MIC.1E/46**

P. Rathmullan
Baptisms, 1854-1954; marriages, 1845-1908.   **MIC.1P/231**

R.C. Killygarvan and Tullyfern (Rathmullen) (Raphoe
diocese)

Baptisms, 1868-80; marriages, 1873-9.   **MIC.1D/85**

KILLYGLEN, GRANGE OF, CO. ANTRIM

C.I. [*see under* **CONNOR**]

M. Killyglen [Wesleyan Methodists]
Baptisms, 1878-1915; marriages, 1863-1906; circuit
schedule books, 1879-93 and 1908-23.   **MIC.1E/39**

R.C. [Grange of Killyglen is part of the Roman Catholic
parish of Larne - *see under* **LARNE**]

KILLYLEA CHURCH OF IRELAND PARISH,
CO. ARMAGH
[Formed out of the parishes of Derrynoose, Tynan and
Armagh - *see under* **TYNAN**]

KILLYLEA METHODIST CHURCH, CO. ARMAGH
[*see under* **TYNAN**]

KILLYLEAGH, CO. DOWN

C.I. Killyleagh (Down diocese)
Baptisms, 1813-72; marriages, 1813-45; burials, 1823-96.   **MIC.1/58**

Documents relating to the parish of Killyleagh,
1600-1850.   **MIC.35**

Baptisms, 1873-; marriages, 1845-; burials, 1897-; vestry
minutes, 1827-; cess applotment, 1827-; churchwardens'
accounts etc., 1875-.   **In local custody**

P. 1st Killyleagh
Baptisms, 1693-1757 and 1835-1881; marriages,
1692-1757, 1833-51 and 1854-72; minute books, 1725-32,
and 1809-70; accounts, 1820-60; communion rolls,
1835-70.   **MIC.1P/53;**
                                                                            D.1759/1D/7-11

P. 2nd Killyleagh
Baptisms, 1840-1968; marriages, 1846-1906; committee
minutes, 1847-84; names and addresses of pew holders,
c.1843-1871.   **MIC.1P/261**

KILLYMADDY METHODIST CHURCH, CO. ARMAGH
[*see under* **EGLISH**]

KILLYMAN, COS ARMAGH AND TYRONE

C.I. Annaghmore
[*see under* **LOUGHGALL**]

C.I. Brackaville
[*see under* **DONAGHENRY**]

C.I. Killyman (Armagh diocese)
Baptisms, 1745-1871; marriages, 1741-1845; burials,
1745-1875; vestry minutes, 1756-1894; confirmations,
1837.   **T.679/383-393**

Baptisms, 1872-; marriages, 1845-; burials, 1876-;
registers of vestrymen, 1870-.   **In local custody**

M. Kinnego
Baptisms, 1874-. (At Moy Church but earlier entries at
Armagh Church)   **In local custody**

M. Laghey
Baptisms, 1830-. (At Dungannon)   **In local custody**

R.C. Killyman
[Forms part of the Roman Catholic parish of
Dungannon - *see under* **DRUMGLASS**]

KILLYMARD, CO. DONEGAL

C.I. Killymard (Raphoe diocese)
Baptisms, 1880-1912; marriages, 1845-1956; burials,
1880-1923.   **MIC.1/145**

C.I. Lough Eske (Raphoe diocese)
Baptisms, 1876-1982.   **MIC.1/297**

P. 2nd Donegal
[After 1885 1st and 2nd Donegal united - *see also under*
DRUMHOME]

Baptisms, 1865-1962; marriages, 1845-1953; session and
committee minutes, 1853-1922.   **MIC.1P/6**

R.C. Killymard (Raphoe diocese)
Baptisms, 1874-81.   **MIC.1D/86**

KILLYMURRIS PRESBYTERIAN CHURCH, CO. ANTRIM
[*see under* **RASHARKIN**]

KILMACRENAN, CO. DONEGAL

C.I. Kilmacrenan (Raphoe diocese)
Baptisms, 1818-32 and 1871-1983; marriages, 1818-30
and 1845-1953; burials, 1818-32 and 1871-1983; vestry
minutes, 1822-1958.   **MIC.1/165**

Register of vestrymen, 1870-.   **In local custody**

C.I. Milford
[Formed out of Kilmacrenan and Tullyaugnish parishes -
see under **AUGHNISH**]

P. Kilmacrenan
Baptisms, 1848-1979; marriages, 1846-1920.   **MIC.1P/141**

R.C. Kilmacrenan (Kilmore diocese)
  Baptisms, 1862-80.   **MIC.1D/85**

KILMAINHAM, CO. MEATH

R.C. Moybologue and Kilmainham Wood
  (Kilmore diocese)

  Baptisms, 1867-81; marriages, 1868-82.   **MIC.1D/82**

KILMEGAN, CO. DOWN

C.I. Castlewellan (Dromore diocese)
  Photograph of drawing of the church, 1850.   **C.R.1/2**

  Baptisms, 1872-; marriages, 1860-; burials,
  1879-; vestry minutes, 1869 and 1897-;
  churchwardens' accounts, 1869-; pew rent
  book, 1888-1906; register of vestrymen, 1870-.   **In local custody**

C.I. Kilmegan (Kilmore diocese)
  Baptisms, 1823-77; marriages, 1823-45; burials, 1823-79;
  vestry minutes, 1827-71; confirmations, 1861, 1865,
  1868, 1871, 1874 and 1877.   **MIC.1/53**

  Marriage notices, 1846-1922.   **D.1563/1-2**

M. Castlewellan
  [No details]   **In local custody**

M. Dundrum
  Baptisms, 1881-; marriages, 1888-.
  (At Newcastle)   **In local custody**

P. Castlewellan
  Baptism, 1845-1964 (with gaps); marriages, 1845-1915;
  session minutes and details of missionary collections,
  1845-8; stipend book, 1836-70; accounts, 1871-4.   **MIC.1P/198**

R.C. Castlewellan (Down and Connor)
  Baptisms, 1859-81.   **MIC.1D/73**

R.C. Drumaroad and Clanvaraghan (Castlewellan)
  (Down and Connor diocese)

  [Partly in Kilmegan parish]

  Baptisms, 1853-81; marriages, 1853-80.   **MIC.1D/72**

KILMOOD, CO. DOWN

C.I. Kilmood (Down diocese)
Baptisms, 1822-1961; marriages, 1822-1928; burials,
1793-1957; preachers' books, 1843-81 and 1906-43.   **MIC.1/59; T.679/60;**
                                                           C.R.1/17

Vestry minutes, 1820-.   **In local custody**

R.C. [Kilmood parish forms part of the Roman Catholic parish
of Carrickmannon and Saintfield - *see under*
SAINTFIELD]

KILMORE, CO. ARMAGH

C. Richhill
Baptisms, 1846-84 and 1922-39; marriages, 1850-76;
attendance lists, 1849-51; lists of members, c.1848-1877,
and minutes, 1848-76.   **C.R.7/7**

C.I. The Diamond (Armagh diocese)
[Partly in Drumcree parish and partly in Kilmore parish]

[Earliest registers destroyed in Dublin]

Baptisms, 1877-; vestry minutes, 1876-; preachers'
books, 1869-.   **In local custody**

C.I. Kilmore (Armagh diocese)
Baptisms, 1789-95 and 1799-1879; marriages,
1799-1845; burials, 1824-71; vestry minutes, 1733-79
and 1813-1944; confirmations, 1824; extracts from
vestry minutes, 1732-79; typescript notes about the
parish from the 5th century.   **MIC.1/8; T.476/1;**
                                                         T.636 pp.73-80;
                                                         T.2706/10 pp.69-98

C.I. Mullavilly (Armagh diocese)
Baptisms, 1821-74; marriages, 1821-45; burials, 1821-76;
vestry minutes, 1814-70.   **MIC.1/70; T.679/23;**
                                                         T.2706/10

Notes about the church from 1750.   **T.2706/10 pp.46-68**

Baptisms, 1875-; marriages, 1845-; burials, 1877-; vestry
minutes, 1875-; preachers' books, 1862-.   **In local custody**

C.I. Richhill (Armagh diocese)
[Earliest registers destroyed in Dublin]

Baptisms, 1878-; marriages, 1845-; vestry minutes,
1870-; preachers' books, 1898-.   **In local custody**

C.I. St Saviour's (Armagh diocese)
    [Partly in Kilmore parish]

    Baptisms, 1858-63.   T.679/54

    Notes about the church from 1856.   T.2706/10 pp.69-98

    Baptisms, 1864-; marriages, 1871-; burials, 1862-; vestry
    minutes, 1870-; preachers' books, 1858-.   **In local custody**

M. Kilmore [Primitive Wesleyan Methodists]
    Baptisms, 1815-. (At Armagh)   **In local custody**

M. Richhill
    Marriages, 1886-1931.   **MIC.1E/6**

    Baptisms, 1815-.   **In local custody**

P. Ahorey
    Baptisms, 1834-50; marriages, 1834-1933; session
    minutes, 1850-57; new communicants, 1837-57; collections
    and accounts, 1834-7.   **MIC.IP/353**

P. Richhill
    Baptisms, 1848-1960; marriages, 1845-1936; communion
    roll, 1889-1950.   **MIC.10/372**

P. Vinecash
    Baptisms, 1838-79; marriages, 1838-1903; list of
    communicants, 1849, 1882-5, 1892-1902 and 1911-24;
    session minutes, 1898, 1904, 1910, 1924-5 and 1931;
    committee minutes, 1937-44; stipend lists, 1879-1922;
    history of the church, 1697-1923; accounts relating to the
    building of new church, 1878-9.   **MIC.1P/348**

R.C. Kilmore (Richhill) (Armagh diocese)
    Baptisms and marriages, 1845-81.   **MIC.1D/38**

R.S.F. Ballyhagen (also includes Richhill)
    Family lists with details of births and burials,
    c.1680-1814 (Ballyhagen and Richhill); marriage
    certificates, 1692-1789 (Ballyhagen); testimonies of
    disunity, 1708-1813 (Ballyhagen and Richhill); wills
    and inventories, 1685-1740 (Ballyhagen); account book
    of Ballyhagen monthly meetings, 1714-66, with details
    about the library of Richhill monthly meeting,
    c.1824-1834.   **MIC.16/39**

R.S.F. Richhill and Grange
    Birth registers, 1812-1919, with an index, 1878-1919;
    marriages, 1816-1913; burials, 1812-1920; men's
    minutes, 1793-1960; women's minutes, 1866-87; minutes
    of monthly meetings of ministry and oversight,
    1914-52.   **MIC.16/39-42**

KILMORE, CO. CAVAN

C.I. Kilmore (Kilmore diocese)
Baptisms, 1702-1950; marriages, 1702-1930; burials,
1702-1974.   **MIC.1/255**

R.C. Kilmore (Kilmore diocese)
Baptisms, marriages and burials, 1859-81.   **MIC.1D/76**

KILMORE, CO. DOWN

C.I. Kilmore (Down diocese)
Baptisms, 1820-56; marriages, 1822-65; burials, 1822-56;
vestry minutes, 1824-92.   **MIC.1/59; T.679/24**

N.S.P. Rademon
Baptisms, 1830-92; marriages, 1832-46 and 1879-82;
accounts, 1898-1944; minute book, 1888-1911; lists of
communicants, 1833-66; list of families, 1836.   **C.R.4/2**

P. Kilmore
Baptisms, 1833-5; marriages, 1833-45.   **D.1759/1D/1**

P. Lissara
Baptisms, 1809-1909; marriages, 1811-1900; burials,
1809-88; session minutes, 1815-1933; committee minutes,
1864-1914; stipend account book, 1867-91; communion
lists, 1881 and 1890-1908; collections, 1815-58; lists of
elders, 1815-72.   **MIC.1P/299;
                                                              D.1759/1D/13**

R.C. Kilmore   **In local custody**

KILMORE, CO. MONAGHAN

C.I. Kilmore (Clogher diocese)
Baptisms, 1826-1984; marriages, 1826-1956; burials,
1826-1982.   **MIC.1/247**

Vestry minutes, 1870-.   **In local custody**

C.I. Stranoodan Chapel of Ease (Clogher diocese)
Baptisms, 1861-1959; marriages, 1861-1945.   **MIC.1/247**

Burials, 1867-.   **In local custody**

R.C. Kilmore
[*see under* **DRUMSNAT**]

KILMOREMOY, CO. MAYO

M. Ballina
Baptisms, 1837-42.   **MIC.429/1/164**

KILMOUNT PRESBYTERIAN CHURCH, CO. CAVAN
[*see under* KILLASHANDRA]

KILRAGHTS, CO. ANTRIM

C.I. Kilraghts (Connor diocese)
[*See under* RASKHARKIN]

Entries are made in Ballymoney registers from 1922.

P. 1st Kilraughts
Baptisms, 1836-.   In local custody

P. 2nd Kilraughts
[Later known as Bushvale]

Baptisms, 1858-1934; marriages, 1848-1909; session
minutes, 1879-1935; lists of communicants, c.1860-1878.   MIC.1P/362

R.C. [Kilraghts parish forms part of the Roman Catholic parish
of Loughguile - *see under* LOUGHGUILE and part of
the Roman Catholic parish of Dunloy and Cloughmills -
see under FINVOY]

R.P. Kilraughts
Baptisms, 1898-1966; marriages, 1864-1914, including
those for Cloughwater Reformed Presbyterian Church;
renewal of the National Covenant of Scotland and the
Solemn League and Covenant by Kilraughts Reformed
Presbyterian Church signed by the elders and others,
1855.   MIC.1C/8

KILREA, CO. LONDONDERRY

C.I. Kilrea (Derry diocese)
Baptisms, 1801-1961; marriages, 1802-05 and 1829-48;
burials, 1802-04 and 1829-96; vestry minutes, 1736-1951;
notes on the parish of Kilrea, 1607-1947, by the
Rev. Edwin G Parke.   MIC.1/54/2, 55;
                                                                   T.679/22; T.799/7

Marriages, 1845-; registers of vestrymen, 1870-;
preachers' books, 1869-.   In local custody

P. 1st Kilrea
Baptisms, 1825-59 and 1862-70; marriages, 1825-99;
session minutes, 1825-52; committee minutes, 1825-67 and
1910-32; communicants' roll, 1865-6 and 1891-1932.   MIC.1P/87

P. 2nd Kilrea
Baptisms, 1840-85 and 1903-1930; marriages, 1845-1929;
committee minutes and accounts, 1860-70 and 1886-94;

correspondence and notes on the history of the church
from 1832 and events in the church, 1938-64; session
minutes, 1840-80 and 1903-1957; session and
committee minutes, 1906-62.

MIC.1P/20

R.C. Kilrea (Derry diocese)
Baptisms, 1846-65; marriages, 1846-77; deaths, 1846-77.

MIC.1D/58-59

KILROOT, CO. ANTRIM

C.I. Kilroot (Connor diocese)
[Formerly united with Ballynure and Templecorran - *see
under* **BALLYNURE** and **TEMPLECORRAN**]

R.C. [Kilroot parish is part of the Roman Catholic parishes of
Carrickfergus and Larne - *see under*
CARRICKFERGUS and **LARNE**]

KILRUSH, CO. CLARE

M. Kilrush
Baptisms, 1844-58.

MIC.429/1/540

KILSARAN, CO. LOUTH

R.C. Kilsaran (Armagh diocese)
Baptisms, 1809-24, 1831-6 and 1853-81; marriages,
1809-26, 1831-6 and 1853-82.

MIC.1D/53

KILSHERDANY ROMAN CATHOLIC PARISH,
CO. CAVAN
[*see under* **KILDRUMSHERDAN**]

KILSKEERY, CO. TYRONE

C.I. Barr (Clogher diocese)
[Partly in Kilskeery parish and partly in Donacavey and
Dromore parishes]

Baptisms, 1880-1982; marriages, 1845-1934; burials,
1885-1921.

MIC.1/223

C.I. Kilskeery (Clogher diocese)
Baptisms, 1767-1938; marriages, 1778-1935; burials,
1796-1973.

MIC.1/6; C.R.1/22-23

Indexes to baptisms, 1767-1844, marriages, 1778-1841,
and burials, 1796-1841.

**In Public Search
Room**

Register of vestrymen, 1870-; vestry book with accounts,
1768 -.   **In local custody**

C.I. Trillick (Clogher diocese)
Baptisms, 1872-1958; marriages, 1904-34; vestry
minutes, 1873-1939.   **C.R. 1/23**

M. Togherdoo (in Irvinestown circuit) [Wesleyan Methodists]
Baptisms, 1829-1913; marriages may be included in
Irvinestown Church marriages, 1863-1918.   **MIC.1E/37**

M. Trillick [Wesleyan Methodists]
Baptisms, 1829-1913; marriages may be included in
Irvinestown Church marriages, 1863-1918.   **MIC.1E/37**

R.C. Kilskeery (Trillick) (Clogher diocese)
Baptisms, 1840-81; marriages, 1840-82.   **MIC.1D/11**

KILTEEVOGUE, CO. DONEGAL

C.I. Kilteevogue (Raphoe diocese)
Baptisms, 1818-79; marriages, 1845-96; burials,
1825-1921.   **MIC.1/168**

Baptisms, 1882-; marriages, 1897-; burials, 1921-;
register of vestrymen, 1870-; preachers' books,
1857-73 and 1884-.   **In local custody**

R.C. Kilteevogue (Cloghan or Glenfin) (Raphoe diocese)
Baptisms, 1855-62 and 1870-80; marriages, 1855-62 and
1870-82.   **MIC.1D/85**

**KILTERMON CHURCH OF IRELAND PARISH,
CO. TYRONE**
[*see under* **AGHALURCHER**]

**KILTYCLOGHER CHURCH OF IRELAND PARISH,
CO. LEITRIM**
[*see under* **CLOONCLARE**]

KILWARLIN CHURCH OF IRELAND PARISH, CO. DOWN
[*see under* **HILLSBOROUGH**]

KILWARLIN MORAVIAN CHURCH, CO. DOWN
[*see under* **HILLSBOROUGH**]

KILWAUGHTER, CO. ANTRIM

C.I. Kilwaughter and Carncastle (Connor diocese)
[Earliest registers destroyed in Dublin]

Baptisms, 1883-; marriages, 1845-; burials, 1883-.   **In local custody**

N.S.P. Larne and Kilwaughter
   [Originally 1st Larne Presbyterian Church - *see under*
   LARNE]

R.C. [*see under* **LARNE** and *under* **DOAGH, GRANGE OF**]

KINAWLEY, COS CAVAN AND FERMANAGH

C.I. Kinawley (Kilmore diocese)
   Baptisms, 1761-3, 1768-83 and 1794-1961; marriages,
   1761-3 and 1768-1913; burials, 1768-1972; publication
   of banns, 1823-7.   **MIC.1/76; C.R.1/62**

C.I. Swanlinbar (Kilmore diocese)
   Baptisms, 1798-1883; marriages, 1798-1895; burials,
   1799-1812, 1822-6 and 1863-83.   **MIC.1/212**

C.I. Trinity, later **Holy Trinity, Crom** (Kilmore diocese)
   Baptisms, 1842-1972; marriages, 1845-1935; burials,
   1869 and 1884-1964.   **C.R. 1/63**

M. Swanlinbar [Wesleyan Methodists]
   Baptisms, 1879-1955; marriages, 1865-1946.   **MIC.1E/11-12**

R.C. Glangevlin (Kilmore diocese)
   [Partly in Kinawley parish and partly in Templeport
   parish - *see under* **TEMPLEPORT**]

R.C. Kinawley (Swanlinbar) (Kilmore diocese)
   Baptisms, 1835-81; marriages, 1835-57; burials, 1853-7.   **MIC.1D/79**

R.C. Knockninny (Kilmore diocese)
   Baptisms and marriages, 1855-70.   **MIC.1D/78**

KINGSMILLS PRESBYTERIAN CHURCH, CO. ARMAGH
   [*see under* **LOUGHGILLY**]

KINGSCOURT METHODIST CHURCH, CO. CAVAN
   [*see under* **ENNISKEEN**]

KINLOUGH CHURCH OF IRELAND PARISH,
CO. LEITRIM
   [*see under* **ROSSINVER**]

KINLOUGH ROMAN CATHOLIC PARISH, CO. LEITRIM
   [*see under* **ROSSINVER**]

KINNEGO METHODIST CHURCH, CO. ARMAGH
[*see under* KILLYMAN]

KIRCUBBIN CHURCH OF IRELAND PARISH, CO. DOWN
[*see under* INISHARGY]

KIRCUBBIN PRESBYTERIAN CHURCH, CO. DOWN
[*see under* INISHARGY]

KIRKINRIOLA, CO. ANTRIM

B. Ballymena
Marriages, 1865-. **In local custody**

C. Ballymena
Baptisms, 1901-; marriages, 1898-; historical account, 1881. **In local custody**

C.I. Kirkinriola (Connor diocese)
Baptisms, 1789-1805 and 1815-71; marriages, 1807, 1809, 1819 and 1822-41; burials, 1780, 1792, 1809, 1815, 1836 and 1841-71; vestry minutes, 1777-1890; confirmations, 1868, 1871, 1874 and 1877. **T.679/186-194**

Baptisms, 1871-; marriages, 1841-; burials, 1871-; preachers' books, 1860-; treasurers' account book, 1878-1922. **In local custody**

M. Ballymena [Wesleyan Methodists]
Baptisms, 1829-1925; marriages, 1836-1931; circuit schedule books, 1860-79; register of members, 1826-91; leaders' and stewards' minutes, 1855-87, with gaps. **MIC.1E/57-58; C.R. 6/4**

Baptisms, 1829-45. **MIC.429/1/490**

N.S.P. Ballymena or **Kirkinriola**
Marriages, 1849-63. **C.R. 4/10**

P. 1st Ballymena
Baptisms, 1812-1938; marriages, 1812-1906; session minutes, 1812-1925, with gaps. **MIC.1P/114**

P. 2nd Ballymena (High Kirk)
Baptisms, 1813-1941; marriages, 1845-1936. **MIC.1P/204**

P. Wellington Street, Ballymena
Baptisms, 1863-1962; marriages, 1864-1920; minute books, 1862-93. **MIC.1P/27; T.513/1**

P. West Church, Ballymena
  Baptisms, 1829-1945; marriages, 1830-32 and 1845-1903.   **MIC.1P/105**

R.C. Kirkinriola (Ballymena) (Down and Connor diocese)
  [Also includes part of Ahoghill parish, part of Racavan
  parish, part of Glenwhirry parish and all of Ballyclug
  parish]

  Baptisms, 1848-81; marriages, 1840-42 and 1847-82.   **MIC.1D/69A**

KNAPPAGH PRESBYTERIAN CHURCH, CO. ARMAGH
  [*see under* **EGLISH**]

**KNOCKBRACKEN REFORMED PRESBYTERIAN
CHURCH, CO. DOWN**
  [*see under* **KNOCKBREDA**]

KNOCKBREDA, CO. DOWN

C.I. Ballymacarrett (Down diocese)
  Baptisms, 1827-69; marriages, 1827-57.   **T.679/29**

C.I. Knockbreda (Down diocese)
  Baptisms, 1785-1978; marriages, 1784-1965; burials,
  1787-1905; vestry minutes, 1791-1983; dispensary book,
  1818-53; register of vestrymen, 1870-1960; preachers'
  books, 1824-1975; graveyard books, 1869-1912;
  statement of accounts, 1871-1965, with gaps; notes on
  parishioners - emigration, communicants etc., 1863-1916;
  plans of the church, c.1890-1898.   **MIC.1/57; C.R. 1/24**

  Census of the congregation, 1873 and 1875;
  confirmations, 1874-1914; communicants, 1880-1910.   **T.2786**

P. 1st Ballymacarrett
  Baptisms, 1837-1921; marriages, 1845-1928.   **MIC.1P/15**

P. Castlereagh
  Baptisms, 1816-1922; marriages, 1816-1904;
  communicants' lists, 1854-93; session minutes, 1859-1942;
  committee minutes, 1870-1916.   **MIC.1P/431**

P. Gilnahirk
  Baptisms, 1797-1954; marriages, 1828-1916; session
  minutes, 1830-44 and 1873-1920; minutes of
  committee and congregational meetings, 1830-66;
  communicants' rolls, 1873, 1885-6 and 1894-1924.   **MIC.1P/432**

P. Newtownbreda
Baptisms, 1846-1986; marriages, 1845-1920;
communicants, 1854-83; session minutes, 1871-1921;
committee minutes, 1847-65 and 1881-94; annual reports
and statements of accounts, 1900-38; issues of
The Chronicle, the magazine of the church, 1925-36.   **MIC.1P/51; C.R.3/49**

R.C. Ballymacarrett, St Matthew's (Down and Connor
diocese)

Baptisms, 1841-81; marriages, 1841-82.   **MIC.1D/65**

R.P. Knockbracken
Annual reports, 1869-1959, with gaps; history of the
church up to 1938.   **C.R.5/16**

KNOCKBRIDE, CO. CAVAN

C.I. Knockbride (Kilmore diocese)
Baptisms, 1825-1917; marriages, 1827-1930; burials,
1817-63, 1866-1910 and 1918-71.   **MIC.1/251**

P. Coronary
Baptisms, 1764-1961; marriages, 1768-87 and 1863-1955;
session minutes, 1764-87; history of the congregation and
details of Sunday collections, 1769-89; typescript and
manuscript notes from the church records, c.1940-1974.   **MIC.1P/179**

R.C. Knockbride (Kilmore diocese)
Baptisms, 1835-79; marriages, 1835-79; deaths, 1835-76.   **MIC.1D/82**

**KNOCKBRIDGE ROMAN CATHOLIC PARISH,
CO. LOUTH**
[*see under* **LOUTH**]

**KNOCKMANOUL METHODIST CHURCH,
CO. FERMANAGH**
[*see under* **MAGHERACROSS**]

**KNOCKNAMUCKLY CHURCH OF IRELAND PARISH,
CO. ARMAGH**
[*see under* **SEAGOE**]

**KNOCKNINNY ROMAN CATHOLIC CHURCH,
CO. FERMANAGH**
[*see under* **KINAWLEY**]

KNOWHEAD PRESBYTERIAN CHURCH, CO. DONEGAL
[*see under* **MUFF**]

**LACK OR COLAGHTY CHURCH OF IRELAND PARISH,
CO. FERMANAGH**
[*see under* **MAGHERACULMONEY**]

LAGHEY CHURCH OF IRELAND PARISH, CO. DONEGAL
[*see under* **DRUMHOME**]

LAGHEY METHODIST CHURCH, CO. ARMAGH
[*see under* **KILLYMAN**]

LAMBEG, COS ANTRIM AND DOWN

C.I. Lambeg (Connor diocese)
Marriages, 1845-1908.   MIC.1/124

Reports and accounts, 1934-5.   C.R. 1/64

Baptisms, 1826-1934; burials, 1826-1906; [earliest
baptism, marriage and burial registers are missing from
the parish]; vestry minutes, 1810-1925; tithe applotment
book, 1824-7; preachers' book, 1861-1931; register of
vestrymen, 1870-.   **In local custody**

P. Hillhall
Baptisms, 1866-1952; marriages, 1845-1907; marriage
notice books, 1871-1901; annual reports and financial
statements, 1930-84, with gaps.   MIC.1P/380;
                                                     MIC.1P/ 230/5;
                                                     C.R. 3/35

R.C. [Part of Lambeg parish is in the Roman Catholic parish of
Blaris - *see under* **BLARIS** and part in the Roman
Catholic parish of Derryaghy - *see under*
DERRYAGHY]

**LANGFIELD LOWER AND UPPER CHURCH OF IRELAND
PARISHES, CO. TYRONE**
[*see under* **LONGFIELD WEST and EAST**]

LANGFIELD ROMAN CATHOLIC PARISH, CO. TYRONE
[*see under* **LONGFIELD WEST and EAST**]

LARAGH METHODIST CHURCH, CO. FERMANAGH
[*see under* **TRORY**]

LARAH, CO. CAVAN

C.I. Laragh (Kilmore diocese)
[United with Drung up to 1855]

Baptisms, 1759-1987; marriages, 1785-1898; burials,
1774-1967.								**MIC.1/300-301**

R.C. Laragh (Kilmore diocese)
Baptisms, 1876-81.							**MIC.1D/75**

LARGY PRESBYTERIAN CHURCH, CO. LONDONDERRY
[*see under* TAMLAGHT FINLAGAN]

LARNE, CO. ANTRIM

C.I. Larne
[*see under* **Inver**]

M. Larne [Wesleyan Methodists]
Baptisms, 1878-1915; marriages, 1863-1906; circuit
schedule books, 1879-93 and 1908-23; printed history of
Larne Methodist Circuit, 1885-1985.				**MIC.1E/39**

N.S.P. Larne and Kilwaughter
Baptisms, 1720-69, 1796, 1801-03 and 1826-1929;
marriages, 1721-69 and 1826-1908; session minutes,
1720-48, 1800-01 and 1828-30; session and committee
minutes, 1864-1929; discipline cases, 1721-49; poor
accounts, 1720-57.							**MIC.1B/6**

Stipend subscription books, 1860-89; cash books,
1863-82; account book relating to the rebuilding of the
church, 1828-38.							**D.2009/1**

P. 2nd Larne or Gardenmore
Baptisms, 1861-1906; marriages, 1846-1906.			**MIC.1P/263**

R.C. Carrickfergus, Larne and Ballygowan
(Down and Connor diocese)

Baptisms, 1821-83; marriages, 1821-82; indexes to
baptisms and marriages, 1828-1960.				**MIC.1D/68, 90**

R.P. Larne
Minutes, 1898-1930.							**C.R.5/10**

LARNE (1ST) PRESBYTERIAN CHURCH, CO. ANTRIM
[*see under* **INVER**]

LAVEY, CO. CAVAN

C.I. Lavey (Kilmore diocese)
Baptisms, 1883-1984; marriages, 1846-98; burials,
1889-1967.　　　　　　　　　　　　　　　　　　MIC.1/301-302

R.C. Lavey (Kilmore diocese)
Baptisms, 1867-81.　　　　　　　　　　　　　　MIC.1D/75

LAVEY ROMAN CATHOLIC CHURCH, CO. LONDONDERRY
[*see under* TERMONEENY]

LAYD, CO. ANTRIM

C.I. Layd (Connor diocese)
Baptisms, 1826-73; marriages, 1826-45; burials, 1826-99;
vestry minutes, 1856-72; list of parishioners, 1823.　　T.679/359-363

Baptisms, 1874-; marriages, 1845-; vestry minutes, 1873-;
preachers' books, 1875-.　　　　　　　　　　In local custody

P. Cushendun and Cushendall
Baptisms, 1854-1947; marriages, 1853-1935; register of
members, 1897-1916; list of communicants, 1880, 1889
and 1897-1963.　　　　　　　　　　　　　　　MIC.1P/352

R.C. Layde and Ardclinis (Cushendall)
(Down and Connor diocese)

Baptisms, 1838-44 and 1858-81; marriages, 1837-44 and
1860-81.　　　　　　　　　　　　　　　　　　MIC.1D/68

LAYD, GRANGE OF, CO. ANTRIM
[*see under* LAYD]

LEARMOUNT, CO. LONDONDERRY

C.I. Learmount (Derry diocese)
Baptisms, 1832-1904; marriages, 1833-93; burials,
1832-1959.　　　　　　　　　　　　　　　　　MIC.1/41

Vestry minutes, 1885-.　　　　　　　　　　　In local custody

R.C. Cumber Upper and Learmount (Derry diocese)
[*see under* CUMBER UPPER]

LECK, CO. DONEGAL

C.I. Leck (Raphoe diocese)
Baptisms, 1878-1975; marriages, 1846-1943; burials,
1878-1901; vestry minutes, 1813-69.   **MIC.1/213-214**

Vestry minutes, 1871-; register of vestrymen, 1870-;
preachers' books, 1868-.   **In local custody**

R.C. [Leck parish is part of the Roman Catholic parish of
Conwall and Leck - *see under* **CONWAL**]

LECKPATRICK, CO. TYRONE

C.I. Leckpatrick (Derry diocese)
[Earliest registers destroyed in Dublin]

Baptisms, 1877-; marriages, 1845-; burials, 1877-;
registers of vestrymen, 1870-; preachers' books, 1872-.   **In local custody**

P. Leckpatrick
Baptisms, 1838-99 and 1901-35; marriages, 1845-1930;
session minutes, 1836-1972; financial statements, 1866,
1870 and 1872-3.   **MIC.1P/49**

P. 2nd Strabane
Baptisms, 1844-1916; marriages, 1864-94.   **MIC.1P/10**

R.C. Leckpatrick (Strabane) (Derry diocese)
[*see also under* **DONAGHEDY**]

Baptisms, 1863-81; marriages, 1863-84.   **MIC.1D/62**

R.C. Mourne (Strabane) (Derry diocese)
Baptisms, 1866-81; marriages, 1866-83.   **MIC.1D/62**

LECUMPHER PRESBYTERIAN CHURCH, CO. LONDONDERRY
[*see under* **DESERTMARTIN**]

LEGACURRY PRESBYTERIAN CHURCH, CO. DOWN
[*see under* **DRUMBEG**]

LEITRIM PRESBYTERIAN CHURCH, CO. DOWN
[*see under* **DRUMGOOLAND**]

LEITRIM ROMAN CATHOLIC CHURCH, CO. DOWN
[*see under* **DRUMGOOLAND**]

**LETTERBREEN METHODIST CHURCH,
CO. FERMANAGH**
    [*see under* **CLEENISH**]

LETTERKENNY METHODIST CHURCH, CO. DONEGAL
    [*see under* **CONWAL**]

**LETTERKENNY (1ST, 2ND AND 3RD) PRESBYTERIAN
CHURCHES, CO. DONEGAL**
    [*see under* **CONWAL**]

**LETTERKENNY ROMAN CATHOLIC CHURCH,
CO. DONEGAL**
    [*see under* **CONWAL**]

LETTERMACAWARD, CO. DONEGAL

    C.I. Lettermacaward (Raphoe diocese)
        Baptisms, 1889-1982; burials, 1890-1981.   **MIC.1/188**

        Marriages, 1846-; vestry minutes, 1890-.   **In local custody**

    R.C. Dungloe (Templecrone Upper and Lettermacaward)
    (Raphoe diocese)

        Baptisms, 1876-81.   **MIC.1D/87**

LIMAVADY METHODIST CHURCH, CO. LONDONDERRY
    [*see under* **DRUMACHOSE**]

**LIMAVADY (1ST AND 2ND) PRESBYTERIAN CHURCHES,
CO. LONDONDERRY**
    [*see under* **DRUMACHOSE**]

LIMERICK, CO. LIMERICK

    C. Henry Street, Limerick
        Baptisms and marriages, 1817-72.   **D.814/1**

    M. Limerick
        Baptisms, 1824-46.   **MIC.429/1/59**

**LISBELLAW CHURCH OF IRELAND PARISH,
CO. FERMANAGH**
    [*see under* **CLEENISH**]

**LISBELLAW METHODIST CHURCHES [PRIMITIVE
WESLEYAN AND WESLEYAN METHODISTS],
CO. FERMANAGH**
  [*see under* **CLEENISH**]

**LISBELLAW PRESBYTERIAN CHURCH,
CO. FERMANAGH**
  [*see under* **CLEENISH**]

**LISBURN CHURCH OF IRELAND CATHEDRAL,
CO. ANTRIM**
  [*see under* **BLARIS**]

**LISBURN [WESLEYAN METHODIST, PRIMITIVE
METHODIST AND NEW CONNEXION] METHODIST
CHURCHES, CO. ANTRIM**
  [*see under* **BLARIS**]

LISLEEN METHODIST CHURCH, CO. TYRONE
  [*see under* **ARDSTRAW**]

**LISLIMNAGHAN CHURCH OF IRELAND PARISH,
CO. TYRONE**
  [*see under* **CAPPAGH**]

LISLOONEY PRESBYTERIAN CHURCH, CO. ARMAGH
  [*see under* **TYNAN**]

LISNADILL, CO. ARMAGH

  C.I. Aghavilly (Armagh diocese)
   Baptisms, 1844-71; burials, 1846-71; confirmations, 1849
   and 1852.   **T.679/106**

   Marriages, 1845-. vestry minutes, 1871-; preachers'
   books, 1845-.   **In local custody**

  C.I. Armaghbreague (Armagh diocese)
   [Partly in Lisnadill parish and partly in Keady parish -
   see under **KEADY**]

  C.I. Lisnadill (Armagh diocese)
   [Earliest registers destroyed in Dublin]

   Baptism and burials, 1877-; marriages, 1845-; vestry
   minutes, 1914-.   **In local custody**

R.C. Ballymacnab (Kilcluney) (Armagh diocese)
[*see under* **KILCLOONEY**]

LISNAGLEER BAPTIST CHURCH, CO. TYRONE
[*see under* **DERRYLORAN**]

**LISNASKEA CHURCH OF IRELAND PARISH,
CO. FERMANAGH**
[*see under* **AGHALURCHER**]

**LISNASKEA METHODIST CHURCH,
CO. FERMANAGH**
[*see under* **AGHALURCHER**]

LISSAN, COS LONDONDERRY AND TYRONE

    C.I. Lissan (Armagh diocese)

Baptisms, 1753-95 and 1803-95; marriages, 1744-94 and 1805-46; burials, 1753-95 and 1805-43; vestry minutes, 1734-1816; publication of banns, 1805-1904; confirmations, 1824 and 1828.	**T.679/9A-B; MIC.1/103**
Parish vestry accounts, 1817-23.	**DIO.4/32/L/2/5/1**
Baptisms, 1895-; marriages, 1845-; burials, 1895-; preachers' books, 1810-44 and 1865-; register of vestrymen, 1870-.	**In local custody**

    P. Claggan

Baptisms and marriages, 1848-.	**In local custody**

    R.C. Lissan (Armagh diocese)

Baptisms, 1839-81; marriages, 1839-80.	**MIC.1D/36**
Fragments of baptisms, 1822-39, and marriages, 1822-30.	**MIC.1D/89**

LISSARA PRESBYTERIAN CHURCH, CO. DOWN
[*see under* **KILMORE, CO. DOWN**]

LOANENDS PRESBYTERIAN CHURCH, CO. ANTRIM
[*see under* **KILLEAD**]

LONDONDERRY CHURCHES
[*see under* **TEMPLEMORE**]

LONGFIELD EAST, CO. TYRONE

C.I. Langfield Upper (Derry diocese)
Marriages, 1845-1931; burials, 1892-1988; register of
vestrymen, 1870-1931.   **MIC.1/303**

Baptisms, 1893-; marriages 1931-; vestry minutes, 1884-;
preachers' book, 1903 -.   **In local custody**

M. Drumquin
Baptisms, 1832-80 (Omagh Circuit); baptisms, 1879-1978
(Newtownstewart Circuit); marriages, 1890-1933
(Newtownstewart Circuit); circuit schedule book, 1866-79;
membership register, 1863-c.1880 (Omagh Circuit) and
1898-1954 (Newtownstewart Circuit).   **MIC.1E/24, 26**

P. Drumquin
Baptisms, 1845-1900; marriages, 1845-1912.   **MIC.1P/65**

R.C. Langfield (Drumquin) (Derry diocese)
Baptisms and marriages, 1846-80; deaths, 1853-6.   **MIC.1D/60**

LONGFIELD WEST, CO. TYRONE

C.I. Langfield Lower (Derry diocese)
[Earliest registers destroyed in Dublin]

Marriages, 1845-1934; burials, 1878-1981; vestry
minutes, 1810-29 and 1870-1900; minute book, 1880-91.   **MIC.1/305**

Baptisms, 1875-; register of vestrymen, 1870-; preachers'
books, 1855-.   **In local custody**

R.C. Langfield (Drumquin)
[*see under* LONGFIELD EAST]

LONGFORD, CO. LONGFORD

M. Longford
Baptisms, 1840-1987; marriages, 1868-1955.   **MIC.1E/48**

Baptisms, 1840-42.   **MIC.429/1/137**

LORDSHIP and BALLYMASCANLON ROMAN CATHOLIC PARISH, CO. LOUTH
[*see under* BALLYMASCANLON]

LOUGHAGHERY PRESBYTERIAN CHURCH, CO. DOWN
[*see under* ANNAHILT]

LOUGHAN, COS CAVAN AND MEATH

C.I. Loughan (Kilmore diocese)
Marriages, 1880-91; vestry minutes, 1896-1900.   **MIC.1/263**

LOUGHBRICKLAND PRESBYTERIAN CHURCH, CO. DOWN
[*see under* **AGHADERG**]

LOUGH ESKE CHURCH OF IRELAND PARISH, CO. DONEGAL
[*see under* **KILLYMARD**]

LOUGHGALL, CO. ARMAGH

C.I. Annaghmore (Armagh diocese)
[Partly in Loughgall parish and partly in Killyman and
Clonfeacle parishes]

Baptisms, 1856-72; burials, 1867-70.   **T.679/120, 122-123**

Baptisms, 1873-; marriages, 1859-; burials, 1871-; vestry
minutes, 1877-.   **In local custody**

C.I. Charlemont (Armagh diocese)
Baptisms, 1880-; marriages, 1845-; burials, 1835-;
preachers' books, 1845-.   **In local custody**

C.I. Loughgall (Armagh diocese)
Baptisms, 1706-29, 1779-1820 and 1830-86; marriages,
1706-29 and 1779-1845; burials, 1706-29 and 1779-94;
publication of banns, 1815-30; confirmations, 1828-63;
vestry minutes, 1774-1885.   **MIC.1/59-60; D.54-56**

Baptisms, 1886-1936; marriages, 1845-; burials, 1894-.   **In local custody**

M. Clonmain
Baptisms, 1874-.   **In local custody**

M. Loughgall
Baptisms, 1815 -. [At Armagh]   **In local custody**

P. Loughgall (Cloveneden)
Baptisms, 1842-1965; marriages, 1845-79 and 1881-1925.   **MIC.1P/287; T.3049/1**

R.C. Loughgall and Tartaraghan (Armagh diocese)
Baptisms, 1835-81; marriages, 1833-80.   **MIC.1D/38**

LOUGHGILLY, CO. ARMAGH

C.I. Balleek (Armagh diocese)
[Earliest records destroyed in Dublin]

Vestry minutes, 1827-70 and 1899-1919.   **MIC.1/113**

C.I. Clare
[Partly in Loughghilly parish - *see under*
BALLYMORE]

C.I. Loughgilly (Armagh diocese)
Baptisms, 1804-89; marriages, 1804-45; burials, 1808
and 1811-1932.   **MIC.1/66-67**

Baptisms, 1889-; marriages, 1845-; burials, 1932-; vestry
minutes, 1797-.   **In local custody**

P. Kingsmills
Baptisms, 1842-.   **In local custody**

P. Mountnorris
Baptisms, 1810-48; marriages, 1804-27.   **MIC.1P/29**

Baptisms, 1813-71.   **In Presbyterian
                                                         Historical Society**

P. Tullyallen
Baptisms, 1834-85; notes on congregational history,
1829-75; communicants' list, 1854-83.   **MIC.1P/29**

Baptisms, 1792-1834; marriages, 1868-.   **In local custody**

R.C. Balleek (Armagh diocese)
Historical account of the church, 1872, which includes
names of those buried in the churchyard, 1871-6, and
those who subscribed to building work, 1846-72.   **MIC.1D/9**

R.C. Loughgilly (Armagh diocese)
[Includes Ballymyre and Balleek]

Baptisms and marriages, 1825-44 and 1849-81.   **MIC.1D/38**

R.P. Ballenon [*sic* Ballenan]
Baptisms, 1860-77; marriages, 1851-65; deaths, 1850-68,
with three references, 1880-95; register of admissions,
1849-67; register of departures, 1849-68; session
minutes, 1820-67; diary entries, 1850-67; stipend list,
1853; collection accounts, 1860-65; session minutes,
accounts and correspondence, 1819-83.   **MIC.1C/16**

LOUGHGUILE, CO. ANTRIM

C.I. Loughguile (Connor diocese)
[Earliest registers destroyed in Dublin]

Baptisms, 1877-; marriages, 1846-; burials, 1879-; vestry
minutes, 1801-; preachers' books, 1843-; register of
vestrymen, 1892-.   **In local custody**

P. Ballyweany
    Baptisms, 1862-1967; marriages, 1845-1900; communion
    roll, 1862-1939.   **MIC.1P/82**

R.C. Loughguile (Down and Connor diocese)
    Baptisms, 1845-81; marriages, 1845-69.   **MIC.1D/69A**

LOUGHINISLAND, CO. DOWN

C.I. Loughinisland (Down diocese)
    Baptisms, 1760-1806 and 1816-37, with indexes;
    marriages, 1760-1800 and 1815-1935, with indexes,
    1760-1800 and 1815-94; burials, 1760-93, 1816-38 and
    and 1858-63, with indexes, 1760-93 and 1816-37; vestry
    minutes, 1773-1828 and 1870-1956; register of
    vestrymen, 1870-1957; register of church wardens,
    1891-1958.   **D.1407/1-10; T.1**

    Baptisms, 1838-; burials, 1863-; preachers' books, 1857-;
    churchwardens' accounts, 1890-.   **In local custody**

N.S.P. Clough
    Baptisms, 1792-1939; marriages, 1791-1942; stipend
    book, 1830-67; list of members, 1851, with
    details about deaths, emigration etc., up to 1867.   **C.R. 4/16; T.1707**

P. Clough
    Baptisms, 1791-1837 and 1842-1953; marriages,
    1791-1890.   **MIC.1P/308**

P. Seaforde
    Baptisms, 1826-1925; marriages, 1827-1936; deaths,
    1839-45; transfer certificates, 1839; session minutes,
    1839-99; new communicants, 1826-38; expenditure
    accounts, 1826-38.   **MIC.1P/355**

R.C. Drumaroad and Clanvaraghan (Down and Connor
    diocese)
    [*see under* **KILMEGAN**]

R.C. Loughinisland (Down and Connor diocese)
    Baptisms, 1806-52; marriages and deaths, 1805-52.   **MIC.1D/73**

LOUGHMORNE PRESBYTERIAN CHURCH, CO. ANTRIM
    [*see under* **CARRICKFERGUS**]

LOUGHMOURNE PRESBYTERIAN CHURCH,
CO. MONAGHAN
  [*see under* **AGHNAMULLEN**]

LOUTH, CO. LOUTH

  C.I. Louth (Armagh diocese)
      Baptisms, 1889-1904; marriages, 1845-98; burials,
      1883-1943.   **MIC.1/275**

      Vestry minutes, 1791-.   **In local custody**

  R.C. Knockbridge (Armagh diocese)
      Baptisms and marriages, 1858-69.   **MIC.1D/45**

  R.C. Louth (Armagh diocese)
      Baptisms, 1833-71 and 1873-81; marriages, 1833-81.   **MIC.1D/44**

LOWER MOURNE ROMAN CATHOLIC PARISH,
CO. DOWN
  [*see under* **KILKEEL**]

LOWTHERSTOWN, CO. FERMANAGH
  [*see under* **DERRYVULLAN** - sometimes known as
  Lowtherstown]

LUCAN, CO. DUBLIN

  P. Lucan
      Marriages, 1899-1920.   **MIC.1P/12**

LURGAN, CO. CAVAN

  C.I. Ballyjamesduff
      [Partly in Lurgan parish but also partly in Castlerahan,
      Crosserlough and Denn parishes - *see under*
      CASTLERAHAN]

  C.I. Lurgan (Kilmore diocese)
      [Also includes Munterconnaught up to 1845]

      Baptisms, 1831-1902; marriages, 1831-1900; burials,
      1831-1901.   **MIC.1/260**

  P. Bellasis
      Baptisms, 1833-1985; marriages, 1845-1951.   **MIC.1P/267**

R.C. Lurgan (Virginia) (Kilmore diocese)
Baptisms, 1755-95 (with gaps 1778-9 and 1785-6), and
1821-81; marriages, 1755-70, 1773-80 and 1821-75;
deaths, 1821-55.   **MIC.1D/80-81**

**LURGAN, HIGH STREET, METHODIST CHURCH,
CO. ARMAGH**
[*see under* **SHANKILL**]

**LURGAN, QUEEN STREET, METHODIST CHURCH,
CO. ARMAGH**
[*see under* **SHANKILL**]

LURGAN (1ST) PRESBYTERIAN CHURCH, CO. ARMAGH
[*see under* **SHANKILL**]

**LURGAN (HILL STREET) PRESBYTERIAN CHURCH,
CO. ARMAGH**
[*see under* **SHANKILL**]

LURGAN ROMAN CATHOLIC PARISH, CO. ARMAGH
[*see under* **SHANKILL**]

**LURGAN RELIGIOUS SOCIETY OF FRIENDS,
CO. ARMAGH**
[*see under* **SHANKILL**]

**LURGANBOY CHAPEL OF EASE (CHURCH OF
IRELAND), CO. LEITRIM**
[*see under* **KILLASNET**]

LYLEHILL PRESBYTERIAN CHURCH, CO. ANTRIM
[*see under* **TEMPLEPATRICK**]

MACOSQUIN, CO. LONDONDERRY

C.I. Camus-Juxta-Bann (Derry diocese)
Vestry minutes, 1793-1869.   **MIC.1/121**

Baptisms, 1878-; marriages, 1845-; burials, 1883-; vestry
minutes, 1870-.   **In local custody**

P. Crossgar
Baptisms, 1839-1927; marriages, 1846-1905.   **MIC.1P/409**

P. Dromore
  Baptisms, 1889-1987; marriages, 1869-1932; session
  minutes, 1868-1941.   **MIC.1P/373**

P. Macosquin
  Baptisms, 1823-45, 1860 and 1867-1924; marriages,
  1885-1918; communicants' roll, 1867-84 and 1888-1909.   **MIC.1P/417**

R.C. [Macosquin parish is part of the Roman Catholic parish of
  Coleraine - *see under* **COLERAINE**]

MAGHENE ROMAN CATHOLIC CHURCH, CO. FERMANAGH
  [*see under* **INISHMACSAINT**]

MAGHERA, CO. DOWN

C.I. Maghera (Dromore diocese)
  [Earliest registers destroyed in Dublin]

  Extracts from registers, 1875-6.   **DIO.1/14/3**

  Baptisms, 1881-; marriages, 1845-; burials, 1877-; vestry
  minutes, 1826-; register of vestrymen, 1870-; preachers'
  books, 1870-.   **In local custody**

R.C. Bryansford and Newcastle (Down and Connor diocese)
  Baptisms, 1845-81; marriages, 1845-85; deaths, 1860-82.   **MIC.1D/73**

MAGHERA, CO. LONDONDERRY

C.I. Maghera (Derry diocese)
  Baptisms, 1785-1869; marriages, 1798-1860; burials,
  1809-1904.   **MIC.1/20, 77**

  Baptisms, 1870-; marriages, 1861-; vestry minutes,
  1870-; register of vestrymen, 1870-.   **In local custody**

M. Maghera
  Baptisms, 1825-; marriages, 1867-. [At Magherafelt]   **In local custody**

P. Curran
  Marriages, 1845-1936. [No pre-1900 baptisms exist]   **MIC.1P/338**

P. Maghera
  Baptisms, 1843-1962; marriages, 1843-1936; burials,
  1861-5, 1891-1916 and 1940-45; communicants' roll books,
  1847-1924.   **MIC.1P/376**

P. Swatragh
  Baptisms, 1851-1902; marriages, 1845-1935.   **MIC.1P/433**

R.C. Maghera and Killylough (Derry diocese)
Baptisms, 1841-81; marriages, 1841-53 and 1857-82;
deaths, 1848-80 and 1887-8.   **MIC.1D/58**

MAGHERACLOONE, CO. MONAGHAN

C.I. Magheracloone (Clogher diocese)
Baptisms, 1806-1984; marriages, 1813-1945; burials,
1806-1984; vestry minutes, 1810-72.   **MIC.1/171**

R.C. Magheracloone (Carrickmacross) (Clogher diocese)
Baptisms, 1836-63 and 1865-81; marriages, 1826-59 and
1866-80.   **MIC.1D/17; C.R.2/17**

MAGHERACROSS, COS FERMANAGH AND TYRONE

C.I. Garvary (Clogher diocese)
[Partly in Magheracross parish - *see under*
ENNISKILLEN]

C.I. Magheracross (Clogher diocese)
Baptisms, 1800-40 and 1846-91; marriages, 1800-1919;
burials, 1800-1979; vestry minutes, 1847-1966; preachers'
books, 1843-65 and 1930-61; register of vestrymen,
1870-1919.   **MIC.1/78; C.R. 1/20;**
T.679/37

Baptisms, 1891-.   **In local custody**

M. Ballinamallard [Wesleyan Methodists]
Baptisms, 1829-1919; marriages, 1882-1937; circuit
schedule books, 1881-91 and 1895-1908; membership
rolls, 1881-92 and 1898-1900; circuit stewards' book,
1879-94.   **MIC.1E/23, 37**

M. Knockmanoul [Wesleyan Methodists]
Baptisms, 1879-1919 [there may be earlier baptisms in
MIC.1E/15]; circuit schedule books, 1866-1908;
membership rolls, 1881-1900; circuit stewards' book,
1879-94.   **MIC.1E/15, 23**

R.C. Whitehill
[*see under* **DERRYVULLAN**]

MAGHERACULMONEY, CO. FERMANAGH

C.I. Lack or Colaghty (Clogher diocese)
Baptisms, 1835-1915; marriages, 1844; accounts,
1835-44; vestry minutes, 1852-70; preachers' book,
1858-68.   **MIC.1/37**

Marriages, 1845-; burials, 1874-.   **In local custody**

C.I. Magheraculmoney or St Mary's (Kesh)
(Clogher diocese)

Baptisms, 1767-1907; marriages, 1767-1818 and
1825-45; burials, 1767-1876; vestry minutes, 1763-1887.   **MIC.1/67-68**

Baptisms, 1907-; marriages, 1845-; burials, 1876; vestry
minutes, 1887-; register of vestrymen, 1870-.   **In local custody**

R.C. Magheraculmany (Culmaine, Ederney)
(Clogher diocese)

Baptisms, 1836-81; marriages, 1837-81.   **MIC.1D/14; C.R.2/1**

MAGHERADROOL, CO. DOWN

C.I. Magheradrool (Dromore diocese)
[Earliest registers destroyed in Dublin]

Baptisms, 1879-99; marriages, 1845-1913; burials
1879-1912; vestry minutes, 1870-1906; lists of
vestrymen, 1874-1903; accounts, 1876-82.   **C.R. 1/41**

Extracts from registers, 1783-1859.   **DIO.1/14/4**

Preachers' books, 1872-.   **In local custody**

P. 1st Ballynahinch
Baptisms, 1841-59, 1869 and 1871-1986; marriages,
1870-1900; communicants' roll, 1884-1907; list of poor
householders, c.1840.   **MIC.1P/302;
                                                     D.1759/1D/1**

P. 2nd Ballynahinch [2nd and 3rd united in 1949 to form
    Edengrove]

Baptisms, 1829-49 and 1880-1986; marriages, 1846-1903;
missionary prayer meeting subscription lists, 1823-7;
session minutes, 1829-34; library subscription list, 1836-7;
register of members, 1829 and 1856; minutes of Down
Missionary Society, 1822-5; lists of communicants, 1848-67;
annual reports, 1887, 1892, 1896 and 1910; typescript and
published histories of the congregation, c.1770-1974; call to
Mr David Edgar to become minister signed by 56 members
of the congregation, 1829.   **MIC.1P/110; C.R. 3/41**

Papers about the history of the congregation, c.1743-c.1900.   **D.1650/2-3**

P. 3rd Ballynahinch
Baptisms, 1820-1948; marriages, 1820-1931; session
minutes, 1849-76 and 1896-1906; communion lists,

1841-93; lists of subscribers, 1832; acceptance certificates, 1830-39.

MIC.1P/110

P. Spa
Baptisms, 1880-1986; marriages, 1875-1936.

MIC.1P/301

R.C. Ballynahinch and Dunmore (Dromore diocese)
Baptisms, 1827-81; marriages, 1829-64.

MIC.1D/25

MAGHERAFELT, CO. LONDONDERRY

C.I. Castledawson (Derry diocese)
[Formed out of Magherafelt parish but added to Ballyscullion parish - *see under* **BALLYSCULLION**]

C.I. Magherafelt (Armagh diocese)
Baptisms, 1718-93 and 1799-1895; marriages, 1720-1845; burials, 1716-71 and 1799-1893; vestry minutes, 1718-95 and 1798-1909; confirmations, 1833.

MIC.1/1A

Baptisms, 1895-; marriages, 1845-; burials, 1893-.

In local custody

M. Magherafelt Circuit [Churches at Magherafelt and Castledawson]

Baptisms, 1825-1941.

MIC.1E/22

Baptisms, 1841-5.

MIC.429/1/384, 493

P. Castledawson
Baptisms, 1805-1901; marriages, 1805-1932; session minutes, 1831-50 and 1905; list of communicants, 1847-8, 1888-94 and 1912.

MIC.1P/90

P. 1st Magherafelt
Baptisms, 1813-1964; marriages, 1845-1963; marriage notice books for Magherafelt Presbytery, 1845-1946; session minutes, 1818-56; committee minutes, 1848, 1852-3 and 1911-45; list of elders in 1828; ministers' visitation books, 1823-32 and 1841; ministers' diaries, 1833-54; ministers' account book, 1889-1904; history of the congregation prepared in 1853.

C.R. 3/13; D.2725/6; D.1926/1-2

Baptisms, 1703-06 and 1771-80; marriages, 1769-82.

In Presbyterian Historical Society

P. Union Road, Magherafelt
Baptisms and marriages, 1867-.

In local custody

R.C. Magherafelt (Armagh diocese)
[The Roman Catholic parish of Magherafelt includes the
parish of Magherafelt, part of Ballyscullion parish and
part of Desertlyn parish]

Baptisms, 1834-80; marriages, 1834-81.   **MIC.1D/30-31**

MAGHERAGALL, CO. ANTRIM

C.I. Magheragall (Connor diocese)
Baptisms, 1776-1820 and 1825-76; marriages, 1772-84
and 1825-45; burials, 1772-81 and 1825-78; vestry
minutes, 1771-1870.   **MIC.1/75A-76;**
                                                          T.679/53

Miscellaneous papers, 1641-1931.   **T.1398**

Notes by Canon Dundas relating to the history of
Magheragall, c.1930.   **T.1349**

Baptisms, 1877-; marriages, 1845-; burials, 1878-; vestry
minutes, 1871-; registers of vestrymen, 1870-;
confirmations, 1976-.   **In local custody**

M. Magheragall
Baptisms, 1827-1975; marriages, 1871-1931; circuit
schedule book, 1923-36.   **MIC.1E/61**

P. Magheragall
Baptisms, 1878-1903; marriages, 1845-1911; committee
minutes, 1883-1929; session minutes, 1909-20.   **MIC.1P/81; C.R. 3/45**

R.C. [Magheragall is part of the Roman Catholic parish of
Blaris or Lisburn - *see under* **BLARIS**]

MAGHERAHAMLET, CO. DOWN

C.I. Magherahamlet (Dromore diocese)
[Earliest registers destroyed in Dublin].

Extracts from parish registers, 1823-63.   **DIO./1/14/5**

Baptisms, 1881-; marriages, 1845-; burials, 1883-; vestry
minutes, 1819-; preachers' book, 1884-; confirmations,
1892-; register of vestrymen, 1925-.   **In local custody**

P. Magherahamlet
Baptisms, 1831-1986; marriages, 1832-1936; deaths, 1909;
committee minutes, 1886-1912.   **MIC.1P/300**

Session book with lists of communicants, 1825-81.   **D.2487/1**

R.C. Ballynahinch and Dunmore
[Includes Magherahamlet parish - *see under*
MAGHERADROOL]

MAGHERALIN, COS DOWN and ARMAGH

C.I. Magheralin (Dromore diocese)
Baptisms, 1692-1871; marriages, 1692-1782 and
1785-1845; burials, 1692-1863; vestry minutes,
1692-1902.   MIC.1/18;
                                                     T.679/365-380

Extracts from diocesan records relating to Magheralin
parish, 1600-1850.   MIC.35

Extracts from parish registers, 1784-1853.   DIO.1/14/6

Subscription list relating to the building of the church,
c.1840; pew register, 1844.   T.1571

Baptisms, 1872-; marriages, 1845-; burials, 1864-;
churchwardens' accounts, 1766-94 and 1862-72; cess
applotment, 1834; registers of vestrymen, 1870-;
preachers' books, 1873-.   In local custody

R.C. Magheralin and Moira (Dromore diocese)
Baptisms, 1815-81; marriages, 1815-82; deaths, 1815-80.   MIC.1D/26

MAGHERALLY, CO. DOWN

C.I. Magherally (Dromore diocese)
[Earliest registers destroyed in Dublin]

Preachers' books, 1899-1954; Sunday School attendance
book, 1845-65.   D.2949/1

Extracts from parish registers, 1784-91 and 1828-65. DIO.1/14/7

Baptisms, 1880-; marriages, 1845-; burials, 1880-;
register of vestrymen, 1885-; preachers' books, 1883-. In local custody

P. Magherally
Baptisms, 1837-57 and 1860-77 [no baptisms exist from
1877-1900]; marriages, 1845-96; account books relating
to stipend, collections and expenses, 1788-1859; session
minutes, 1825-35; lists of committed members, 1818,
1833 and 1839; list of stipend payers, 1820-22.   MIC.1P/211;
                                                     T.2551/10-11

R.C. [Magherally parish is in the Roman Catholic parish of
Tullylish - *see under* **TULLYLISH**]

**MAGHERAMASON PRESBYTERIAN CHURCH,
CO. TYRONE**
   [*see under* **DONAGHEDY**]

MAGHERAMESK, CO. ANTRIM

   C.I. Magheramesk (Connor diocese)
      [*see under* **AGHALEE**]

   R.C. [Magheramesk parish forms part of the Roman Catholic
      parish of Blaris - *see under* **BLARIS**]

**MAGHERAMORNE PRESBYTERIAN CHURCH,
CO. ANTRIM**
   [*see under* **GLYNN**]

MAGHEROSS, CO. MONAGHAN

   C.I. Ardragh (St Patrick's) (Clogher diocese)
      Baptisms, 1865-71; marriages, 1869-1942; burials,
      1869-1984.   MIC.1/172

   C.I. Carrickmacross or Magheross (Clogher diocese)
      Baptisms, 1796-1984; marriages, 1798-1920; burials,
      1798-1983; preachers' books, 1834-75; accounts,
      1825-36; clothing fund book, 1859-82; poor collection
      and expenditure book, 1852-70; notes on parishioners,
      1883-1910.   MIC.1/173

      Minute book of Carrickmacross Men's Society, 1910-14,
      continued as a rector's visitation book, 1915-42.   D.2222/9

   P. Corvalley or Carrickmaclin
      Baptisms, 1832-1955; marriages, 1838-1955; session
      minutes, 1848-84.   MIC.1P/214

   R.C. Machaire Rois (Carrickmacross) (Clogher diocese)
      Baptisms, 1858-70 and 1878-80; marriages, 1838-44 and
      1858-81.   MIC.1D/21

MAGILLIGAN OR TAMLAGHTARD, CO. LONDONDERRY

   C.I. Tamlaghtard (Derry diocese)
      Baptisms, 1747-68, 1817-18, 1831-9 and 1844-1961;
      marriages, 1747-53, 1820-26 and 1832-4; burials,
      1768-75, 1824-9, 1832-4, 1837 and 1844-1962; vestry
      minutes, 1747-1897; list of the poor, 1773; census, 1843.   MIC.1/86

      Statistical account of the parish, 1824.   T.3239/1

Registers of vestrymen, 1870-; preachers' books, 1864-8,
1875-80 and 1902-.   **In local custody**

P. Magilligan
    Baptisms, 1814-1920; marriages, 1814-1923; some deaths,
    1890s; session and committee minutes, 1823-8; session
    minutes, 1872-7 and 1899-1905; list of committee
    members, 1814-45; lists of communicants, 1854-1911;
    details on the founding of the church, 1813-76; a census
    of the congregation, c.1850, with details up to 1876.   **MIC.1P/215**

R.C. Tamlaghtard or Magilligan and part of Aghanloo
    (Derry diocese)

    Baptisms, 1863-81; marriages, 1863-81; deaths,
    1863-80.   **MIC.1D/56**

**MAGUIRESBRIDGE CHURCH OF IRELAND PARISH,
CO. FERMANAGH**
    [*see under* **AGHALURCHER**]

**MAGUIRESBRIDGE METHODIST CHURCH,
CO. FERMANAGH**
    [*see under* **AGHALURCHER**]

**MAGUIRESBRIDE PRESBYTERIAN CHURCH,
CO. FERMANAGH**
    [*see under* **AGHALURCHER**]

MAHON METHODIST CHURCH, CO. ARMAGH
    [*see under* **DRUMCREE**]

MALIN PRESBYTERIAN CHURCH, CO. DONEGAL
    [*see under* **CLONCA**]

MALL, THE, PRESBYTERIAN CHURCH, ARMAGH
    [*see under* **ARMAGH**]

MALLOW, METHODIST CHURCH, CO. CORK
    [*see under* **FERMOY**]

**MANORHAMILTON CHURCH OF IRELAND PARISH,
CO. LEITRIM**
    [*see under* **CLOONCLARE**]

**MANORHAMILTON METHODIST CIRCUIT,
CO. LEITRIM**
[*see under* **CLOONCLARE**]

MARKETHILL METHODIST CHURCH, CO. ARMAGH
[*see under* **MULLAGHBRACK**]

**MARKETHILL (1ST and 2ND) PRESBYTERIAN CHURCH,
CO. ARMAGH**
[*see under* **MULLAGHBRACK**]

MARYBOROUGH, Co. LEIX (QUEEN'S COUNTY)

  M. Maryborough
    Baptisms, 1846-54.   MIC.429/1/124

MAYNE METHODIST CHURCH, CO. TYRONE
[*see under* **CAPPAGH**]

MAZE PRESBYTERIAN CHURCH, CO. DOWN
[*see under* **BLARIS**]

MEENGLASS PARISH CHURCH, CO. DONEGAL
[*see under* **DONAGHMORE, CO. DONEGAL**]

MELLIFONT ROMAN CATHOLIC PARISH, CO. LOUTH
[*see under* **TULLYALLEN**]

MEVAGH, CO. DONEGAL

  C.I. Mevagh (Holy Trinity, Carrigart) (Raphoe diocese)
    Baptisms, 1876-1983; marriages, 1846-1908; burials,
    1877-1984; index to gravestone inscriptions and to
    Protestant families in the parish, compiled 1960.   MIC.1/193

  P. Carrigart
    Baptisms, 1844-1984; marriages, 1846-1954; communion
    roll, 1885-1984.   MIC.1P/216

  R.C. Mevagh (Carrigart) (Raphoe diocese)
    Baptisms, 1871-8.   MIC.1D/87

**MIDDLETOWN CHURCH OF IRELAND PARISH,
CO. ARMAGH**
[*see under* **TYNAN**]

MIDDLETOWN PRESBYTERIAN CHURCH, CO. ARMAGH
　　[*see under* **TYNAN**]

**MILFORD CHURCH OF IRELAND PARISH,
CO. DONEGAL**
　　[*see under* **AUGHNISH**]

MILFORD PRESBYTERIAN CHURCH, CO. DONEGAL
　　[*see under* **TULLYFERN**]

**MILFORD REFORMED PRESBYTERIAN CHURCH,
CO. DONEGAL**
　　[*see under* **TULLYFERN**]

MILLISLE PRESBYTERIAN CHURCH, CO. DOWN
　　[*see under* **DONAGHADEE**]

**MILLROW (OR 1ST) PRESBYTERIAN CHURCH,
CO. ANTRIM**
　　[*see under* **ANTRIM**]

**MILLTOWN CHURCH OF IRELAND PARISH,
CO. ARMAGH**
　　[*see under* **TARTARAGHAN**]

MINTERBURN PRESBYTERIAN CHURCH, CO. TYRONE
　　[*see under* **AGHALOO**]

MOHILL, CO. LEITRIM

　M. Mohill
　　　　[Later known as Ballinamore and Newtowngore]

　　　　Baptisms, 1882-1961; marriages, 1888-1905; quarterly
　　　　meeting minute books, 1897-1936.　　　　　　　　　　**MIC.1E/55**

MOIRA, CO. DOWN

　C.I. Kilwarlin
　　　　[Partly in Moira parish - *see under* **HILLSBOROUGH**]

　C.I. Moira (Dromore diocese)
　　　　Baptisms, 1725-56 and 1823-71; marriages, 1725-56 and
　　　　1823-45; burials, 1725-56 and 1823-77; vestry minutes,
　　　　1758-1899; minute book, 1725-55; accounts, 1745-8.　　**MIC.1/79-80**

Extracts from parish registers, 1784-1860.   **DIO.1/14/8**

Plan of Moira graveyard with reference table, c.1925.   **T.2645/1**

Registers of vestrymen, 1870-; preachers' books, 1885-.   **In local custody**

M. Moira
Baptisms, 1827-44.   **MIC.429/1/496**

Baptisms, 1827-; marriages, 1843-.   **In local custody**

P. Moira
Baptisms, 1866-; marriages, 1845-.   **In local custody**

R.C. [Moira parish is part of the Roman Catholic parish of
Magheralin and Moira - *see under* **MAGHERALIN**]

MONAGHAN, CO. MONAGHAN

C.I. Monaghan (Clogher diocese)
Baptisms, 1802-1907; marriages, 1802-1918; burials,
1802-45.   **MIC.1/248**

Burials, 1846-; vestry minutes, 1802-; register of
vestrymen, 1870-; preachers' books, 1857-.   **In local custody**

M. Castleblaney and Monaghan
Baptisms, 1838-42.   **MIC.429/1/179**

P. 1st Clontibret
Baptisms, 1825-98; marriages, 1827-42 and 1845-1919.   **MIC.1P/176**

P. 1st Monaghan
Baptisms, 1821-31 and 1861-1983; marriages, 1821-31,
1834 and 1845-1907; census, 1821.   **MIC.1P/199**

R.C. Monaghan (St Macartan's Cathedral) (Clogher diocese)
Baptisms, 1835-47 and 1849-81, with an index;
marriages, 1827-80; plans of the cathedral, c.1850.   **MIC.1D/13; C.R. 2/6**

Account book containing baptisms, marriages and
funerals, 1865-86.   **DIO.(RC)1/11D**

MONAGHAN (2ND) PRESBYTERIAN CHURCH,
CO. MONAGHAN
[*see under* **TEDAVNET**]

MONASTERBOICE, CO. LOUTH

R.C. Monasterboice (Armagh diocese)
[Formerly Ballymakenny]

Baptisms, 1814-30 and 1834-81; marriages, 1814-72;
deaths, 1814-50, with gaps, and some for 1857-8 and
1876-7.   **MIC.1D/51-52**

MONELLAN CHURCH OF IRELAND CHAPEL OF EASE, CO. DONEGAL
[*see under* **DONAGHMORE, CO. DONEGAL**]

MONEYDIG PRESBYTERIAN CHURCH, CO. LONDONDERRY
[*see under* **DESERTOGHILL**]

MONEYMORE (1ST and 2ND) PRESBYTERIAN CHURCHES, CO. LONDONDERRY
[*see under* **ARTREA**]

MONEYREAGH NON-SUBSCRIBING PRESBYTERIAN CHURCH, CO. DOWN
[*see under* **COMBER**]

MONKSTOWN, CO. DUBLIN

C.I. Monkstown (Dublin diocese)
Extracts from parish registers, 1685-1860.   **T.921/1**

Extracts from parish registers, 1669-1800.   **T.808/15028, 15032, 15034-15035**

MONREAGH PRESBYTERIAN CHURCH, CO. DONEGAL
[*see under* **TAUGHBOYNE**]

MONTIAGHS, CO. ARMAGH

C.I. Moyntaghs or Ardmore (Dromore diocese)
Baptisms, 1822-37 and 1842-75; marriages, 1823-45;
burials, 1822-79.   **MIC.1/79; T.679/39**

Extracts from parish registers, 1789-1863.   **DIO.1/14/9**

Vestry minutes, 1822-1933; registers of vestrymen,
1874-1905 and 1917-; preachers' books, 1874-.   **In local custody**

M. Bannfoot
Baptisms, 1823-1950; marriages, 1864-1918; circuit
schedule books, 1867-1909; registers of members,
1819-1905; quarterly leaders' meetings minute books,
1867-1915.   **MIC.1E/33**

P. Bellville
    Baptisms, 1863-1980; marriages, 1875-1934.   **MIC.1P/271**

R.C. [Montiaghs parish is part of the Roman Catholic parish of
    Seagoe - *see under* **SEAGOE**]

MOSSIDE PRESBYTERIAN CHURCH, CO. ANTRIM
    [*see under* **BILLY**]

MOSSTOWN CHURCH OF IRELAND PARISH, CO. LOUTH
    [*see under* **COLLON**]

**MOUNTCHARLES CHURCH OF IRELAND PARISH,
CO. DONEGAL**
    [*see under* **INVER**]

**MOUNTFIELD CHURCH OF IRELAND CHURCH,
CO. TYRONE**
    [*see under* **CAPPAGH**]

MOUNTJOY PRESBYTERIAN CHURCH, CO. TYRONE
    [*see under* **CAPPAGH**]

**MOUNTNORRIS PRESBYTERIAN CHURCH,
CO. ARMAGH**
    [*see under* **LOUGHGILLY**]

**MOUNTRATH METHODIST CHURCH, CO. LEIX
(QUEEN'S COUNTY)**
    [*see under* **CLONENAGH and CLONAGHEEN**]

MOURNE PRESBYTERIAN CHURCH, CO. DOWN
    [*see under* **KILKEEL**]

MOURNE ROMAN CATHOLIC PARISH, CO. TYRONE
    [*see under* **LECKPATRICK**]

**MOURNE (LOWER) ROMAN CATHOLIC PARISH,
CO. DOWN**
    [*see under* **KILKEEL**]

MOVILLE LOWER, CO. DONEGAL

C.I. Moville Lower (St Columb's) and St Finian's, Greencastle (Raphoe diocese)

Baptisms, 1876-1982, with gaps (St Columb's and St Finian's); marriages, 1867-1955, (St Columb's); marriages, 1845-1933 (St Finian's); vestry minutes, 1783-1918; preachers' book containing Sunday School returns for both churches, 1853-62; lists of confirmations, 1853, 1857 and 1861; tithe applotment, 1830-32; lists of parishioners, 1812 and 1820; history of the parish of Lower and Upper Moville with lists of prebendaries and incumbents, 1781-1923, compiled c.1930.　　　　**MIC.1/138**

Burials, 1893-.　　　　**In local custody**

R.C. Moville (Derry diocese)
Baptisms and marriages, 1847-80; deaths, 1847-54.　　　　**MIC.1D/55**

MOVILLE UPPER, CO. DONEGAL

C.I. Moville Upper (Raphoe diocese)
Baptisms, 1804-1981; marriages, 1814-1931; burials, 1815-1981, with some entries for 1812 and 1813; register, of church members and emigration details, 1870-1942; confirmation registers, 1886-1944; publication of banns, 1814-29 and 1833-91.　　　　**MIC.1/139; T.1823/4**

List of clergymen, 1615-1870.　　　　**DIO.3/26**

P. Moville
Baptisms, 1833-1984; marriages, 1845-1956; marriage notice books, 1845-1984.　　　　**MIC.1P/241; MIC.1P230/2B**

R.C. [*see under* **MOVILLE LOWER**]

MOY CHURCH OF IRELAND PARISH, CO. TYRONE
[*see under* **CLONFEACLE**]

MOY METHODIST CHURCH, CO. TYRONE
[*see under* **CLONFEACLE**]

MOY PRESBYTERIAN CHURCH, CO. TYRONE
[*see under* **CLONFEACLE**]

MOY ROMAN CATHOLIC CHAPEL, CO. TYRONE
[*see under* **CLONFEACLE**]

MOYBOLOGUE, COS CAVAN AND MEATH

R.C. Moybologue and Kilmainham Wood
[*see under* **KILMAINHAM**]

MUCKAMORE, GRANGE OF, CO. ANTRIM

C.I. Muckamore (Connor diocese)
Baptisms, 1847-71; burials, 1848-1921.   **T.679/55-56**

Baptisms, 1872-; marriages, 1853-; vestry minutes, 1884-;
register of vestrymen, 1870-1954.   **In local custody**

P. Muckamore
Baptisms, 1861-1985; marriages, 1845-1936.   **MIC.1P/277**

MUCKNO, CO. MONAGHAN

C.I. Muckno (Clogher diocese)
Baptisms, 1810-1983; marriages, 1811-1919; marriage
notice book, 1871-1973; burials, 1811-1976; vestry
minutes, 1802-1948; parochial accounts, 1895-1916;
accounts, 1882-5; confirmation roll, 1882-1983.   **MIC.1/151**

M. Castleblaney and Monaghan
Baptisms, 1838-42.   **MIC.429/1/179**

P. 1st Castleblaney
Baptisms, 1827-1934; marriages, 1829-38 and 1845-1922.   **MIC.1P/196**

P. 2nd Castleblaney or Frankford
Baptisms, 1820-1981; marriages, 1845-1916; list of
ministers, 1755-1956.   **MIC.1P/191**

R.C. Muckno (Castleblaney) (Clogher diocese)
Baptisms and marriages, 1835-81.   **MIC.1D/19-20**

MUCKROSS CHURCH OF IRELAND PARISH, CO. FERMANAGH
[*see under* **TEMPLECARN**]

MUFF, CO. DONEGAL

C.I. Muff (Derry diocese)
Baptisms, 1837-1986; marriages, 1837-1956; burials,
1847-75.   **MIC.1/249**

Vestry minutes, 1856-; church wardens' accounts, 1873-;
register of vestrymen, 1872-; preachers' books, 1851-.   **In local custody**

P. Greenbank
    Baptisms, 1862-1985; marriages, 1864-1932.   **MIC.1P/240**

P. Knowhead
    Baptisms, 1826-1948; marriages, 1846-1909; session
    minutes, 1855-1935; committee minutes, 1856-1918.   **MIC.1P/238**

R.C. Iskaheen (Derry diocese)
    Baptisms, 1858-80.   **MIC.1D/55**

MULLAGH, CO. CAVAN

C.I. Mullagh (Kilmore diocese)
    Baptisms, 1877-1984; marriages, 1846-1948; burials,
    1877-1980; vestry minutes, 1826-70; collection book for
    services held in Graughlough School houses, 1879-1909,
    with a list of preachers, 1876-7, and a list of members of
    Mullagh Temperance Society, c.1900; accounts,
    1870-1900.   **MIC.1/254, 261**

R.C. Mullagh (Kilmore diocese)
    Baptisms, 1760-90; marriages, 1766-89.   **MIC.1D/82**

    Baptisms and marriages, 1842-72; deaths, 1842-57.   **MIC.1D/80**

MULLAGHBAWN ROMAN CATHOLIC CHURCH, CO. ARMAGH
    [*see under* **FORKHILL**]

MULLAGHBRACK, CO. ARMAGH

C.I. Clare (Armagh diocese)
    [Partly in Mullaghbrack parish - *see under*
    BALLYMORE]

C.I. Kilcluney (Armagh diocese)
    [Part of Mullaghbrack parish before 1794 - *see under*
    MULLAGHBRACK below]

    Baptisms, 1821-; marriages, 1835-; burials, 1837-.   **In local custody**

C.I. Mullabrack (Armagh diocese)
    [Earliest registers destroyed in Dublin i.e. baptisms,
    1737-63 and 1813-75, marriages, 1737-63 and 1812-45,
    and burials, 1737-60 and 1813-74]

    Baptisms, 1764-83 and 1799-1803; marriages, 1767-83
    and 1798-1811; vestry minutes, 1764-89 and 1826-1905;
    preachers' books, 1842-74 and 1907-21; subscription

book, 1901-22; Sunday School attendance book, 1917-32;
notes on families in Mullaghbrack parish, 1847-51.

**MIC.1/83-85;
T.1075/19;
T.636/153-156**

Extracts from baptisms, marriages and deaths relating to
the Beck family, 1804-48.

T.1202/1

Baptisms and burials, 1875-1935; marriages, 1845-1935.

In local custody

M. Markethill [Wesleyan Methodists]
   Marriages, 1866-1918.

MIC.1E/4

   Baptisms, 1830-.

In local custody

P. 1st Markethill
   Baptisms, 1843-89; marriages, 1845-1936.

**MIC.1P/428;
T.2853/3-5**

P. 2nd Markethill
   Baptisms, 1821-1926; marriages, 1821-1924; communion
   roll, c.1860-c.1907.

**MIC.1P/429;
T.2853/1**

R.C. [Partly in the Roman Catholic parish of Ballymore and
      Mullabrack (Tandragee) and partly in Ballymacnabb
      (Kilcluney) - *see under* **BALLYMORE** and
      KILCLOONEY]

**MULLAGHDUN CHURCH OF IRELAND PARISH,
CO. FERMANAGH**
   [*see under* **CLEENISH**]

**MULLAGHFAD CHURCH OF IRELAND PARISH,
CO. FERMANAGH**
   [*see under* **AGHALURCHER**]

**MULLAGLASS CHURCH OF IRELAND PARISH,
CO. ARMAGH**
   [*see under* **KILLEVY**]

**MULLANADARAGH ROMAN CATHOLIC CHURCH,
CO. LEITRIM**
   [*see under* **CARRIGALLEN**]

**MULLARTOWN CHURCH OF IRELAND CHURCH,
CO. DOWN**
   [*see under* **KILKEEL**]

**MULLAVILLY CHURCH OF IRELAND PARISH,
CO. ARMAGH**
[*see under* **KILMORE, CO. ARMAGH**]

**MULVIN REFORMED PRESBYTERIAN CHURCH,
CO. TYRONE**
[*see under* **ARDSTRAW**]

MUNTERCONNAUGHT, CO. CAVAN

C.I. Munterconnaught (Kilmore diocese)
[*see also under* **LURGAN**]

Baptisms, 1857-1901; marriages, 1845-99; burials,
1878-1901; vestry minutes with accounts, 1861-1900;
lists of vestrymen, 1888, 1896, 1898-9, 1901 and 1903-04.   **MIC.1/259**

R.C. [Munterconnaught parish is part of the Roman Catholic
parish of Castlerahan and Munterconnaught - *see under*
CASTLERAHAN]

**MYROE, ST JOHN THE BAPTIST, CHAPEL OF EASE,
CO. LONDONDERRY**
[*see under* **TAMLAGHT FINLAGAN**]

MYROE PRESBYTERIAN CHURCH, CO. LONDONDERRY
[*see under* **TAMLAGHT FINLAGAN**]

NAAS, CO. KILDARE

P. Naas
Marriages, 1861-1930.   **MIC.1P/12**

**NEWBLISS CHURCH OF IRELAND PARISH,
CO. MONAGHAN**
[*see under* **KILLEEVAN** and *see also under* **AGHABOG**]

NEWBLISS PRESBYTERIAN CHURCH, CO. MONAGHAN
[*see under* **KILLEEVAN**]

NEWCASTLE CHURCH OF IRELAND PARISH, CO. DOWN
[*see under* **KILCOO**]

NEWCASTLE METHODIST CHURCH, CO. DOWN
[*see under* **KILCOO**]

NEWCASTLE PRESBYTERIAN CHURCH, CO. DOWN
   [*see under* **KILCOO**]

NEWCASTLE ROMAN CATHOLIC CHURCH, CO. DOWN
   [*see under* **MAGHERA, CO. DOWN**]

NEWMILLS PRESBYTERIAN CHURCH, CO. DOWN
   [*see under* **TULLYLISH**]

NEWMILLS PRESBYTERIAN CHURCH, CO. TYRONE
   [*see under* **TULLYNISKAN**]

**NEW ROW, COLERAINE, PRESBYTERIAN CHURCH,
CO. LONDONDERRY**
   [*see under* **COLERAINE**]

NEWRY, COS DOWN and ARMAGH

  C.I. Newry (formerly St Patrick's and then St Mary's)
     (Dromore diocese)

     Baptisms, 1804-14, 1817, 1819 and 1822-94; marriages
     1784-1963; burials, 1824-76; index to baptisms,
     marriages and burials, 1784-c.1910; vestry minutes,
     1775-1948; select vestry minutes, 1877-1909; registers
     of vestrymen, 1870-1935; preachers' books, 1878-1957;
     registers of pews occupied, 1886-1926, and of
     subscribers, 1886-1959.   **MIC.1/46-48; D.2034**

  C.I. St Patrick's (Dromore diocese)
     [Restored as a chapel of ease and became a separate
     parish in 1870]

     Baptisms, 1847-1926; burials, 1862-1919.   **MIC.1/120; D.2034**
     [For marriages, *see above*]

  M. Newry
     Baptisms, 1826-44.   **MIC.429/1/410**

     Baptisms, 1830-; marriages, 1892-.   **In local custody**

  N.S.P. Newry
     Baptisms, 1779-97, 1809-63, 1900, 1909-12 and
     1934; marriages, 1781-95, 1809-45 and 1892; list of
     communicants, 1810-42; minutes and accounts, 1877-98
     and 1938-66, with lists of pew holders, c.1820; notes on
     ministers and the congregation, c.1690-1909. **C.R.4/1, 3; T.699/7**

P. Katesbridge
[United with Ballydown in 1938]

Baptisms, 1866-1929; marriages, 1867-1935; lists of
communicants, 1867, 1869-70, 1873 and 1876-1901;
session minutes, 1872, 1876 and 1899; deaths, 1909-41. **MIC.1P/170**

P. 1st Newry
[*see also under* Non-Subscribing Presbyterian Church
above]

Baptisms, 1829-; marriages, 1830-. **In local custody**

P. Newry, Downshire Road
Baptisms, 1849-1965; marriages, 1845-1909;
communicants' roll, 1884-99. **MIC.1P/106**

P. Ryans
Baptisms, 1851-. **In local custody**

R.C. Newry (Dromore diocese)
Baptisms, 1818-84; index to baptisms, 1858-; marriages,
1820-1917; funerals, 1818-62. **MIC.1D/26-28**

NEWTOWNARDS, CO. DOWN

C.I. Newtownards (Down diocese)
[Earliest registers destroyed in Dublin]

Baptisms, 1884-; marriages, 1845-; vestry minutes,
1909-; registers of vestrymen, 1870-; preachers' book,
1897-. **In local custody**

M. Regent Street, Newtownards [Wesleyan Methodists]
Baptisms, 1870-1945; marriages, 1863-1963; account
books, 1854-1956; minutes of leaders' meetings,
1850-1926; circuit schedule books, 1870-1936; membership
registers and quarterly class rolls, 1899-1943. **D.2687**

M. Zion, Newtownards [Methodist New Connexion]
Baptisms, 1847-68, 1880-93 and 1901-06; marriages,
1864-1907; treasurers' account book, 1901-07; minutes of
quarterly meetings, 1866-1901, with accounts, 1869-1905,
and lists of members, 1869-1905; minutes of leaders'
meetings, 1834-54, with seatholders' accounts, 1839-57;
circuit schedule books, 1905-36. **D.2687**

N.S.P. Newtownards
Baptisms, 1827-1978; marriages, 1827-1919; deaths,
1898-1923; minutes, 1888-1923; history of the
congregation, c.1638-c.1919. **C.R. 4/7**

P. Ballyblack
 Baptisms, 1821-1948; marriages, 1820-1915; deaths,
 1821-52; communicants' roll book, 1869-89; session
 minutes, 1821-43; transfer certificates, 1824-8; census,
 1821-39; collections, subscriptions and accounts, 1822-49.   **MIC.1P/318**

P. 1st Newtownards
 Marriages, 1845-1909; marriage notice books, 1879-1906.   **MIC.1P/390;**
                                                                    MIC.1P/230/6

 Baptisms, 1833-.   **In local custody**

P. 2nd Newtownards
 Baptisms, 1832-1940; marriages, 1833-42; marriage notice
 books, 1879-1906; communion roll, 1876-1929.   **MIC.1P/333;**
                                                                    MIC.1P/230/6

P. 4th Newtownards
 Baptisms, 1854-1906; marriages, 1855-1905.   **MIC.1P/389**

P. Greenwell Street, Newtownards
 Baptisms, 1866-99 and 1946; marriages, 1870-1903;
 marriage notice books, 1879-1906; index to marriages,
 1870-1936; deaths, 1821-52; list of members, c.1920;
 communion roll, 1909-10.   **MIC.1P/317; MIC.1P/**
                                                                    230/6; D.1195/1/50,69,
                                                                    125

P. Regent Street, Newtownards
 Baptisms, 1835-1961; marriages, 1835-1927; burials,
 1892-1901.   **T.2811**

P. Strean
 Baptisms, 1888-1943; marriages, 1867-1935.   **MIC.1P/361**

R.C. Newtownards (Down and Connor diocese)
 [Newtownards Roman Catholic parish consists of the
 parishes of Newtownards, Donaghadee, Comber,
 Dundonald and Bangor]

 Baptisms, 1864-81.   **MIC.1D/63**

R.P. Newtownards
 Account books, 1931-75; pledge book of the Total
 Abstinence Association, 1869-1906.   **C.R. 5/11**

NEWTOWNBARRY METHODIST CHURCH,
CO. WEXFORD
 [*see under* **ST MARY'S, NEWTOWNBARRY**]

NEWTOWNBREDA PRESBYTERIAN CHURCH,
CO. DOWN
 [*see under* **KNOCKBREDA**]

NEWTOWNBUTLER METHODIST CHURCH, CO. FERMANAGH
[*see under* GALLOON]

NEWTOWNBUTLER ROMAN CATHOLIC CHURCH, CO. FERMANAGH
[*see under* GALLOON]

NEWTOWN CROMMELIN, CO. ANTRIM

C.I. Newtown Crommelin (Connor diocese)
[Earliest registers destroyed in Dublin]

Baptisms, 1831-41 and 1873-1961; extracts from baptisms, 1841-79; burials, 1843-1955; extracts from burials, 1841-79; register of vestrymen, 1922-37.	**MIC.1/123, 299**
Copy of baptisms, 1843-73; marriages, 1832-7 (1839-41 and 1845-1930 in baptism register); vestry minutes, 1829-; cess applotment, 1833; preachers' books, 1872-1923 and 1925-.	**In local custody**

P. Newtowncrommelin
Baptisms, 1835-1954; marriages, 1836-99; session minutes, 1836-76; communicants' roll, 1861.　　　　**MIC.1P/319**

R.C. Glenravel and Braid (Down and Connor diocese)
[Includes Newtown Crommelin parish - *see under* DUNAGHY]

NEWTOWNCUNNINGHAM CHURCH OF IRELAND PARISH, CO. DONEGAL
[*see under* ALL SAINTS]

NEWTOWNCUNNINGHAM PRESBYTERIAN CHURCH, CO. DONEGAL
[*see under* ALL SAINTS]

NEWTOWNGORE CHURCH OF IRELAND PARISH, CO. LEITRIM
[*see under* CARRIGALLEN]

NEWTOWNGORE METHODIST CHURCH, CO. LEITRIM
[*see under* CARRIGALLEN]

NEWTOWNHAMILTON, CO. ARMAGH

C.I. Newtownhamilton (Armagh diocese)
[Earliest registers destroyed in Dublin, c.1825-c.1875]

Baptisms, 1823-6.

T.1075/15;
T.808/14963

Baptisms, 1871-; marriages, 1845-; burials, 1876-; vestry
minutes, 1877-; preachers' books, 1845-.

In local custody

P. Clarkesbridge
Baptisms, 1822-50; marriages, 1840-45; communicants,
1822 and 1862.

T.2523

P. 1st Newtownhamilton
Baptisms, 1822-1954.

**In Presbyterian
Historical Society**

P. 2nd Newtownhamilton
Baptisms and marriages, 1823-.

In local custody

R.C. [Newtownhamilton parish forms part of the Roman
Catholic parish of Lower Creggan - *see under*
CREGGAN]

NEWTOWNKELLY METHODIST CHURCH, CO. TYRONE
[*see under* **DONAGHENRY**]

**NEWTOWNSAVILLE CHURCH OF IRELAND PARISH,
CO. TYRONE**
[*see under* **CLOGHER, CO. TYRONE**]

**NEWTOWNSTEWART METHODIST CHURCH,
CO. TYRONE**
[*see under* **ARDSTRAW**]

**NEWTOWNSTEWART (1ST and 2ND) PRESBYTERIAN
CHURCH, CO. TYRONE**
[*see under* **ARDSTRAW**]

NILTEEN, GRANGE OF, CO. ANTRIM
[*see under* **DONEGORE**]

**OLD RANDALSTOWN PRESBYTERIAN CHURCH,
CO. ANTRIM**
[*see under* **DRUMMAUL**]

**OMAGH (1ST and 2ND) PRESBYTERIAN CHURCHES,
CO. TYRONE**
[*see under* **DRUMRAGH**]

OMAGH METHODIST CHURCH, CO. TYRONE
  [*see under* **DRUMRAGH**]

OMAGH ROMAN CATHOLIC CHURCH, CO. TYRONE
  [*see under* **DRUMRAGH**]

OMEATH CHURCH OF IRELAND PARISH, CO. LOUTH
  [*see under* **CARLINGFORD**]

ORRITOR PRESBYTERIAN CHURCH, CO. TYRONE
  [*see under* **KILDRESS**]

OUGHTERAGH, CO. LEITRIM

  R.C. Oughteragh (Ballinamore) (Kilmore diocese)
    Baptisms, 1869-81; marriages, 1870-81.   **MIC.1D/79-80**

PETTIGO METHODIST CHURCH, CO. FERMANAGH
  [*see under* **DRUMKEERAN**]

PETTIGO PRESBYTERIAN CHURCH, CO. FERMANAGH
  [*see under* **DRUMKEERAN**]

PETTIGO ROMAN CATHOLIC PARISH, CO. DONEGAL
  [*see under* **TEMPLECARN**]

POMEROY, CO. TYRONE

  B. Lisnaglear
    [*see under* **DERRYLORAN**]

  C.I. Altedesert
    [Partly also in Desertcreat parish]

    Baptisms, 1877-; marriages, 1846-; burials, 1877-; vestry
    minutes, 1852-.   **In local custody**

  C.I. Pomeroy (Armagh diocese)
    [Earliest registers destroyed in Dublin]

    Baptisms, 1876-; marriages, 1845-; burials, 1876-;
    Sunday School roll book, 1899-1915.   **In local custody**

  P. Pomeroy
    Baptisms, 1841-1967; marriages, 1845-1936; session
    minutes, 1864-1967.   **MIC.1P/120**

R.C. Pomeroy (Armagh diocese)
Baptisms, 1837-52, 1857-65 and 1869-81; marriages, 1837-65 and 1869-82; deaths, 1837-40, 1857-61 and 1871-81.   **MIC.1D/36**

PORTADOWN CHURCH OF IRELAND PARISH (ST MARK'S), CO. ARMAGH
[*see under* **DRUMCREE**]

PORTADOWN METHODIST CHURCHES, CO. ARMAGH
[*see under* **DRUMCREE**]

PORTADOWN (1ST) PRESBYTERIAN CHURCH, CO. ARMAGH
[*see under* **SEAGOE**]

PORTADOWN (2ND) or ARMAGH ROAD, PORTADOWN PRESBYTERIAN CHURCH, CO. ARMAGH
[*see under* **DRUMCREE**]

PORTADOWN ROMAN CATHOLIC PARISH, CO. ARMAGH
[*see under* **DRUMCREE**]

PORTAFERRY METHODIST CHURCH, CO. DOWN
[*see under* **BALLYPHILIP**]

PORTAFERRY PRESBYTERIAN CHURCH, CO. DOWN
[*see under* **BALLYPHILIP**]

PORTAFERRY ROMAN CATHOLIC CHURCH, CO. DOWN
[*see under* **BALLYPHILIP**]

PORTCLARE (ST MARY'S) CHURCH OF IRELAND PARISH, CO. TYRONE
[*see under* **ERRIGAL TROUGH**]

PORTGLENONE, CO. ANTRIM

C.I. Portglenone (Connor diocese)
[Earliest registers destroyed in Dublin]

Baptisms, 1873-; marriages, 1845-1923 and 1927-32;
burials, 1877-1912; vestry minutes, 1879-; register of
vestrymen, 1870-; preachers' books, 1896-.   **In local custody**

P. 1st Portglenone
Baptisms, 1826-46 and 1852-1923; marriages, 1845-1933;
marriage notice books, 1859-1936; marriage licence books,
1906-20; marriage declarations, 1895-1920; consents for the
marriage of minors, 1908-43; marriage declarations in
cases of a minor, 1886-1918; committee minutes, 1869-75
and 1903-21; accounts, 1856-87 and 1912-31; session
minutes, 1903-20; communion rolls, 1859-1951.   **MIC.1P/24**

Marriage licences, 1845-56.   **D.2594/1**

P. 2nd Portglenone
Baptisms, 1821-67 and 1881-1910; marriages, 1822-1910;
session minutes, 1881-1901, with a list of communicants,
1880-83; temperance pledges, 1899-1900; communicants'
roll, 1886-96; Sunday School roll book, 1821-67;
stipend lists, 1829-34; stipend accounts, 1829-51.   **MIC.1P/357**

P. 3rd Portglenone
Baptisms, 1869-1944; marriages, 1845-1911;
communicants' roll book, 1869-1909.   **MIC.1P/334**

R.C. Portglenone (Down and Connor diocese)
Baptisms, 1864-81; marriages, 1864-82.   **MIC.1D/71**

PORTRUSH METHODIST CHURCH, CO. ANTRIM
[*see under* **BALLYWILLIN**]

PORTRUSH PRESBYTERIAN CHURCH, CO. ANTRIM
[*see under* **BALLYWILLIN**]

**PORTRUSH REFORMED PRESBYTERIAN CHURCH,
CO. ANTRIM**
[*see under* **BALLYWILLIN**]

PORTRUSH ROMAN CATHOLIC PARISH, CO. ANTRIM
[*see under* **BALLYWILLIN**]

**PORTSTEWART PRESBYTERIAN CHURCH,
CO. LONDONDERRY**
[*see under* **BALLYAGHRAN**]

POYNTZPASS BAPTIST CHURCH, CO. ARMAGH
[*see under* **BALLYMORE**]

POYNTZPASS PRESBYTERIAN CHURCH, CO. ARMAGH
[*see under* **BALLYMORE**]

**PRIESTHILL METHODIST NEW CONNEXION CHURCH
AND PRIESTHILL WESLEYAN METHODIST CHURCH,
CO. DOWN**
[*see under* **BLARIS**]

PUBBLE METHODIST CHURCH, CO. FERMANAGH
[*see under* **ENNISKILLEN**]

**QUEEN'S PARADE METHODIST CHURCH, BANGOR,
CO. DOWN**
[*see under* **BANGOR**]

QUIVVY CHURCH OF IRELAND PARISH, CO. CAVAN
[*see under* **DRUMLANE**]

RACAVAN, CO. ANTRIM

C.I. Skerry and Racavan (Connor diocese)
[*see under* **SKERRY**]

P. 1st Broughshane
Baptisms, 1827-32 and 1836-94; marriages, 1845-1905;
accounts, 1842-66; communicants' lists, 1845-53;
communicants' roll, 1871-91.   **MIC.1P/76**

P. 2nd Broughshane
Baptisms, 1868-1986; marriages, 1864-1906.   **MIC.1P/77**

P. Buckna
Baptisms, 1836-93; marriages, 1836-40 and 1845-1907;
communion roll, 1862-3, 1869 and 1880-82; pew rent book,
c.1890-1917.   **MIC.1P/322; T.859/1;
                                                 T.1389**

Index to baptisms, 1828-36 and 1841-65, and marriages,
1830 and 1845-99.   **T.3054/B/1**

R.C. Braid
Baptisms and marriages, 1878-81.   **MIC.1D/69A**

R.C. Glenravel and Braid (Down and Connor diocese)
Baptisms, 1825-56 and 1864-81; marriages, 1825-41,
1864-9 and 1878-82; funerals, 1825-41 and 1864-9.   **MIC.1D/70**

[Part of Racavan parish is in the Roman Catholic parish
of Ballymena - *see also under* **KIRKINRIOLA**]

RADEMON NON-SUBSCRIBING PRESBYTERIAN CHURCH, CO. DOWN
[*see under* **KILMORE, CO. DOWN**]

RAFFREY PRESBYTERIAN CHURCH, CO. DOWN
[*see under* **KILLINCHY**]

RAILWAY STREET PRESBYTERIAN CHURCH, LISBURN, CO. ANTRIM
[*see under* **BLARIS**]

RALOO, CO. ANTRIM

C.I. Raloo (Connor diocese)
[Earliest registers destroyed in Dublin]

Printed list of seatholders, with names of committee members, and income/expenditure for the year ending January 1872.　　　　D.1788/4

N.S.P. Raloo
Baptisms, 1859-; marriages, 1846-; congregation minute book, 1839-.　　　　**In local custody**

P. Raloo
Baptisms, 1842-1927; marriages, 1841-1900; lists of new communicants, 1859-82; pew register, c.1860; Sustentation Fund accounts recording names and payments, 1875.　　　　MIC.1P/354

R.C. Ballyclare (Down and Connor diocese)
[Raloo parish was formerly in the Roman Catholic parish of Larne and Carrickfergus - *see also under* **LARNE**, and then became part of the Roman Catholic parish of Ballyclare]

Baptisms, 1869-81; marriages, 1870-82.　　　　MIC.1D/63

RAMELTON (1ST, 2ND and 3RD) PRESBYTERIAN CHURCHES, CO. DONEGAL
[*see under* **AUGHNISH**]

RAMELTON METHODIST CIRCUIT and CHURCH, CO. DONEGAL
[*see under* **AUGHNISH**]

RAMOAN, CO. ANTRIM

C.I. Ramoan (Connor diocese)
[Earliest registers destroyed in Dublin]

[United to Culfeitrin before 1831]

Burials, 1805-31.   **MIC.1/109**

Baptisms, 1879-; marriages, 1845-; burials, 1879-; vestry
minutes, 1802-; churchwardens' accounts, 1872-94;
register of vestrymen, 1870-; preachers' books, 1838-47
and 1879-1935.   **In local custody**

M. Ballycastle
Marriages, 1865-1925.   **MIC.1E/63**

Baptisms, 1843.   **MIC.429/1/184**

P. Ballycastle
Baptisms, 1829-1967; marriages, 1829-44 and
1848-1922; census, 1846; committee minutes, 1827-1932;
session minutes, 1867-1953; communion roll, 1868-1922.   **MIC.1P/115**

P. Ramoan
[No pre-1900 baptisms exist]; marriages, 1845-1910.   **MIC.1P/366**

R.C. Ramoan (Ballycastle) (Down and Connor diocese)
Baptisms, 1838-81; marriages, 1838-83.   **MIC.1D/72**

RANDALSTOWN METHODIST CHURCH, CO. ANTRIM
[*see under* **DRUMMAUL**]

**RANDALSTOWN (1ST, 2ND and OLD) PRESBYTERIAN
CHURCHES, CO. ANTRIM**
[*see under* **DRUMMAUL**]

**RANDALSTOWN ROMAN CATHOLIC CHURCH,
CO. ANTRIM**
[*see under* **DRUMMAUL**]

RAPHOE, CO. DONEGAL

C.I. Raphoe (St Eunan's Cathedral) (Raphoe diocese)
Baptisms, 1771-83 and 1808-93; marriages, 1771-1896;
burials, 1771-83 and 1820-1900; register of vestrymen,
1870-1964; vestry book, 1673-1870; list of
communicants, 1820; cess lists, 1841-2; graveyard
inscription book, compiled in 1970.   **MIC.1/95, 143**

Preachers' books, 1842-.   **In local custody**

P. 1st Raphoe
Baptisms, 1829-1982; marriages, 1829-96.   **MIC.1P/1, 183**

P. 2nd Raphoe
Baptisms, 1860-1923; marriages, 1829-45 and 1860-1939.   **MIC.1P/1, 184**

R.C. Raphoe (Raphoe diocese)
Baptisms and marriages, 1876-81.   **MIC.1D/85**

RASHARKIN, CO. ANTRIM

C.I. Rasharkin (Connor diocese)
[Earliest registers destroyed in Dublin]

Baptisms, 1871-; marriages, 1845-; burials, 1878; vestry
minutes, 1902-; churchwardens' accounts, 1883-; register
of vestrymen, 1870-; preachers' book, 1901-.   **In local custody**

P. Killymurris
[Was originally 1st and 2nd Killymurris but united in 1884]

Baptisms, 1862-84 (1st); baptisms, 1878-84 (2nd);
baptisms, 1884-1925 (1st and 2nd); marriages,
1855-84 (2nd); marriages, 1887-1908 (1st and 2nd);
communion rolls, 1875 (1st) and 1888 (1st and 2nd).   **MIC.1P/309**

P. Rasharkin
Baptisms, 1834-1919; marriages, 1845-1919.   **MIC.1P/292**

R.C. Rasharkin (Down and Connor diocese)
[The Roman Catholic Parish of Rasharkin contains part
of the parishes of Finvoy and Rasharkin. The other part
of Rasharkin parish is in the Roman Catholic parish of
Dunloy and Cloughmills - *see under* **FINVOY**]

Baptisms and marriages, 1848-81.   **MIC.1D/72**

RASHEE, CO. ANTRIM

C.I. [*see under* **BALLYCOR**]

R.C. [Rashee parish forms part of the Roman Catholic parish
of Ballyclare - *see under* **RALOO**]

RATHASPICK, CO. WESTMEATH

C.I. Rathaspeck (Ardagh diocese)
Census for the united parish of Rathaspick and Russagh,
made by the Rev. H W Stewart, 1863-71.   **T.2786**

RATHFRILAND (1ST, 2ND and 3RD) PRESBYTERIAN CHURCHES, CO. DOWN
[*see under* **DRUMGATH**]

RATHFRILAND REFORMED PRESBYTERIAN CHURCH, CO. DOWN
[*see under* **DRUMGATH**]

RATHLIN ISLAND, CO. ANTRIM

C.I. Rathlin Island (Connor diocese)
[Earliest registers destroyed in Dublin]

Baptisms, 1845-1954; marriages, 1845-1922; burials, 1845-1962; vestry minutes, 1769-95.	**MIC.1/114; T.861; T.897**
Vestry minutes, 1911-34; churchwardens' accounts, 1932-4 and 1940-; register of vestrymen, 1911-34; preachers' book, 1908-34; receipt for Rev. Gage's institution, 1824.	**In local custody**

R.C. Rathlin Island (Down and Connor diocese)

Baptisms, 1856-80; marriages, 1857-80.	**MIC.1D/92**

RATHMULLAN, CO. DOWN

C.I. Killough (Down diocese)
[Earliest registers destroyed in Dublin]

Baptisms, 1893-; marriages, 1876-; burials, 1892-; vestry minutes, 1880-; register of vestrymen, 1870-; preachers' book, 1879-.	**In local custody**

C.I. Rathmullan (Down diocese)
[Earliest registers destroyed in Dublin]

Marriage notices, 1845-1957.	**D.1563**
Baptisms, 1876-; marriages, 1845-1935; burials, 1878-1928; vestry minutes, 1870-1924; register of vestrymen, 1870-.	**In local custody**

R.C. [Part of Rathmullan belongs to the Roman Catholic parish of Bright, Rossglass and Killough - *see under* **BRIGHT** and part belongs to Tyrella and Ballykinler - *see under* **TYRELLA**]

Baptisms and marriages, 1856-80.	**MIC.1D/74**

RATHMULLAN PRESBYTERIAN CHURCH, CO. DONEGAL
[*see under* **KILLYGARVAN**]

RATHMULLEN METHODIST CHURCH, CO. DONEGAL
[*see under* **KILLYGARVAN**]

**RAY (1ST and 2ND) PRESBYTERIAN CHURCHES,
CO. DONEGAL**
[*see under* **RAYMOGHY**]

RAYMOGHY, CO. DONEGAL

C.I. Raymochy (Raphoe diocese)
Baptisms, 1844-1986; marriages, 1845-83 and 1888-1952;
burials, 1878-1986; register of vestrymen, 1870-1986.   **MIC.1/284**

P. 1st Ray
Baptisms, 1855-1982; marriages, 1845-1928.   **MIC.1P/187**

P. 2nd Ray
Baptisms, 1882-1982; marriages, 1845-1937.   **MIC.1P/186**

R.C. [*see under* **ALL SAINTS**]

RAYMUNTERDONEY, CO. DONEGAL

C.I. Raymunterdoney (Myra Church) (Raphoe diocese)
Baptisms, 1878-1983; marriages, 1845-1955; burials,
1880-1983.   **MIC.1/161**

Vestry minutes, 1870-1934.   **In local custody**

R.C. [*see under* **TULLAGHOBEGLEY**]

REDROCK PRESBYTERIAN CHURCH, CO. ARMAGH
[*see under* **KILCLOONEY**]

**REGENT STREET, NEWTOWNARDS, METHODIST
CHURCH, CO. DOWN**
[*see under* **NEWTOWNARDS**]

**REGENT STREET, NEWTOWNARDS, PRESBYTERIAN
CHURCH, CO. DOWN**
[*see under* **NEWTOWNARDS**]

RICHHILL CHURCH OF IRELAND PARISH, CO. ARMAGH
[*see under* **KILMORE, CO. ARMAGH**]

RICHHILL CONGREGATIONAL CHURCH, CO. ARMAGH
[*see under* **KILMORE, CO. ARMAGH**]

RICHHILL METHODIST CHURCH, CO. ARMAGH
[*see under* **KILMORE, CO. ARMAGH**]

RICHHILL PRESBYTERIAN CHURCH, CO. ARMAGH
[*see under* **KILMORE, CO. ARMAGH**]

**RICHHILL RELIGIOUS SOCIETY OF FRIENDS,
CO. ARMAGH**
[*see under* **KILMORE, CO. ARMAGH**]

**RINGSEND PRESBYTERIAN CHURCH,
CO. LONDONDERRY**
[*see under* **AGHADOWEY**]

ROCK ROMAN CATHOLIC CHURCH, CO. ANTRIM
[*see under* **DERRYAGHY**]

**ROCKCORRY CHURCH OF IRELAND PARISH,
CO. MONAGHAN**
[*see under* **EMATRIS**]

ROCKCORRY METHODIST CHURCH, CO. MONAGHAN
[*see under* **EMATRIS**]

**ROCKCORRY PRESBYTERIAN CHURCH,
CO. MONAGHAN**
[*see under* **EMATRIS**]

ROSCREA, CO. TIPPERARY

 M. Roscrea
  Baptisms, 1830-42.   **MIC.429/1/83**

ROSEYARDS PRESBYTERIAN CHURCH, CO. ANTRIM
[*see under* **BALLYMONEY**]

ROSSGLASS ROMAN CATHOLIC CHURCH, CO. DOWN
[*see under* **BRIGHT**]

ROSSINVER, CO. LEITRIM

 C.I. Ballaghameehan (Kilmore diocese)
  Baptisms, 1877-1985; marriages, 1859-1936; burials,
  1877-1982.   **MIC.1/232**

C.I. Kiltyclogher
[Partly in Rossinver parish - *see under* **CLOONCLARE**]

C.I. Rossinver or Kinlough (Kilmore diocese)
Baptisms, 1876-1986; marriages, 1845-1944; burials,
1879-1983.   MIC.1/296

R.C. Glenade (Kilmore diocese)
Baptisms, 1867-81; marriages, 1873-80.   MIC.1D/77

R.C. Kinlough (Kilmore diocese)
Baptisms, 1835-81; marriages, 1840-81.   MIC.1D/77

R.C. Rossinver (Kilmore diocese)
Baptisms, 1851-75; marriages, 1844-70.
[Many pages missing]   MIC.1D/83

ROSLEA ROMAN CATHOLIC PARISH, CO. FERMANAGH
[*see under* **CLONES**]

ROSSNOWLAGH CHURCH OF IRELAND PARISH, CO. DONEGAL
[*see under* **DRUMHOME**]

ROSSORY, CO. FERMANAGH

C.I. Rossory (Clogher diocese)
Baptisms, 1796-7 and 1799-1956; marriages, 1799-1950;
burials, 1799-1923; vestry minutes, 1763-1870.   MIC.1/22; C.R. 1/45

Marriage notice book, 1845-70; burials, 1923-.   In local custody

R.C. [Rossory parish forms part of the Roman Catholic parish
of Enniskillen - *see under* **ENNISKILLEN**]

ROSTREVOR PRESBYTERIAN CHURCH, CO. DOWN
[*see under* **KILBRONEY**]

RYANS PRESBYTERIAN CHURCH, CO. DOWN
[*see under* **NEWRY**]

ST ANDREW'S or BALLYHALBERT, CO. DOWN

C.I. Ballyhalbert (St Andrew's) (Down diocese)
Baptisms, 1846-76; burials, 1855-1922.   T.679/184-185

M. Glastry
Baptisms, 1870-c.1878; circuit schedule book, 1870-78.   D.2687

Baptisms, 1879-; marriages, 1864-.   **In local custody**

P. Glastry
Baptisms, 1728-1966; marriages, 1750-1914;
communicants' roll, 1860-63 and 1871.   **MIC.1P/111**

R.C. [*see under* **ARDKEEN**]

**ST ANNE'S, SIXTOWNS, CHURCH OF IRELAND PARISH,
CO. LONDONDERRY**
[*see under* **BALLYNASCREEN**]

**ST COLUMB'S CHURCH OF IRELAND CATHEDRAL,
LONDONDERRY**
[*see under* **TEMPLEMORE**]

**ST COLUMB'S ROMAN CATHOLIC CHURCH,
LONDONDERRY**
[*see under* **TEMPLEMORE**]

ST EUGENE'S CATHEDRAL, LONDONDERRY
[*see under* **TEMPLEMORE**]

SAINTFIELD, CO. DOWN

C.I. Saintfield (Down diocese)
Baptisms, 1724-57 and 1793-1847; marriages, 1724-57,
1798 and 1813-45; burials, 1824-1831 and 1834-78;
vestry minutes, 1730-1824; vestry book, 1812-1920;
minutes of Saintfield Auxiliary Bible Society, 1837-57.   **MIC.1/69; C.R.1/4;
                                                                        D.1759/1D/1**

Churchwardens' accounts, 1871-; cess applotment,
1833-; register of vestrymen, 1870-; preachers' books,
1849-69 and 1877-1924.   **In local custody**

P. 2nd Boardmills
Baptisms, 1846-1950; marriages, 1847-1902; session
minutes, 1857-1908 and 1931-66, [session minutes,
1931-66, relate to the congregations of 2nd Boardmills
and Killaney].   **MIC.1P/102;
                                                                        D.1759/1D/2**

Marriage notice books, 1871-1901.   **MIC.1P/230/5/1-2**

P. 1st Saintfield
Baptisms, 1854-1986; marriages, 1845-1905; marriage
notice book, 1871-7.   **MIC.1P/298; MIC.1P/
                                                                        230/5/1; T.2320**

Session minutes, 1845-69; treasurers' book containing a
list of seatholders, 1855-60.   **T.1184**

Volume of manuscript notes giving dates and places of
death of members, c. 1950-c.1961.   **D.1693/3**

P. 2nd Saintfield
Baptisms, 1831-1902; marriages, 1831-1930; burials,
1831-84; details of elders, 1831-9.   **MIC.1P/289**

R.C. Carrickmannon and Saintfield (Down and Connor
diocese)

Baptisms, 1837-81; marriages, 1845-83.   **MIC.1D/63**

ST JAMES', BALLYMONEY, PRESBYTERIAN CHURCH, CO. ANTRIM
[*see under* **BALLYMONEY**]

ST JOHN'S POINT METHODIST CHURCH, CO. DONEGAL
[*see under* **KILLAGHTEE**]

ST JOHNSTON PRESBYTERIAN CHURCH, CO. DONEGAL
[*see under* **TAUGHBOYNE**]

ST MACARTAN'S CATHEDRAL, MONAGHAN, CO. MONAGHAN
[*see under* **MONAGHAN**]

ST MARY'S (KESH) CHURCH OF IRELAND PARISH, CO. FERMANAGH
[*see under* **MAGHERACULMONEY**]

ST MARY'S, NEWTOWNBARRY, CO. WEXFORD

M. Newtownbarry
Baptisms, 1833-42.   **MIC.429/1/536**

ST PATRICK'S, NEWRY, CHURCH OF IRELAND PARISH, CO. DOWN
[*see under* **NEWRY**]

ST PETER'S, CO. LOUTH

C.I. St Peter's, Drogheda (Armagh diocese)
Baptisms, 1654-1886; marriages, 1654-1956; burials,
1653-1864.   **MIC.1/207**

Vestry minutes, 1747-; register of vestrymen, 1870-.   **In local custody**

M. Drogheda
Baptisms, 1829-50.   **MIC.429/1/1**

R.C. St Peter's, Drogheda (Armagh diocese)
Baptisms, 1744-57, 1764-71, 1777-8, 1781-95, 1803-04
and 1815-81; marriages, 1815-80.   **MIC.1D/48-49**

**ST SAVIOUR'S CHURCH OF IRELAND PARISH,
CO. ARMAGH**
[*see under* **KILMORE, CO. ARMAGH**]

**SALLAGHY CHURCH OF IRELAND PARISH,
CO. FERMANAGH**
[*see under* **GALLOON**]

SALTERSTOWN PRESBYTERIAN CHURCH, CO. TYRONE
[*see under* **ARTREA**]

SANDHOLES PRESBYTERIAN CHURCH, CO. TYRONE
[*see under* **DESERTCREAT**]

SAUL, CO. DOWN

C.I. Saul (Down diocese)
[Earliest registers destroyed in Dublin]

Marriage notices, 1845-63.   **D.2319**

Baptisms, 1876-; marriages, 1845-; burials, 1877-; vestry
minutes, 1849-; register of vestrymen, 1870-.   **In local custody**

R.C. Saul (Down and Connor diocese)
[Includes part of Ballyculter parish]

Baptisms, 1868-80; marriages, 1868-81.   **MIC.1D/74**

SCARVA CHURCH OF IRELAND PARISH, CO. DOWN
[*see under* **AGHADERG**]

SCARVA PRESBYTERIAN CHURCH, CO. DOWN
[*see under* **AGHADERG**]

**SCARVA STREET PRESBYTERIAN CHURCH,
BANBRIDGE, CO. DOWN**
[*see under* **SEAPATRICK**]

**SCOTSHOUSE ROMAN CATHOLIC CHURCH,
CO. MONAGHAN**
[*see under* **DRUMMULLY**]

**SCOTSTOWN PRESBYTERIAN CHURCH,
CO. MONAGHAN**
[*see under* **TEDAVNET**]

SCRABBY, CO. CAVAN

    C.I. Gowna or Ballymacaleny (Kilmore diocese)
        Baptisms, 1875-1986; marriages, 1840-1955; burials,
        1881-1986.   **MIC.1/289**

**SCRIGGAN PRESBYTERIAN CHURCH,
CO. LONDONDERRY**
[*see under* **DUNGIVEN**]

SEAFIN PRESBYTERIAN CHURCH, CO. CAVAN
[*see under* **KILLINKERE**]

SEAFORDE PRESBYTERIAN CHURCH, CO. DOWN
[*see under* **LOUGHINISLAND**]

SEAGOE, CO. ARMAGH

    C.I. Knocknamuckly (Dromore diocese)
        Baptisms, 1838-76; marriages, 1838-45; burials, 1853-80.   **MIC.1/99**

        Extracts from parish registers, 1841-57.   **DIO.1/14/2**

        Vestry minutes, 1871-; churchwardens' account book,
        1854-91; preachers' books, 1853-88 and 1925-34;
        register of vestrymen, 1870-.   **In local custody**

    C.I. Seagoe (Dromore diocese)
        Baptisms, 1672-1731, 1735-1821 and 1829-76;
        marriages, 1672-1731, 1735-1821 and 1826-45; burials,
        1672-1731, 1735-1821 and 1829-81; vestry minutes,
        1734-1900.   **MIC.1/73-75**

        Analysis of register of baptisms, marriages and burials,
        1672-1904.   **T.2588**

        Index to baptisms, marriages and burials, 1672-1919.   **In Public Search
                                                                     Room**

        Preachers' books, 1877-; visiting book, 1879.   **In local custody**

M. Ballinacor [Wesleyan Methodists]
Baptisms, 1845-1950; circuit schedule books, 1867-1909;
registers of members, 1845-1905; quarterly leaders'
meetings, 1867-1915.   **MIC.1E/33**

M. Bluestone [Wesleyan Methodists]
Baptisms, c.1839-1950; marriages, 1842-4, 1855 and
1864-1918; circuit schedule books, 1867-1909; register
of members, 1819-1905; minutes of quarterly leaders'
meetings, 1867-1915.   **MIC.1E/33**

P. 1st Portadown
Baptisms, 1839-1954; marriages, 1838-1900; session
minutes, 1855-80.   **MIC.1P/52**

R.C. Seagoe (Dromore diocese)
Baptisms, 1836-81 (October 1837-19 December 1837
missing); marriages, 1836-81; deaths, 1837-80.   **MIC.1D/23-24**

SEAPATRICK, CO. DOWN

B. Banbridge
Marriages, 1864-; minute book, 1887-.   **In local custody**

C.I. Seapatrick (Holy Trinity) (Dromore diocese)
Baptisms, 1802-82; marriages, 1802-45; burials, 1802-76;
vestry minutes, 1802-46.   **MIC.1/83**

Vestry minutes, 1880-88 and 1901-34.   **D.2573**

Register of vestrymen, 1870-; preachers' book, 1871-.   **In local custody**

M. Banbridge
Baptisms, 1866-; marriages, 1863-.   **In local custody**
[Earlier baptismal registers kept at Tandragee]

N.S.P. 1st Banbridge
Baptisms, 1756-94 and 1814-1971; marriages, 1756-94
and 1814-45; session and committee minutes, 1848-1933. **T.2995/1-4; C.R. 4/6;**
                                                        C.R. 3/53

P. Ballydown [United with Katesbridge in 1938]
Baptisms, 1875-1985; marriages, 1845-1911.   **MIC.1P/169**

P. Bannside, Banbridge
Baptisms, 1867-1915; marriages, 1867-1909;
communicants' roll, 1875-1918; stipend list, 1891-1910;
committee minutes, 1871-1903; session minutes,
1869-1973.   **MIC.1P/386; C.R. 3/47**

P. Katesbridge
[Although Katesbridge is in the Seapatrick area, it is in a
townland which is an outlying part of Newry parish - *see
under* **NEWRY**]

P. Scarva Street, Banbridge
[In 1828 this church split and part became the
Non-Subscribing Presbyterian Church - *see under* **N.S.P.**
above for earlier baptisms and marriages].

Baptisms, 1872-1946; marriages, 1867-1909;
communicants' roll, 1875-1918; stipend list, 1891-1910.   **MIC.1P/386**

R.C. Seapatrick (Banbridge) (Dromore diocese)
Baptisms, 1843-81; marriages, 1850-82; deaths, 1833-80.   **MIC.1D/26**

[Earlier entries may be in with Tullylish - *see under*
TULLYLISH]

SESKINORE PRESBYTERIAN CHURCH, CO. TYRONE
[*see under* **CLOGHERNEY**]

SHANKILL, COS ARMAGH and DOWN

C.I. Shankill (Christ Church) (Dromore diocese)
Baptisms, 1681-1872; marriages, 1676-1845; burials,
1675-1857 and 1866-77; vestry minutes, 1672-1960.   **MIC.1/18, 24-25**

Baptisms, 1873; marriages, 1845-; burials, 1858-;
Churchwardens' accounts, 1790-1828 and 1854-96;
parish reports, 1873; register of vestrymen, 1870-94;
census of parish, 1868-; preachers' books, 1865-9
and 1881-; list of churchwardens, 1760-1831; charitable
bequests, 1854.   **In local custody**

M. Lurgan, High Street [Wesleyan Methodists]
Baptisms, 1823-1950; marriages, 1864-1902; circuit
schedule book, 1867-1909; register of members in circuit,
1819-60 and 1863-1905; minute books of quarterly
leaders' meetings, 1867-1915; Sunday School roll books,
1892-5 and 1897-8; minute book of Sunday School
teachers' meetings, 1895-1905; leaders' accounts,
1860-1909; collection book arranged by pew number and
name, 1892-1907.   **MIC.1E/33**

M. Lurgan, Queen Street [Primitive Wesleyan Methodists]
Baptisms, 1873-1986.   **MIC.1E/21A/1**

Baptisms, 1823-44.   **MIC.429/1/439**

Marriages, 1874-.   **In local custody**

P. 1st Lurgan
Baptisms, 1746-1965, with index, 1746-1877; marriages,
1746, 1754, 1759 and 1845-1929.   **MIC.1P/71**

P. Hill Street, Lurgan
    Baptisms, 1861-1961; marriages, 1864-1916; committee
    and congregational minutes, 1861-1922.   **MIC.1P/109**

R.C. Shankill (Lurgan) (Dromore diocese)
    Baptisms, 1822-81; marriages and funerals, 1866-81.   **MIC.1D/23**

R.S.F. Lurgan
    Births, 1632-1806 and 1809-1979; marriages, 1632-1936;
    burials, 1632-1806 and 1812-1979; minutes of men's
    meetings, 1675-1954; minutes of women's meetings,
    1794-1864; removal certificates, 1796-1955; removal
    and admission registers, 1863-1902; testimonies of
    disownment, 1688-1796; list of members, c.1810-c.1883;
    accounts of sufferings, 1812-c.1868; testimonies against
    Quakers, 1673-1700.   **MIC.16; C.R. 8/1**

SHERCOCK, CO. CAVAN

C.I. Shercock (Kilmore diocese)
    Baptisms, 1881-1979; marriages, 1846-1955; burials,
    1881-1976.   **MIC.1/253**

M. Shercock
    Baptisms, 1835-6 and 1843-78; marriages may be in
    Cootehill Circuit, 1871-8; register of members, 1847-72.   **MIC.1E/54**

P. Glasleck or Shircock or Shercock
    Baptisms, 1836-1974; marriages, 1845-1956.   **MIC.1P/219**

R.C. [Shercock parish is united to Bailieborough parish to form
      the Roman Catholic parish of Killann - *see under*
      BAILLIEBOROUGH]

SHILVODAN, GRANGE OF

C.I. [*see under* **DRUMMAUL** and **CONNOR**]

R.P. Eskylane
    [Joined the Irish Presbyterian Church in 1902/03]

    Marriages, 1874-1902.   **MIC.1P/311**

SION MILLS CHURCH OF IRELAND PARISH, CO. TYRONE
    [*see under* **URNEY, COS TYRONE** and **DONEGAL**]

SION or SION MILLS PRESBYTERIAN CHURCH, CO. TYRONE
    [*see under* **URNEY, COS TYRONE** and **DONEGAL**]

**SIXMILECROSS CHURCH OF IRELAND PARISH,
CO. TYRONE**
[*see under* **TERMONMAGUIRK**]

SIXMILECROSS PRESBYTERIAN CHURCH, CO. TYRONE
[*see under* **TERMONMAGUIRK**]

**SIXTOWNS, ST ANNE'S, CHURCH OF IRELAND PARISH,
CO. LONDONDERRY**
[*see under* **BALLYNASCREEN**]

SKERRY, CO. ANTRIM

C.I. Skerry and Racavan (Connor diocese)
Baptisms, 1805-67; marriages, 1826-45; burials, 1828-91;
publication of banns, 1828-47, 1934, 1943 and 1947.   **MIC.1/78**

Baptisms, 1805-1906; index to burials, 1805-1929.   **T.3054/B/1/11, 28**

Baptisms, 1867-; vestry minutes, 1873-; preachers' books,
1824-8, 1869-1902 and 1914-; confirmation roll, 1869.   **In local custody**

P. Cloughwater
Baptisms, 1852-1955; marriages, 1845-1923; session
minutes with discipline cases and lists of new
communicants, 1855-65; session minutes, 1878-1905.   **MIC.1P/320**

R.C. [Part of Skerry parish is in the Roman Catholic parish
of Glenravel - *see under* **DUNAGHY** and part is in
the Roman Catholic parish of the Braid - *see under*
RACAVAN]

SKIBBEREEN, CO. CORK

M. Skibereen
Baptisms, 1833-44.   **MIC.429/1/500**

SLANES, CO. DOWN

C.I. Slanes (Down diocese)
[*See under* **BALLYPHILIP**]

R.C. [Slanes parish is in the Roman Catholic parish of
Ballygalget - *see under* **ARDQUIN**]

**SLAVIN CHURCH OF IRELAND PARISH,
CO. FERMANAGH**
[*see under* **INISHMACSAINT**]

SLIGO, CO. SLIGO

    C. Sligo (Elphin diocese)
        Deed of settlement, 1857.   C.R. 7/10

    M. Sligo
        Baptisms, 1819-42.   MIC.429/1/143

**SLOAN STREET, LISBURN, PRESBYTERIAN CHURCH,
CO. DOWN**
    [*see under* **BLARIS**]

**SMITHBOROUGH PRESBYTERIAN CHURCH,
CO. MONAGHAN**
    [*see under* **CLONES**]

SPA PRESBYTERIAN CHURCH, CO. DOWN
    [*see under* **MAGHERADROOL**]

SPRINGFIELD METHODIST CHURCH, CO. FERMANAGH
    [*see under* **DEVENISH**]

STAGHALL ROMAN CATHOLIC CHURCH, CO. CAVAN
    [*see under* **DRUMLANE**]

**STEWARTSTOWN (1ST and 2ND) PRESBYTERIAN
CHURCH, CO. TYRONE**
    [*see under* **DONAGHENRY**]

**STEWARTSTOWN ROMAN CATHOLIC PARISH,
CO. TYRONE**
    [*see under* **DONAGHENRY**]

**STONEBRIDGE PRESBYTERIAN CHURCH,
CO. MONAGHAN**
    [*see under* **CLONES**]

**STONEYFORD CHURCH OF IRELAND PARISH,
CO. ANTRIM**
    [*see under* **DERRYAGHY**]

**STRABANE METHODIST CIRCUIT AND CHURCH,
CO. TYRONE**
    [*see under* **CAMUS**]

**STRABANE (1ST), PRESBYTERIAN CHURCH,
CO. TYRONE**
    [*see under* **CAMUS**]

**STRABANE (2ND), PRESBYTERIAN CHURCH,
CO. TYRONE**
    [*see under* **LECKPATRICK**]

STRAID CONGREGATIONAL CHURCH, CO. ANTRIM
    [*see under* **BALLYNURE**]

STRAND PRESBYTERIAN CHURCH, LONDONDERRY
    [*see under* **TEMPLEMORE**]

STRANGFORD PRESBYTERIAN CHURCH, CO. DOWN
    [*see under* **BALLYCULTER**]

STRANGFORD ROMAN CATHOLIC PARISH, CO. DOWN
    [*see under* **KILCLIEF**]

**STRANOODAN CHAPEL OF EASE (CHURCH OF
IRELAND), CO. MONAGHAN**
    [*see under* **KILMORE, CO. MONAGHAN**]

STRANORLAR, CO. DONEGAL

    C.I. Kilteevogue (Raphoe diocese)
        [Up to 1835 it was a perpetual curacy in Stranorlar parish
        but was then made a separate parish - *see under*
        KILTEEVOGUE]

    C.I. Stranorlar (Raphoe diocese)
        Baptisms, 1802-84; marriages, 1821-93; burials,
        1821-1976; confirmations, 1832, 1840, 1845, 1853, 1857
        and 1861.   **MIC.1/170**

        Vestry minutes, 1816-.   **In local custody**

    M. Stranorlar
        Baptisms, 1829-67; marriages, 1865-1935 [may be
        included in Strabane register]; circuit schedule books,
        1865-1909; membership register and quarterly class
        roll, 1897-1947; minutes of quarterly leaders' meetings,
        1880-1910; circuit steward's book, 1872-86.   **MIC.1E/46**

        Baptisms, 1830-41.   **MIC.429/1/504**

P. 1st Stranorlar
Baptisms, 1821-59, 1861-74 and 1881-1932; marriages,
1846-1914.   **MIC.1P/218**

R.P. Stranorlar
[Formerly 2nd Stranorlar Presbyterian Church which in
1871 became Stranorlar Reformed Presbyterian Church]

Marriages, 1846-69 and 1872-1926.   **MIC.1C/7**

STREAN PRESBYTERIAN CHURCH, CO. DOWN
[*see under* NEWTOWNARDS]

SWANLINBAR CHURCH OF IRELAND PARISH, CO. CAVAN
[*see under* KINAWLEY]

SWANLINBAR METHODIST CIRCUIT AND CHURCH, CO. CAVAN
[*see under* KINAWLEY]

SWANLINBAR ROMAN CATHOLIC CHURCH, CO. CAVAN
[*see under* KINAWLEY]

SWATRAGH PRESBYTERIAN CHURCH, CO. LONDONDERRY
[*see under* MAGHERA]

TALLANSTOWN, CO. LOUTH

R.C. Tallanstown (Armagh diocese)
Baptisms, 1817-25 and 1830-81; marriages, 1804-63
and 1867-84.   **MIC.1D/50**

TAMLAGHT, COS LONDONDERRY AND TYRONE

C.I. Ballyeglish
[Partly in Tamlaght parish - *see under* ARTREA]

C.I. Tamlaght (Armagh diocese)
Baptisms, 1801-07 and 1821-70; marriages, 1829-45;
burials, 1834-71; vestry minutes, 1835-1931 (gap
1920-29); communicants' roll, 1847.   **T.679/46, 173, 181**

Returns to the Primate of sums levied by the parish
vestry, 1812-23.   **DI0.4/32/T/1/4/1**

P. Ballygoney
    Baptisms, 1834-.   **In local custody**

P. Coagh
    Typescript extracts from session minutes, 1858.   **C.R. 3/40**

    Baptisms, 1839-; marriages, 1845-.   **In local custody**

    Committee minutes, 1848-69; session minutes, 1850-1915.   **In Presbyterian
                                                                        Historical Society**

R.C. Coagh (Armagh diocese)
    Baptisms, 1865-82; marriages, 1865-81 and 1884-91.   **MIC.1D/33**

TAMLAGHTARD CHURCH OF IRELAND PARISH, CO. LONDONDERRY
    [*see under* MAGILLIGAN]

TAMLAGHT FINLAGAN, CO. LONDONDERRY

C.I. Myroe, St John the Baptist, Chapel of Ease
    (Derry diocese)

    [*See also under* TAMLAGHT FINLAGAN below]

    Preachers' book, 1863-.   **In local custody**

C.I. Tamlaght Finlagan (Derry diocese)
    Baptisms, 1796-1875; marriages, 1796-1846; burials,
    1796-1946; vestry minutes, 1748-1881.   **MIC.1/38**

    Index to the registers, 1796-1861.   **C.R.1/8**

    Baptisms, 1876; marriages, 1845-; parochial visiting
    register, 1850-70; confirmation register, 1850-70;
    preachers' book, 1858-; register of vestrymen, 1870-;
    churchwardens' accounts, 1871-98; vestry minutes, 1881-.   **In local custody**

P. Ballykelly
    Baptisms, 1699-1709, 1805-19 and 1826-1983; indexes to
    baptisms, 1699-1709 and 1805-19, and to marriages,
    1699-1740 and 1805-11; marriages, 1699-1740, 1805-11
    and 1845-1920; session minutes, 1826 and 1846-68; list
    of communicants, 1804-18, 1826-55 and 1859-62.   **MIC.1P/208**

P. Largy
    Baptisms, 1848-72 and 1913-46; marriages, 1845-1936;
    communicants' roll, 1848-77; committee minutes,
    1882-1905; stipend book, 1867-1919.   **MIC.1P/180**

P. Myroe
    Baptisms, 1850-1919; marriages, 1845-1917.   **MIC.1P/411**

R.C. [*see under* DRUMACHOSE]

TAMLAGHT O'CRILLY, CO. LONDONDERRY

C.I. Tamlaght O' Crilly Lower (Derry diocese)
[Earliest registers destroyed in Dublin]

Baptisms, 1881-; marriages, 1849-; burials, 1881 and
1908-; vestry minutes, 1889-; preachers' book, 1899-;
grave book.   **In local custody**

C.I. Tamlaght O'Crilly Upper (Derry diocese)
[Earliest registers destroyed in Dublin]

Burials, 1934-60 (incomplete).   **D.1208/1**

Baptisms, 1895-; marriages, 1845-; burials, 1895-;
vestry minutes, 1870-; preachers' books, 1899-1910
and 1930-.   **In local custody**

P. Boveedy
Baptisms, 1841-1929; marriages, 1842-1929; session
minutes, 1842-1925; accounts, 1855-80; communicants'
roll, 1857-70 and 1888-1929.   **MIC.1P/18**

P. Churchtown
Baptisms, 1840-1970; marriages, 1839-45 and 1877-1936.   **MIC.1P/347**

R.C. Greenlough (Tamlaght O'Crilly) (Derry diocese)
Baptisms, 1846-81; marriages, 1846-82; deaths, 1846-70.   **MIC.1D/58**

R.P. Drumbolg or Drimbolg
Baptisms, 1895-1956; marriages, 1864-1925; session book
with discipline cases, 1809-59; committee minutes,
1887-1919.   **MIC.1C/15**

TANDRAGEE METHODIST CHURCH, CO. ARMAGH
[*see under* BALLYMORE]

TANDRAGEE PRESBYTERIAN CHURCH, CO. ARMAGH
[*see under* BALLYMORE]

TARTARAGHAN, CO. ARMAGH

C.I. Milltown (Armagh diocese)
Baptisms, 1840-1917; marriages, 1840-45; burials, 1845-89. **MIC.1/89**

Baptisms, 1917-; marriages, 1845-; burials, 1889-; vestry
minutes, 1876-.   **In local custody**

C.I. Tartaraghan (Armagh diocese)
  Baptisms, 1825-88; marriages, 1824-45; burials, 1828-82;
  confirmations, 1840.   **MIC.1/77-78; T.679/26**

  Baptisms, 1889-; marriages, 1845-; burials, 1883-; vestry
  minutes, 1828-.   **In local custody**

M. Cranagill
  Baptisms, 1871-; marriages, 1884-.   **In local custody**

M. Derrylee
  Baptisms, 1874-.   **In local custody**

P. Tartaraghan
  Baptisms, 1853-1962; marriages, 1845-1921.   **MIC.1P/288**

R.C. [Tartaraghan parish is linked with Loughgall - *see under*
  LOUGHGALL]

TASSAGH PRESBYTERIAN CHURCH, CO. ARMAGH
  [*see under* **KEADY**]

**TATTYKEERAN CHURCH OF IRELAND PARISH,
CO. FERMANAGH**
  [*see under* **AGHAVEA**]

TAUGHBOYNE, CO. DONEGAL

C.I. Craigadooish (Raphoe diocese)
  Baptisms, 1871-1907; preachers' book, 1862-71.   **MIC.1/177**

C.I. Taughboyne (Raphoe diocese)
  [Earliest registers destroyed in Dublin]

  Baptisms, 1820-1983; marriages, 1820-1906; burials,
  1820-1982; vestry minutes, 1791 and 1804-76; preachers'
  book, 1841-9.   **MIC.1/174**

  Vestry minutes, 1877-; register of vestrymen, 1870-.   **In local custody**

P. 1st Ballylennon
  Baptisms, 1829-39 and 1861-73; marriages, 1831-9 and
  1845-1915; burials, 1830-38; notes on the history of the
  church, 1829.   **MIC.1P/207**

P. 2nd Ballylennon
  Marriages, 1845-78.   **MIC.1P/207**

P. Ballylennon (1st and 2nd united)
  Baptisms, 1878-1983.   **MIC.1P/207**

P. Monreagh
  Baptisms, 1845-1984; marriages, 1894-1933; marriage
  notice books, 1845-84.   **MIC.1P/233; MIC.1P/
                                                            230/2B/1**

P. St Johnston
  Baptisms, 1838-1949; marriages, 1835-45 and 1864-1901;
  session minutes, 1838-69.   **MIC.1P/206**

R.C. [Taughboyne parish records are with All Saints, etc. -
  see under **ALL SAINTS**]

**TAWNAWILLY ROMAN CATHOLIC PARISH,
CO. DONEGAL**
  [*see under* **DONEGAL**]

TEDAVNET, CO. MONAGHAN

  C.I. Tydavnet (Clogher diocese)
    Baptisms, 1822-98; marriages, 1822-1950; burials,
    1822-1906.   **MIC.1/246**

    Baptisms, 1898-; vestry minute books (dates unknown);
    preachers' books, 1858-.   **In local custody**

  P. Ballyalbany or 2nd Monaghan
    Baptisms, 1802-1948; marriages, 1807-30, 1845-74 and
    1876-1920.   **MIC.1P/146**

  P. Scotstown
    Baptisms, 1855-1963; marriages, 1846-1935.   **MIC.1P/203**

  R.C. Tydavnet (Clogher diocese)
    Baptisms, 1835-81; marriages, 1825-65 and 1876-81.   **MIC.1D/2, 16-17**

TEHALLEN, CO. MONAGHAN

  C.I. Tyholland (Clogher diocese)
    Baptisms, 1806-80; marriages, 1806-1951; burials,
    1806-1912.   **MIC.1/126**

    Baptisms, 1881-; vestry minutes, 1712-.   **In local custody**

  R.C. Tyholland (Clogher diocese)
    Baptisms, 1835-81; marriages, 1827-82.   **MIC.1D/3, 15**

TEMPLECARN, COS FERMANAGH AND DONEGAL

  C.I. Muckross (Clogher diocese)
    [Baptisms, 1868-1908, destroyed in Dublin]

Marriages, 1869-1930; burials, 1892-1985.   **MIC.1/216**

C.I. Templecarn (Clogher diocese)
Baptisms, 1825-1931 and 1936; marriages, 1825-1906;
burials, 1825-1985.   **MIC.1/217**

Vestry minutes, 1777-; register of vestrymen, 1870-.   **In local custody**

R.C. Carn (Devenish West, Belleek and Pettigo)
(Clogher diocese)

[Templecarn parish forms part of the Roman Catholic
parish of Carn or Pettigo]

Baptisms, 1851-81; marriages, 1836-81.   **MIC.1D/12-13**

TEMPLECORRAN, CO. ANTRIM

C.I. Templecorran and Kilroot (Connor diocese)
Baptisms, 1848-1901; burials, 1848-1962.   **MIC.1/98; T.679/51**

Deed of consecration, 1854.   **T.928/1**

Marriages, 1848-; vestry minutes, 1848-; registers of
vestrymen (kept in St Patrick's, Whitehead).   **In local custody**

C.I. Whitehead (Connor diocese)
Deed of consecration of St Patrick's Church, 1908.   **T.929/1**

N.S.P. Ballycarry
[Part of this Church seceded from the Synod of Ulster in
1829]

Session minutes, 1704-80.   **C.R. 4/18**

P. Ballycarry
Baptisms, 1832-1969; marriages, 1832-1945;
session minutes, 1704-80.   **MIC.1P/330; C.R.3/31**

P. Whitehead
Registers, 1900-.   **In local custody**

R.C. [*see under* **LARNE and CARRICKFERGUS**]

TEMPLECRONE, CO. DONEGAL

C.I. Gweedore, (Bunbeg) (Raphoe diocese)
[Previously known as Ardangligger]

[Earliest registers destroyed in Dublin]

Baptisms, 1880-1980 [also includes Carrickfin];
marriages, 1855-1952; burials, 1881-1982.   **MIC.1/196**

Vestry minutes, 1872-; preachers' books, 1858-.   **In local custody**

C.I. Templecrone (Raphoe diocese)
Baptisms, 1878-1982; burials, 1879-1980.   **MIC.1/198**

Marriages, 1845-; vestry minutes, 1776-; register of
vestrymen, 1870-.   **In local custody**

R.C. Dungloe (Templecrone Upper and Lettermacaward)
(Raphoe diocese)

[*see under* **LETTERMACAWARD**]

TEMPLEMORE, CO. LONDONDERRY

B. Londonderry
Marriages, 1899-; church and deacons' meeting book, 1897-.   **In local custody**

C.I. Christ Church, Londonderry [Episcopal Free Church]
(Derry diocese)

Baptisms, 1855-97.   **MIC.1/88; T.679/27**

Baptisms, 1898-; marriages, 1882-; burials, 1891-;
confirmations, 1880-; vestry minutes, 1870-; register of
vestrymen, 1870-; preachers' books, 1862-.   **In local custody**

C.I. Culmore (Derry diocese)
Baptisms, 1867-1920; marriages, 1868-1935.   **MIC.1/250**

Burials, 1869-; vestry minutes, 1869-; registers of
vestrymen, 1872-; preachers' books, 1867-.

C.I. Mission Church, Londonderry (Derry diocese)
Preachers' book, 1903-.   **In local custody**

C.I. St Augustine's Chapel of Ease, Londonderry
(Derry diocese)

[Earliest registers destroyed in Dublin]

Baptisms, 1878-; marriages, 1886-; vestry minutes, 1878-;
register of vestrymen, 1870-; preachers' book, 1850-68
and 1888-.   **In local custody**

C.I. Templemore (St Columb's) (Derry diocese)
Baptisms, 1642-1876; marriages, 1649-1843; burials,
1642-1775 and 1829-74; vestry minutes, 1741-93 and
1823-1937; acts of vestry, 1741-3 and 1750-60; lists of

cess payers, 1743-9, 1756-60 and 1772-93; tithe
applotment book, 1772-84 and 1786-93; book of
tombstone inscriptions, c.1800-c.1880; choir committee
book, 1830-31; book of meetings of trustees of Stanley's
Charity, 1827-1924; chapter book, 1801-26.   **MIC.1/18-20, 26-31**

Transcript of baptisms, marriages and deaths, 1703-32,
with an index.   **C.R.1/6**

Parish cess applotments and lists, 1751-6.   **T.1020/1**

Extracts from vestry book, 1772-84.   **T.945/1; T.946/1**

Preachers' books, 1834-60 and 1870-; confirmation
register, 1884-92 and 1905-; select vestry minutes, 1870-.   **In local custody**

M. Carlisle Road, Londonderry
Circuit stewards' account book, 1846-62.   **C.R. 6/2**

Baptisms, 1820-; marriages, 1863-; minute book of circuit
quarterly meetings, 1862-.   **In local custody**

Baptisms, 1820-42.   **MIC.429/1/230**

M. Londonderry City Mission
Baptisms, 1896-; marriages, 1897-.   **In local custody**

P. Ballyarnett
Baptisms, 1848-91; marriages, 1848-1903; marriage
notices, 1845-84; session minutes, 1850-67 and 1892-1963;
pew rent book, 1864-88; list of communicants, 1848-51.   **MIC.1P/239;**
                                                                   MIC.1P/230/2B/1

P. Carlisle Road, Derry [formerly 4th Derry]
Baptisms, 1838-1921; marriages, 1839-91; session and
committee minutes, 1840-42, 1894 and 1907-23; stipend
accounts, 1840-43; communicants, 1840-96.   **MIC.1P/67**

P. 1st Derry
Baptisms, 1815-1928; marriages, 1815-98; deaths, 1857-86;
minutes, 1810-1949; communicants' roll, 1842-1931;
financial reports, 1848-86.   **MIC.1P/294; T.2711/2**

P. 2nd Derry or Strand
Baptisms, 1847-1918; marriages, 1868-1909.   **MIC.1P/293**

P. Great James' Street, Derry or Kilfennan
Baptisms, 1838-1984; marriages, 1837-1928.   **MIC.1P/150**

R.C. St Columb's, Long Tower, Derry (Derry diocese)
Baptisms, 1823-6 and 1836-81; marriages, 1823-6,
1835-6 and 1841-63; deaths, 1863.   **MIC.1D/57**

Printed history of church, 1841-1991.   **C.R. 2/18**

R.C. St Eugene's Cathedral, Derry (Derry diocese)
Baptisms, 1873-81. **MIC.1D/57**

R.P. Clarendon Street, Londonderry
Marriages, 1864-1929; session minutes, 1848-1955;
committee minutes, 1895-1906; congregational minutes,
1860-61, 1871-4, 1890-96, 1904-05 and 1940-59; minutes of
the building committee, 1856-9; list of members with
details of baptisms, marriages, deaths and emigration,
1848; statements of accounts, 1891. **MIC.1C/12; C.R. 5/13**

R.P. Waterside, Londonderry
Marriages, 1868-1905. **MIC.1C/23**

TEMPLEPATRICK, CO. ANTRIM

C.I. Templepatrick (Connor diocese)
Baptisms, 1827-1908; marriages, 1827-56; burials,
1828-1928; publication of banns, 1827-66; vestry
minutes, 1826-74. **MIC.1/82**

Marriages, 1856-; burials, 1877-; vestry minutes, 1875-;
confirmation register, 1930-. **In local custody**

M. Hydepark
Baptisms, 1843(?)-; marriages, 1864- (at Ligoniel Church,
Belfast). **In local custody**

N.S.P. Templepatrick
[Prior to 1830, when a branch of the Church split away
to form the Non-Subscribing Presbyterian Church, the
records relate to Templepatrick Presbyterian Church of
the General Synod]

Baptisms, 1796-1980; marriages, 1797-1848; burials,
1966-78; lists of communicants, 1811-47; accounts,
1799-1812; list of persons in each family connected
with the church, 1854-5; session minutes, 1646-1743
and 1878-1962. **C.R.4/12**

P. Hydepark
Baptisms, 1861-79; marriages, 1863-1902. **C.R.3/18**

P. Lylehill
Baptisms, 1830-76 and 1881-1966; marriages, 1889-1936;
communion lists, 1859-84; session minutes, 1857-81. **MIC.1P/98**

Marriages, 1830-89; stipend books, 1768-92, 1832-4 and
1857-83. **In Presbyterian Historical Society**

P. Templepatrick
[*see also under* **N.S.P.** above]

Baptisms, 1831-1965; marriages, 1831-1910; register of
families, 1831 and 1857; new communicants' lists,
1831-1919; communicants' lists, 1845-67.   **MIC.1P/325; C.R.3/14**

Baptisms, 1758-1853; marriages, 1797-1829.   **In Presbyterian
                                                            Historical Society**

R.C. [Templepatrick parish is partly in the Roman Catholic
parish of Antrim - *see under* **ANTRIM** and
DRUMMAUL and partly in the Roman Catholic parish
of Whitehouse - *see under* **CARNMONEY**]

TEMPLEPORT, CO. CAVAN

C.I. Templeport (Kilmore diocese)
Baptisms, 1874-1986; marriages, 1845-1954; burials,
1878-1988.   **MIC.1/286**

R.C. Glangevlin (Kilmore diocese)
[Partly in Kinawley parish and partly in Templeport
parish]

Baptisms and marriages, 1867-81.   **MIC.1D/78**

R.C. Templeport (Kilmore diocese)
Baptisms, 1836-80; marriages, 1836-82; burials,
1827-45 and 1870-80.   **MIC.1D/78**

R.C. Corlough (Kilmore diocese)
Baptisms, 1877-81; marriages, 1877-82; deaths, 1877-81.   **MIC.1D/79**

TEMPO CHURCH OF IRELAND PARISH, CO. FERMANAGH
[*see under* **ENNISKILLEN**]

TEMPO METHODIST CHURCH, CO. FERMANAGH
[*see under* **ENNISKILLEN**]

TEMPO PRESBYTERIAN CHURCH, CO. FERMANAGH
[*see under* **ENNISKILLEN**]

TEMPO ROMAN CATHOLIC CHURCH, CO. FERMANAGH
[*see under* **ENNISKILLEN**]

TERMONAMONGAN, CO. TYRONE

C.I. Termonamongan (Derry diocese)
Baptisms, 1812-81 (gap 1834-8); marriages, 1812-46;
burials, 1829-1939; vestry minutes, 1813-51.   **MIC.1/100; T.800**

Baptisms, 1882-; marriages, 1845-; register of vestrymen,
1870-.   **In local custody**

M. Augheyarren [*sic* Aghyaran]
Baptisms, 1822-1961; marriages, 1876-1937.   **MIC.1E/62**

P. Killeter
Baptisms, 1839-1981; marriages, 1839-1911.   **MIC.1P/252**

R.C. Termonamongan (Derry diocese)
Baptisms, 1863-81; marriages, 1863-80.   **MIC.1D/60**

TERMONEENY, CO. LONDONDERRY

C.I. Termoneeny (Derry diocese)
Baptisms, 1821-39 and 1846-82; marriages, 1821-38;
burials, 1833, 1846 and 1855-1961; vestry minutes,
1805-42 and 1863-1939.   **MIC.1/61; T.679/73**

Baptisms, 1882-; marriages, 1845-; preachers' books,
1862-85 and 1889-; register of vestrymen, 1870-.   **In local custody**

R.C. Termoneeny (Lavey) (Derry diocese)
Baptisms, 1837-9, 1852-65 and 1867-81; marriages,
1837-9, 1852-65, 1868-71 and 1873-80; funerals, 1837-9.   **MIC.1D/58**

[Termoneeny parish is partly in the Roman Catholic
parish of Maghera - *see also under* **MAGHERA**]

TERMONFECKIN, CO. LOUTH

R.C. Termonfeckin (Armagh diocese)
Baptisms and marriages, 1823-81; deaths, 1827-33.   **MIC.1D/51**

TERMONMAGUIRK, CO. TYRONE

C.I. Cooley or Sixmilecross (Armagh diocese)
Baptisms, 1836-71; marriages, 1836-46; burials, 1837-71;
confirmations, 1837, 1840, 1843, 1846, 1866, 1870 and
1873.   **T.679/75**

Baptisms, 1872; marriages, 1847; burials, 1872-; vestry
minutes, 1838-.   **In local custody**

C.I. Dunmoyle
Baptisms, 1873-; burials, 1879-.   **In local custody**

C.I. Drumnakilly (Armagh diocese)
[Earliest records destroyed in Dublin]

Baptisms and burials, 1877-; marriages, 1845-.   **In local custody**

C.I. Termonmaguirk (Armagh diocese)
[Earliest registers destroyed in Dublin]

Vestry minutes, 1786-1825; preachers' book, 1845-61.　　　**C.R. 1/46**

List of churchwardens, 1824-1954.　　　**T.1404**

Baptisms, 1880-; marriages, 1845-; burials, 1880-; vestry
minutes, 1825-; preachers' books, 1862-; list of
parishioners made in 1866 by the Rev. Samuel Alexander.　　　**In local custody**

P. Sixmilecross
[No pre-1900 records - destroyed in fire]

R.C. Termonmaguirk (Carrickmore) (Armagh diocese)
Baptisms and marriages, 1834-57.　　　**MIC.1D/33**

TERRACE ROW, COLERAINE, PRESBYTERIAN CHURCH, CO. LONDONDERRY
[*see under* **COLERAINE**]

TERWINNEY METHODIST CHURCH, CO. FERMANAGH
[*see under* **DRUMKEERAN**]

TICKMACREVAN, CO. ANTRIM

C.I. Tickmacrevan or Glenarm (Connor diocese)
Baptisms, 1719-23, 1727 and 1788-1961; indexes to
baptisms, 1788-1941; marriages, 1719, 1723, 1727-8
and 1789-1844; indexes to marriages, 1719-28 and
1788-1922; burials, 1824-1961; indexes to burials,
1846-1941; preachers' book, 1824-43; vestry minutes,
1718-1872; accounts, 1845-74; Sustentation Fund
accounts, 1871-4.　　　**MIC.1/72-73; T.3054**

Transcript of vestry minutes, 1718-1872, with marriages,
1719, 1723, 1727-8, and baptisms, 1719-23.　　　**T.3054**

M. Glenarm [Wesleyan Methodists]
Baptisms, 1878-1915; marriages, 1863-1906; circuit
schedule books, 1879-1923.　　　**MIC.1E/39**

N.S.P. Glenarm
Baptisms, 1833-1922; marriages, 1845-1929; index to
marriages, 1845-1925.　　　**MIC.1B/4;
T.3054/B/1/30**

P. Cairnalbana
Baptisms, 1862-1949; indexes to baptisms, 1862-1953;
marriages, 1867-1936; indexes to marriages, 1867-1952.　　　**MIC.1P/351;
T.3054/B/1/1, 14**

P. Glenarm
　　Baptisms, 1836-1949; indexes to baptisms, 1836-1949;
　　marriages, 1840 and 1845-1914.　　　　　　　　　　　　　　**MIC.1P/350;**
　　　　　　　　　　　　　　　　　　　　　　　　　　　　　　T.3054/B

R.C. Glenarm or Tickmacrevan (Down and Connor diocese)
　　[Part of Tickmacrevan parish is in the Roman
　　Catholic parish of Carnlough - *see also under*
　　ARDCLINIS]

　　Baptisms, 1865-80; marriages, 1825-80; deaths, 1831-8.　　**MIC.1D/71**

TIPPERARY, CO. TIPPERARY

M. Baptisms, 1837-45.　　　　　　　　　　　　　　　　　**MIC.429/1/542**

TOBERDONEY PRESBYTERIAN CHURCH, CO. ANTRIM
　　[*see under* **BILLY**]

TOBERKEIGH PRESBYTERIAN CHURCH, CO. ANTRIM
　　[*see under* **BALLINTOY**]

TOBERMORE BAPTIST CHURCH, CO. LONDONDERRY
　　[*see under* **KILCRONAGHAN**]

**TOBERMORE PRESBYTERIAN CHURCH,
CO. LONDONDERRY**
　　[*see under* **KILCRONAGHAN**]

TOGHER ROMAN CATHOLIC PARISH, CO. LOUTH
　　[*see under* **CLONMORE**]

TOGHERDOO METHODIST CHURCH, CO. FERMANAGH
　　[*see under* **KILSKEERY**]

TOMREGAN, COS FERMANAGH AND CAVAN

C.I. Tomregan (Kilmore diocese)
　　Baptisms, 1797-1984; marriages, 1802-1913; burials,
　　1805-1986.　　　　　　　　　　　　　　　　　　　　　　**MIC.1/218**

M. Ballyconnell
　　Baptisms, 1880-1974; marriages, 1880-1955.　　　　　　　**MIC.1E/53**

R.C. Knockninny (Kilmore diocese)
[Tomregan parish is partly in the Roman Catholic parish
of Knockninny - *see under* **KINAWLEY**. It is also partly
in the Roman Catholic parish of Kildallon - *see under*
KILDALLON, and partly in Drumlane - *see under*
DRUMLANE]

TRALEE, CO. KERRY

M. Tralee
Baptisms, 1833-44.   MIC.429/1/53

TRENTA PRESBYTERIAN CHURCH, CO. DONEGAL
[*see under* **CONWAL**]

TRILLICK CHURCH OF IRELAND PARISH, CO. TYRONE
[*see under* **KILSKEERY**]

TRILLICK METHODIST CHURCH, CO. TYRONE
[*see under* **KILSKEERY**]

TRILLICK ROMAN CATHOLIC CHURCH, CO. TYRONE
[*see under* **KILSKEERY**]

**TRINITY, AHOGHILL, PRESBYTERIAN CHURCH,
CO. ANTRIM**
[*see under* **AHOGHILL**]

**TRINITY, BAILIEBOROUGH, PRESBYTERIAN CHURCH,
CO. CAVAN**
[*see under* **BAILIEBOROUGH**]

**TRINITY, BALLYMONEY, PRESBYTERIAN CHURCH,
CO. ANTRIM**
[*see under* **BALLYMONEY**]

**TRINITY, BANGOR, PRESBYTERIAN CHURCH,
CO. DOWN**
[*see under* **BANGOR**]

**TRINITY, CROM, CHURCH OF IRELAND PARISH,
CO. FERMANAGH**
[*see under* **KINAWLEY**]

TRORY, CO. FERMANAGH

C.I. Killadeas (Clogher diocese)
Baptisms, 1880-1974; marriages, 1883-1935; burials,
1888-1986.   **MIC.1/283**

C.I. Trory, St Michael's (Clogher diocese)
Baptisms, 1779, 1784 and 1796-1922; marriages, 1779,
1799, 1801-32 and 1835-1905; burials, 1802-32 and
1835-1915; vestry minutes, 1778-1959.   **MIC.1/94; C.R. 1/19**

M. Laragh
Baptisms may be in with Enniskillen Circuit baptisms,
1823-, and with Ballinamallard baptisms, 1879-; marriages
may be in with Enniskillen marriages, 1864-1906, and with
Ballinamallard marriages, 1882-; minutes of quarterly
meetings, 1877-93; circuit schedule book, 1866-80
(Enniskillen); circuit schedule book, 1881-91
(Ballinamallard); circuit stewards' book, 1879-94;
membership registers, 1881-1900.   **MIC.1E/15, 23**

TULLAGHOBEGLEY, CO. DONEGAL

C.I. Ardangligger (Raphoe diocese)
[Early marriage entries are in Gweedore Parish Church
records - *see under* **TEMPLECRONE**].

C.I. Dunlewey (Raphoe diocese)
Marriages, 1853-82.   **MIC.1/197**

C.I. Tullaghobegley (Raphoe diocese)
Baptisms, 1821-37 and 1848-1976; marriages, 1821-35
and 1845-1954; burials, 1850-1979; vestry minutes,
1821-1908.   **MIC.1/162**

P. North Donegal Mission Stations
Baptisms, 1865-82.   **C.R. 3/12**

R.C. Tullaghobegley West (Gweedore) (Raphoe diocese)
Baptisms, 1868-71 and 1873-81.   **MIC.1D/87**

R.C. Tullaghobegley East and Raymunterdoney
(Gortahork) (Raphoe diocese)

Baptisms, 1849-61 and 1871-80; marriages, 1861-80;
deaths, 1849-69.   **MIC.1D/87**

TULLAMORE METHODIST CHURCH, CO. OFFALY
(KING'S COUNTY)
[*see under* **KILBRIDE, CO. OFFALY (KING'S
COUNTY)**]

TULLANISKIN CHURCH OF IRELAND PARISH, CO. TYRONE
[*see under* TULLYNISKAN]

TULLYALLEN, COS LOUTH AND MEATH

R.C. Mellifont (Tully) (Armagh diocese)
Baptisms, 1821-81; marriages, 1821-82.   MIC.1D/53

TULLYALLEN PRESBYTERIAN CHURCH, CO. ARMAGH
[*see under* LOUGHGILLY]

TULLYAUGHNISH CHURCH OF IRELAND PARISH, CO. DONEGAL
[*see under* AUGHNISH]

TULLYCORBET, CO. MONAGHAN

C.I. Tullycorbet (Clogher diocese)
Baptisms, 1796-1814, 1829-31 and 1886-1963;
marriages, 1822-31 and 1846-1950; burials, 1822-31
and 1894-1970; vestry minutes, 1809-1936.   MIC.1/153

Indexes to baptisms, 1796-1831, marriages, 1822-30,
and burials, 1814-31.   C.R. 1/44

P. Cahans
Baptisms, 1751-9 and 1767-1971; marriages, 1845-95;
communicants' list, 1816-26 and 1841-1905; session
minutes with discipline cases, 1751-1836; indexes to
baptisms and session minutes, 1751-1894.   MIC.1P/172;
                                                         C.R. 3/25

P. 2nd Clontibret
Baptisms, 1858-1905; marriages, 1845-1956.   MIC.1P/175

R.C. Tullycorbet (Ballybay) (Clogher diocese)
Baptisms, 1862-81; marriages, 1862-76.   MIC.1D/16

Index to baptisms, 1876-1918.   C.R. 2/16

R.P. Creevagh
Baptisms, 1882-1939; session minutes, 1884-1939;
committee minutes, 1884-1911.   MIC.1C/18; C.R. 5/12

TULLYFERN, CO. DONEGAL

C.I. [*see under* AUGHNISH]

P. Fannet
> Baptisms, 1827-1952; marriages, 1827-42 and 1846-1955;
> communicants' roll, 1805-1901 and 1933-42; register of
> stipend payers and seatholders, 1860-1904.   **MIC.1P/232**

P. Milford
> Baptisms, 1839-1902; marriages, 1845-1927.   **MIC.1P/244**

R.C. Tullyfern
> [*see under* **KILLYGARVAN**]

R.P. Milford
> Baptisms, 1870-99 and 1905-85; marriages, 1864-93 and
> 1903-41.   **MIC.1C/14**

TULLYLISH, CO. DOWN

C.I. Gilford (Dromore diocese)
> Baptisms, 1869-95.   **MIC.1/53**

> Baptisms, 1896-; marriages, 1869-; vestry minutes, 1869-;
> preachers' books, 1869-.   **In local custody**

C.I. Tullylish (Dromore diocese)
> Baptisms, 1820-83; marriages, 1820-48; burials, 1829-33
> and 1849-85; vestry minutes and accounts, 1792-1960.   **MIC.1/70-71**

> Register of vestrymen, 1870-; preachers' books, 1879-.   **In local custody**

M. Blackscull
> Baptisms, 1919-; marriages, 1911-.
> [At Donacloney Church]   **In local custody**

M. Gilford
> Marriages, 1886-1935.   **MIC.1E/7**

> Baptisms, 1836-; marriages, 1838-.
> [At Tandragee Church]   **In local custody**

P. Gilford
> Baptisms, 1851-1917; marriages, 1845-1904.   **MIC.1P/384**

P. Newmills
> Baptisms, 1838-1931; marriages, 1838-43 and 1845-99;
> session minutes, 1838-1957.   **MIC.1P/398**

P. Tullylish
> Baptisms, 1813 and 1821-1937; marriages, 1817, 1820-42
> and 1845-1918; session minutes, 1811-26, 1836-7 and
> 1845.   **MIC.1P/385; T.2957**

R.C. Tullylish (Dromore diocese)
> Baptisms, marriages and burials, 1833-81.   **MIC.1D/25**

TULLYNAKILL, CO. DOWN

C.I. Tullynakill (Down diocese)
[Earliest registers destroyed in Dublin]

Baptisms, 1827-1966; marriages, 1829, 1831 and
1845-1935; deaths, 1828 and 1840; burials, 1848-1923;
copy of vestry book, 1827-70, which includes accounts
for poor money collected and lists of Sunday School
pupils, 1827-8; preachers' book, 1923-70.   **C.R. 1/18**

TULLYNISKAN, CO. TYRONE

C.I. Brackaville
[Partly in Tullyniskan - *see under* **DONAGHENRY**]

C.I. Tullaniskan (Armagh diocese)
[*see also under* **DRUMGLASS** for entries prior to 1794]

Baptisms, 1794-1955; marriages, 1794-1845; burials,
1809-1918; vestry minutes, 1791-1870; confirmations,
1824-88.

Marriages, 1845-; vestry minutes, 1871-; preachers'
books, 1822-; registers of vestrymen, 1870-.   **In local custody**

P. Newmills
Baptisms, 1850-1952; marriages, 1846-1923.   **MIC.1P/295**

R.C. [Tullyniskan parish forms part of the Roman Catholic
parish of Dungannon - *see under* **DRUMGLASS**]

TULLYROAN METHODIST CHURCH, CO. TYRONE
[*see under* **KILDRESS**]

TULLYRUSK, CO. ANTRIM

C.I. Tullyrusk (Connor diocese)
[*see under* **GLENAVY**]

P. Dundrod
Baptisms, 1829-1950; marriages, 1829-1930; session
minutes, 1809-91; collections and poor accounts, 1829-46.   **MIC.1P/416**

TYDAVNET CHURCH OF IRELAND PARISH,
CO. MONAGHAN
[*see under* **TEDAVNET**]

TYDAVNET ROMAN CATHOLIC PARISH,
CO. MONAGHAN
   [*see under* **TEDAVNET**]

TYHOLLAND CHURCH OF IRELAND PARISH,
CO. MONAGHAN
   [*see under* **TEHALLEN**]

TYHOLLAND ROMAN CATHOLIC PARISH,
CO. MONAGHAN
   [*see under* **TEHALLEN**]

TYNAN, CO. ARMAGH

C.I. Killylea (Armagh diocese)
   Baptisms, 1845-1901; burials, 1845-1914.   **MIC.1/85**

   Baptisms, 1901-; burials, 1914-; marriages, 1846-; vestry
   minutes, 1829-; preachers' books, 1845-; parish visiting
   book, 1860-88; orphan register, 1876-8.   **In local custody**

C.I. Middletown (Armagh diocese)
   Vestry minutes, 1812-1948.   **MIC.1/13**

   Baptisms, 1880-; marriages, 1845-; burials, 1879-;
   register of vestrymen, 1870-.   **In local custody**

C.I. Tynan (Armagh diocese)
   Baptisms, 1686-1725 and 1806-97; marriages, 1683-1723,
   1806-18, 1821-45 and 1886-1923; burials, 1683-1723 and
   1806-97; vestry minutes, accounts etc., 1699-1960.   **MIC.1/12-13, 18**

   Accounts, c.1830-1835.   **DIO.4/32/T/7/6/1-9**

   Baptisms, 1686-95; marriages, 1683-1723; burials,
   1683-1723.   **T.808/15294**

M. Killylea
   Baptisms, 1815-. [At Armagh]   **In local custody**

P. Drumhillery
   Baptisms, 1829-; marriages, 1834-.   **In local custody**

P. Lislooney
   Baptisms, 1836-1923; marriages, 1845-1919.   **MIC.1P/401**

P. Middletown
   Baptisms, 1829-1984; marriages, 1847-1936.   **MIC.1P/212**

R.C. Tynan (Armagh diocese)
Baptisms, 1822-34, 1838-42 and 1845-84; marriages,
1822-34 and 1845-77.   **MIC.1D/40**

TYRELLA, CO. DOWN

C.I. Tyrella (Down diocese)
[Earliest registers destroyed in a fire]

Fragment of a parish register, c.1900.   **D.357**

Baptisms, marriages and burials, 1933-; vestry minutes,
1840-; register of vestrymen, 1870-.   **In local custody**

R.C. Tyrella and Ballykinlar (Dundrum)
(Down and Connor diocese)

[The Roman Catholic parish of Tyrella and Ballykinlar
contains the parishes of Ballykinlar, Tyrella, part of
Rathmullan and part of Loughinsland]

Baptisms and marriages, 1854-81.   **MIC.1D/72**

TYRONE'S DITCHES PRESBYTERIAN CHURCH, CO. ARMAGH
[*see under* **BALLYMORE**]

UNION ROAD, MAGHERAFELT, PRESBYTERIAN CHURCH, CO. LONDONDERRY
[*see under* **MAGHERAFELT**]

URNEY, CO. CAVAN

C.I. Urney and Annageliffe (Kilmore diocese)
[*see under* **ANNAGELLIFF**]

M. Cavan Mission Station/Cavan Circuit
[Wesleyan Methodists]

Baptisms, 1839-1902; marriages, 1869-1923.   **MIC.1E/51**

Baptisms, 1838-42.   **MIC.429/1/93**

R.C. Urney and Annageliffe
[*see under* **ANNAGELLIFF**]

URNEY, COS TYRONE AND DONEGAL

C.I. Castlederg or Derg (Derry diocese)
Baptisms, 1807-87; marriages, 1807-45; burials, 1839-81. **MIC.1/16**

Vestry minutes, 1807-; register of vestrymen, 1870-;
preachers' books, 1890-.   **In local custody**

C.I. Sion Mills (The Good Shepherd) (Derry diocese)
Baptisms, 1853-; marriages, 1931-; preachers' book,
1953-.   **In local custody**

C.I. Urney (Christ Church) (Derry diocese)
Baptisms, 1813-77; marriages, 1814-44; burials, 1815-19
and 1827-77; vestry book, 1822-38; notes on parishioners,
1860s and 1870s, and Sustentation Fund accounts,
c.1870; list of townlands and number of Episcopalian
Protestant families, 1849.   **MIC.1/81**

Baptisms, 1877-; marriages, 1845-; burials, 1877-; vestry
minutes, 1870-; register of vestrymen, 1870-; preachers'
books, 1850-58 and 1860-; confirmation register, 1859-;
list of parishioners, schools etc., 1849 and 1871; sermon
preached by Rev. William Henry, 1745.   **In local custody**

M. Castlederg [Wesleyan Methodists]
Baptisms, 1822-1961; marriages, 1864-1937; circuit
stewards' book, 1866-86.   **MIC.1E/45, 62**

P. Alt
Marriages, 1845-1955; stipend and account book, 1860-84.   **MIC.1P/249**

P. 2nd Castlederg
Baptisms, 1880-1985; marriages, 1861-1935; session and
committee minutes, 1875-1923.   **MIC.1P/248**

P. Sion or Sion Mills
Baptisms, 1866-81; marriages, 1866-84.   **MIC.1P/251**

P. Urney
[In 1881 Urney and Sion Mills were united]

Baptisms, 1837-81; marriages, 1866-81.   **MIC.1P/250**

P. Urney and Sion
Baptisms, 1881-1957; marriages, 1881-1926.   **MIC.1P/250-251**

R.C. Urney
Baptisms and marriages, 1866 -.   **In local custody**

VINECASH PRESBYTERIAN CHURCH, CO. ARMAGH
[see under **KILMORE**]

VIRGINIA ROMAN CATHOLIC CHURCH, CO. CAVAN
[see under **LURGAN**]

**WALSHESTOWN ROMAN CATHOLIC CHURCH,
CO. LOUTH**
 [*see under* **CLOGHER**]

WARINGSTOWN PRESBYTERIAN CHURCH, CO. DOWN
 [*see under* **DONAGHCLONEY**]

WARRENPOINT, CO. DOWN

 C.I. Warrenpoint (Dromore diocese)
  Baptisms, 1825-78; marriages, 1826 and 1829-46; burials,
  1845-1914; vestry minutes, 1826-70; confirmations,
  1853-89.   **MIC.1/85; T.679/50**

  Extracts from parish registers, 1829-66.   **DIO.1/14/11**

 M. Warrenpoint
  Baptisms, 1878-; marriages, 1889-.   **In local custody**

 N.S.P. Warrenpoint
  Minutes, 1840-70 and 1939-53; stipend and seatholders'
  account books, 1832-49; stipend/collection account book,
  1937-63; poor account book, 1836-9; account book,
  1942-60.   **C.R. 4/4**

 P. Warrenpoint
  Baptisms, 1832-1986; marriages, 1823-1907. **MIC.1P/307**

 R.C. [Warrenpoint parish is in the Roman Catholic parish of
  Clonallon - *see under* **CLONALLAN**]

WATERFORD, CO. WATERFORD

 M. Waterford
  Baptisms, 1825-42.   **MIC.429/1/19**

WATERSIDE PRESBYTERIAN CHURCH, LONDONDERRY
 [*see under* **CLONDERMOT**]

**WATERSIDE REFORMED PRESBYTERIAN CHURCH,
LONDONDERRY, CO. LONDONDERRY**
 [*see under* **TEMPLEMORE**]

**WESLEY CENTENARY METHODIST CHURCH, BANGOR,
CO. DOWN**
 [*see under* **BANGOR**]

WEXFORD, CO. WEXFORD

M. Quarterly leaders' minutes, 1858-1943; building
committee minutes, 1833-6, with accounts, 1834-41 etc.   **C.R. 6/8**

**WHITEABBEY CONGREGATIONAL CHURCH,
CO. ANTRIM**
    [*see under* **CARNMONEY**]

WHITEABBEY PRESBYTERIAN CHURCH, CO. ANTRIM
    [*see under* **CARNMONEY**]

**WHITEHEAD CHURCH OF IRELAND PARISH,
CO. ANTRIM**
    [*see under* **TEMPLECORRAN**]

WHITEHEAD PRESBYTERIAN CHURCH, CO. ANTRIM
    [*see under* **TEMPLECORRAN**]

**WHITEHILL ROMAN CATHOLIC PARISH,
CO. FERMANAGH**
    [*see under* **DERRYVULLAN**]

**WHITEHOUSE CHURCH OF IRELAND PARISH,
CO. ANTRIM**
    [*see under* **CARNMONEY**]

WICKLOW, CO. WICKLOW

M. Wicklow [Wesleyan Methodists]
    Leaders' and stewards' quarterly meeting minutes,
    1889-1906.   **C.R. 6/9**

    Baptisms, 1828-44.   **MIC.429/1/13**

WOODBURN PRESBYTERIAN CHURCH, CO. ANTRIM
    [*see under* **CARRICKFERGUS**]

**WOODS CHAPEL CHURCH OF IRELAND PARISH,
CO. LONDONDERRY**
    [*see under* **ARTREA**]

**YELLOW CHURCH METHODIST CHURCH,
CO. FERMANAGH**
    [*see under* **DERRYVULLAN**]

YOUGHAL, CO. CORK

M. Youghal
Baptisms, 1833-42.   **MIC.429/1/543**

**ZION METHODIST CHURCH, NEWTOWNARDS,
CO. DOWN**
[*see under* **NEWTOWNARDS**]